PIMLICO

546

A LIFE OF WALTER SCOTT

A.N. Wilson was born in 1950 and educated at Rugby and New College, Oxford. A Fellow of the Royal Society of Literature, he has held a prominent position in the world of letters and has been Literary Editor of both the *Evening Standard* and the *Spectator*.

An award-winning biographer, he has written lives of John Milton, Tolstoy (Whitbread Award for biography), C.S. Lewis and Hilaire Belloc. In 1992 he caused a sensation with his bestselling *Jesus* and this he followed with his equally controversial *Paul*. He is also a celebrated novelist, winning prizes for much of his fiction, and *The Victorians* is his most recent book.

A LIFE OF
WALTER SCOTT

The Laird of Abbotsford

———

A.N. WILSON

PIMLICO

Published by Pimlico 2002

4 6 8 10 9 7 5

First published in Great Britain by Oxford University Press 1980
Pimlico edition 2002

Pimlico
Random House, 20 Vauxhall Bridge Road,
London SW1V 2SA

www.rbooks.co.uk

Addresses for companies within
The Random House Group Limited can be found at:
www.randomhouse.co.uk/offices.htm

The Random House Group Limited Reg. No. 954009

A CIP catalogue record for this book
is available from the British Library

ISBN 9780712697545

The Random House Group Limited supports The Forest Stewardship
Council (FSC), the leading international forest certification organisation.
All our titles that are printed on Greenpeace approved FSC certified paper
carry the FSC logo. Our paper procurement policy can be found at:
www.rbooks.co.uk/environment

Printed and bound in Great Britain by
CPI Antony Rowe, Chippenham, Wiltshire

To Helen Gardner

Preface and Acknowledgements

Scott was not only a great writer; he was also a great man. The following essay would be ten times longer if it were to begin to do justice to its subject. It is an attempt to read Scott's life and work as complementary to one another. Between the work and the life, as between the works themselves—poems, historical novels and medieval romances—I find harmonies where other critics see only unevenness and discord; but I am grateful to all writers on the subject, contemporary and modern, to whom acknowledgement is made in the notes. So often one owes more to a critic with whom one disagrees than to a writer whose views merely reflect one's own.

The range of my survey is obviously limited, but where a poem or novel is not discussed, it does not mean that I regard them as unimportant. I have said very little about the later poems; nothing of *The Siege of Malta*; and my comments on the medieval fiction have been very selective.

Anyone working on Scott owes much to Edgar Johnson's huge biographical study, *The Great Unknown*. I would also like to record how especially helpful I still find two earlier biographies: John Buchan's *Sir Walter Scott*, and Hesketh Pearson's *Sir Walter Scott: His Life and Personality*.

Many friends, relations, colleagues and pupils have lit up areas of Scott's life and work which would have remained obscure for me without the benefit of their conversation. I am particularly grateful to Lord Dacre who read the chapter on *Old Mortality* and made illuminating suggestions. I have had the privilege to number two Scott enthusiasts among my immediate colleagues: Anne Barton and Marilyn Butler, among other acts of friendship, read the entire book in manuscript. Both 'thrust their sharp wit quite through my ignorance' at many points and saved me from innumerable errors of taste or fact.

Professor John Bayley and Mr Mark Hamilton were the book's begetters. Mr Jeremy Lewis and Miss Judith Chamberlain have been an invaluable help in the course of its completion.

The Reverend Allan Maclean of Dochgarroch has not only provided great hospitality in Scotland, but also been my guide in Scott's
'homes and haunts', and opened to me the funds of an immense
knowledge of Scottish life and history.

My greatest debt is, of course, to Scott himself. My acquaintance
with his life and work has provided me with much more than merely
the subject of a book. No one can meditate on Scott for long without a
sense that life is richer and fuller for his having lived; that his sheer
goodness, as a man and as an artist, have permanently extended the
limits which human genius and virtue may hope to touch.

I hope that this essay might have the result of causing some readers
to look at Scott again, so that he need no longer be, in our generation,
'the Great Unknown'.

New College, Oxford
June 1979

Contents

Chronology of the Life of Sir Walter Scott

1771 15 August (?): born in the College Wynd, Edinburgh, the ninth child (fourth surviving) of Walter Scott, Writer to the Signet, and Anne Rutherford.

1773 Contracts polio, and is lame for the rest of his life. Sent to the farm of his grandfather Robert Scott at Sandyknowe in the Borders.

1775 In January, Robert Scott dies. Walter Scott returns briefly to Edinburgh to his father's new house at 25 George Square.

In the summer, his aunt Janet Scott takes the boy south for a cure. He visits London and Bath, where he sees *As You Like It*.

1776 Returns to Edinburgh.

1779 Enters the High School in Edinburgh.

1783 'I left the High School with a great quantity of general information, ill-arranged, indeed, and collected without system, yet deeply impressed upon my mind.' Spends a year in Kelso with his Aunt Janet. At Kelso Grammar School he meets and befriends the Ballantyne brothers.

In November, he enrols in the College at Edinburgh.

1784–5 Ill again. Sent to Kelso. All formal studies are now interrupted. All treatments, including electrical shocks, are unsuccessful; his lameness becomes worse.

1786 31 March: apprenticed to his father's legal firm.

1786–7 Meets Burns.

On business of his father's, he sees the Highlands for the first time, including Loch Katrine and the Trossachs. Meets a client of his father's Alexander Stewart of Invernahyle, who had fought a duel with Rob Roy and fought in the '15 and the '45.

Breaks a blood vessel in the lower bowel, and is on a vegetarian diet for six months. Convalescence at Kelso.

1789–91 Reads law at Edinburgh University.

1790(?) Meets Williamina Belsches and falls in love.

1791 4 January: admitted to the Speculative Society.

1792 6 July: called to the Bar. Makes his first appearance as counsel in a criminal court at Jedburgh, where he successfully defends a sheep-stealer and poacher. ('You're a lucky scoundrel,' he whispered. 'I'm just o' your mind and I'll send ye a maukin [a hare] the morn, man.')

1792–6 Practises as an advocate in Edinburgh.

1797 19 January: Williamina Belsches marries William Forbes of Pitsligo.

WS brushes up his German and reads Goethe and Schiller.

14 February: with Skene and others, he forms the Royal Edinburgh Volunteer Light Dragoons. WS is made Quartermaster and is nick-named 'Earl Walter'.

Translates three poems by Goethe.

Visits the Lake District and meets Charlotte Charpentier, whom he marries, on Christmas Eve, in Carlisle Cathedral. From now on, he regards himself as an Episcopalian. His marital homes are a cottage in Lasswade, and 39 Castle Street, Edinburgh.

1798 His friend Will Erskine shows his German translations to 'Monk' Lewis, who asks for more. WS writes 'The Eve of Saint John'.

1799 In March, accompanied by his wife, he visits London. In April, while he is still away, his father dies. He renews his friendship, formed the previous year, with Richard Heber, the MP for the University of Oxford.

16 December: becomes Sheriff-Deputy for the County of Selkirk.

1800 With Heber's encouragement, he starts to collect material for *The Minstrelsy of the Scottish Border*, to be published by Ballantyne.

1802 First edition of the *Minstrelsy*.

1803 Expanded, three-volume edition of the *Minstrelsy* is published, including many of his own 'imitations'. Visits Oxford and London. Meets Rogers, W. S. Rose, Matt Lewis *et al*.

1804 Moves to Ashiestiel, where Wordsworth visits him.
Writes *The Lay of the Last Minstrel*.

1805 Publication of *The Lay of the Last Minstrel*: it is an instant success.
Becomes a Principal Clerk to the Court of Sessions in Edinburgh. From now on, he has a steady source of income from the law without having to practise as an advocate.
Enters secret business partnership with the Ballantyne brothers.
Contributes to the *Edinburgh Review*.

1805–8 Plans a complete edition of one hundred English poets with Archibald Constable, the Edinburgh publisher. Edits Dryden.
In 1807, finishes Joseph Strutt's historical romance, *Queenhoo Hall*, published by John Murray. Writes Essay on Chivalry for the *Encyclopaedia Britannica*.
In November 1807, Constable pays him 1,000 guineas for a poem he has not yet written. It is *Marmion*: by 1811, it has passed through many editions and sold 28,000 copies.

1809 WS is involved in the foundation of the *Quarterly*, a rival to the Whig *Edinburgh Review*. He starts to edit Swift.

1810 WS wants to visit the Peninsular War; instead, he makes his first journey to the Hebrides.
Publication of *The Lady of the Lake*. After only eight months, 25,000 copies have been sold. Loch Katrine and the Trossachs become a popular tourist attraction.
On 5 December, Williamina Forbes dies, aged thirty-four.

1811 The lease expires on Ashiestiel. WS buys the nearby farm of Clarty Hole where he builds a *cottage ornée*, renamed Abbotsford.

1812 Byron publishes the first two cantos of *Childe Harold*: 'Byron beat me'.

1812–13 Publishes *Rokeby* and *The Bridal of Triermain*. Meets Byron.

1813 WS is offered the Poet Laureateship, which he declines on the grounds that he feels incapable of writing on a regular basis.

1814 Publication of *Waverley*, anonymously.

WS visits Orkney, and returns to find *Waverley* the most successful novel ever before published in English (four editions and profits of £2,100 by the end of the year).

1815 Publication of *The Lord of the Isles* and *Guy Mannering*.

WS visits the field of Waterloo, and Paris, where he meets the Tsar.

Reviews *Emma* for the *Quarterly*.

Publication of *The Field of Waterloo*.

1816 Inherits the fortune of his brother, Major Scott.

Publication of *Tales of My Landlord, First Series* (*The Black Dwarf* and *Old Mortality*)

1817 Publication of *Harold the Dauntless*, his last long poem, and *Rob Roy*

Reviews Mary Shelley's *Frankenstein* for the *Quarterly*.

Publication of Maria Edgeworth's *Harrington*.

1818 *Tales of My Landlord, Second Series* (*The Heart of Midlothian*). WS accepts baronetcy.

1819 Prince Leopold and Prince Gustavus visit Abbotsford.

Death of WS's mother.

During two weeks of the summer, delirious with pain from gallstones, WS dictates *The Bride of Lammermoor*, which is published, together with *A Legend of Montrose*, as *Tales of My Landlord, Third Series*.

Later in the same illness, he dictates *Ivanhoe*, which is published at the end of the year and sells 10,000 copies in a fortnight.

1820 Publication of *The Monastery* and *The Abbot*. WS becomes an Honorary DCL at Oxford and Cambridge. Elected President of Royal Society of Edinburgh.

1821 Publication of *Kenilworth* and *The Pirate*.

1822 Publication of *The Fortunes of Nigel*.

WS helps to stage-manage the visit of George IV to Edinburgh, the first by a Hanoverian monarch to Scotland.

1823 Publication of *Peveril of the Peak*, *Quentin Durward*, and *St. Ronan's Well*.

WS shows the first symptoms of apoplexy.

1824 Death of Lord Byron; and of Maida, WS's favourite dog, to whom he builds a monument.

Publication of *Redgauntlet*.

1825 His elder daughter marries John Gibson Lockhart, his future biographer.

Publication of *Tales of the Crusaders*, *The Betrothed* and *The Talisman*.

In the summer, WS visits Maria Edgeworth in Ireland.

In November, he starts his Journal.

By Christmas, he is suffering from gallstones and fears financial ruin.

1826 The extent of his ruin becomes apparent: his personal liability amounts to £130,000. Sells 39 Castle Street, and resolves to pay his creditors by the work of his pen—'My own hand shall do it.'

15 May: his wife dies, and is buried in Dryburgh Abbey.

October–November: WS is in Paris, where he sees an opera of *Ivanhoe* by Rossini.

Publication of *Woodstock*.

1827 Publication of *Chronicles of the Canongate, First Series*; and the first volume of *The Life of Napoleon*.

At a Theatrical Fund dinner, avows the authorship of the novels.

Death of Archibald Constable.

1828 Publication of *The Fair Maid of Perth* and further volumes of *Napoleon*. Prepares *Opus Magnum*, a complete annotated edition of his works.

Dr Pusey breakfasts at Abbotsford and falls in the Tweed.

WS visits Stratford.

1829 Publication of *Anne of Geierstein* and *Tales of My Landlord, Fourth Series (Count Robert of Paris)*.

WS suffers from haemorrhages.

Death of Tom Purdie, WS's favourite servant.

1830 WS declines offer of Civil List pension and rank of Privy Councillor. Electioneering at Jedburgh before hostile mobs.

1831 A. W. Pugin designs sets for the ballet *Kenilworth*.

WS pays for the erection of a memorial to Helen Walker, the original of Jeanie Deans.

WS has his first stroke.

In September, visits Yarrow with Wordsworth. Last visits to Smailholm and Bemersyde.

Apoplectic paralysis. Lockhart takes him to Italy.

15 December: death of WS's grandson, Johnnie Lockhart, aged ten: the news reaches Naples a month later.

1832 Publication of *Castle Dangerous*.

WS returns from the Continent to die at Abbotsford on 21 September. He is buried beside his wife in Dryburgh Abbey.

CHAPTER ONE

Introductory

Every man's work, whether it be literature or music or pictures or architecture or anything else, is always a portrait of himself.

Samuel Butler: *The Way of All Flesh*

Beneath every king's reign Papa expects Sophia to write down neatly and in good spelling . . . whether he was a good man or a bad.

Undated letter from Sir Walter Scott
to his elder daughter (1810?)

By the age of sixty, Sir Walter Scott was worn out. In the previous five years he had suffered bankruptcy, the loss of his wife and all his best friends, and persistent illness, which culminated in two strokes, brought on in the summer of 1831 by disregarding medical advice and drinking champagne. Now, his abnormally large head, which had been covered with a mop of hair the colour of pale straw, was shaven and skull-like. The honest, doggy face was half-frozen with paralysis. He spoke with difficulty. His black coat, striped waistcoat and tweed trousers, like giant's robes, hung loosely on what had been a stocky, muscular frame. Death, now longed for so passionately, still eluded him.

His son-in-law Lockhart, in most other respects perfectly odious, was a most conscientious nurse during that final phase. He arranged for a recuperative visit to Italy. By now there would have been no question of slipping away quietly. The servants were lined up; the dogs which were always clustering around his legs were patted, as if for the last time; the local aristocracy paid final calls of courtesy; his younger daughter, who had inherited her mother's nerves, had hysterics; and the whole party left Abbotsford on the 23rd of September, with all the clutter of a royal progress, and a bad sonnet from Wordsworth to speed them on their way:

> . . . the might
> Of the whole world's good wishes with him goes;
> Blessings and prayers, in nobler retinue
> Than sceptred king or laurelled conqueror knows
> Follow this wondrous Potentate. . . .

Perhaps the lines were hyperbolic. In his later years, Scott's political views veered rather to the right of Dr Johnson's, and the industrial mobs from Galashiels had not taken kindly to having Shakespeare's tag of 'unwash'd artificers' applied to themselves in a public speech. But further south, he had indeed 'the world's good wishes'.

By the time he reached London, more than half-dead with tiredness, Scott was invited out as much as when, in middle-age, he had been lionized as the author of *The Lay of the Last Minstrel*. Inquiries after his health came from the Palace of St. James. Duchesses and poets clamoured for his company. Invitations poured in. He had known *everyone*, and had an extraordinary genius for friendship: shepherds and princes of the blood, scholars and dukes, poets and soldiers had all felt his charm and his easy intimacy. But it was all over now. Dinners were out of the question, but he felt up to breakfast with friends, and on 8 October he presented himself at Amen Corner to see his old friend Mrs Hughes and her husband, who was a Canon of St. Paul's.

When he met Hughes, Scott held out his hand, exclaiming 'You see me a broken man in every sense, my dear Doctor!' But he was able to eat breakfast, his very salt taste particularly appreciating the excellence of the Yarmouth bloaters. As they left, Scott's elder daughter, Mrs Lockhart, asked her hostess if she could procure 'half a hundred' for their own consumption; and Mrs Hughes took on the task.

As soon as they drove away, I went to Mr Bateman, a great salesman in Billingsgate, and I gave the order: he replied that such a number would not suit a private family, for owing to the manner in which these fish are cured they will only keep good a short time: I then desired half the quantity to be sent to Sussex Place: he answered decidedly but civilly, that it was not their custom to send so far: I do not know what prompted me, but I said, almost involuntarily, 'I am very sorry the order cannot be complied with—it was for Sir Walter Scott'—The rough fishmonger started back and pushing forward to me through his piles of fish cried out almost loudly—'Sir Walter Scott!—did you say madam? Sir Walter Scott!—God bless my soul! He shall have them directly if I carry them myself—Sir Walter Scott! they shall be with him tonight'—then pausing—'No, not tonight—for tomorrow morning at 7 o'clock a fresh cargo comes in, and he shall have them for his breakfast—Sir Walter Scott!' Then with a very grave look and in as soft a tone as his loud voice could be lowered to, he said, 'They say he has been ill, and is not well now—*how* is he?' Mr Bateman kept his word and Sir Walter was more pleased than I can describe when I related the words I have been writing; he laughed and said, 'I don't think my works ever produced an effect so much to my taste before.'[1]

The whole anecdote is entirely believable and convincing: Scott, scarcely able to hold food down at this stage, ordering more bloaters than 'would suit a private family'; extravagant yet self-deprecating, as his genuine delight in the fishmonger's testimony shows. Even in Billingsgate market, he had 'the world's good wishes'.

If one tries to picture the reaction of a fishmonger nowadays when asked for bloaters on behalf of a famous novelist, it is hard to imagine even our most popular and illustrious writers inspiring a similar response. The nineteenth century differed in that respect from our own. One thinks of Tennyson's admirers storming him as he walked down Piccadilly, or of the crowds who flocked to Dickens's lectures. Yet even by the standards of the age, Scott was distinct. The Victorians canonized him. Indeed, he was scarcely cool in his grave, five years before the Queen's accession, before his fellow-citizens had planned the vast Gothic memorial in Princes Street, which would dwarf an average-sized cathedral spire. The encrustations of his cult expanded and grew. We approach him through it, like Armada gold thick with barnacles: something over a thousand paintings inspired by his work and well over fifty operas, not to mention the Gothic residences, all partaking a little of the quality of Abbotsford, which sprawl in unending lines through Great Malvern, Leamington Spa and north Oxford.

Scott's fantasies became the reality of the succeeding generation. The stag at eve not merely drank his fill in thousands of limp suede-bound editions, but sprouted antlers over the furniture at Osborne. The moonlight which Scott never actually saw shining down upon the ruins of Melrose casts its eery glow on the nineteenth-century Gothic monasteries of Llanthony and Mount St. Bernard. Every well-educated Victorian and Edwardian schoolboy learnt inner cleanliness not only through organized games and syrup of figs, but through imbibing Scott's *Tales of the Crusaders*. And even today, the pibroch sounds and the tartan is worn not just by Highland-men, but in dining-rooms all over the world from Balmoral to Minneapolis.

All this led to the inevitable reaction. Scott's art became confused with the bizarre range of life-styles and fantasies which it inspired.

Even if it had deserved its fate, it should still be studied; for without a knowledge of it, how can we understand the Victorians, who lived and breathed Scott's poems and novels?

But, of course, Scott was much more than the greatest single popular imaginative inspiration of the nineteenth century. He was a genius of extraordinary range, depth and intelligence. Had he merely been crippled since infancy, perpetually afflicted by bile and gall-stones, jaundice and rheumatism, financially ruined and occupied by almost full-time activity as a judge, a businessman and a conscientious landowner, his collapse at the age of sixty would have been unsurprising. But a glance at our bookshelves shows us that this was not all. Booksellers deal in Scott by the yard, more often than in individual volumes: a four-volume collection of ballads; editions of Dryden and Swift; a poetical output the size of Shelley's; twenty-seven novels; numerous tales; a child's history of Scotland in three volumes; a nine-volume life of Napoleon, twelve large volumes of correspondence, and as many again of miscellaneous essays and reviews; a Journal which runs to over seven hundred pages.

It would have been a large achievement if he had started writing in adolescence and continued until his first stroke. But that was not the pattern. He hardly wrote anything before he was thirty, and the huge bulk of his work belongs to the last fifteen years of his life, when he was chronically ill, and most occupied with his professional concerns. He was never a 'full-time writer'.

This again, like his almost fabulous influence on the whole of European culture in the nineteenth century, would make him worthy of wonder and admiration (not only to Byron was he 'the Monarch of Parnassus'; Ruskin, Hugo, Balzac, Pushkin, Manzoni all acknowledged him as their master). It does not make him unique—Trollope, Balzac and Tolstoy wrote on a comparable scale—but few can have written so much with so little time to spare, and so little physical health to sustain them.

Every so often, someone publishes a book suggesting that we have another look at Scott. The notices appear, each reviewer praising Scott to the skies for his personal courage, his historical intelligence, his influence not merely on art but on history, his Shakespearean ability to create character. The Scott readers go on reading Scott. And the huge majority of intelligent readers have another go at starting *The Heart of Midlothian* and then go back to Dickens or Trollope or D. H. Lawrence. What is the justification for yet another book on

Scott? And what hopes can the present author have, where others, more scholarly and imaginative, have failed?

None at all. This is a work of pure self-indulgence. It arose during a period of illness when I had a chance to re-read my favourite Scott, and to look at the works I had not read before. I started to write this book to provide myself with an excuse for reading them all again. And now I feel like Lady Louisa Stuart, one of Scott's most appreciative correspondents, who was in the secret of the authorship of the novels from the beginning: 'They are to me less like books, than like letters one treasures up, "pleasant, yet mournful to the soul" . . . how many hours of mine have they soothed and softened! and still do soothe and soften, for I can read them over and over again.'[2]

Byron, in his Ravenna Journal (5 January 1821) makes exactly the same point: that an addiction to Scott is bound up with an addiction to his personality: 'Read the conclusion, for the fiftieth time (I have read all W. Scott's novels at least fifty times) of the third series of "Tales of my Landlord",—grand work—Scotch Fielding, as well as great English poet—wonderful man! I long to get drunk with him.'[3]

What Byron and Lady Louisa Stuart both imply is that the experience of reading Scott brings one into touch not merely with great art, but with the greatness of the man. They knew him, of course. But so, in a sense, do all his dedicated readers. He was not only one of the greatest of our novelists. He was also one of those rare writers—Byron himself was one, Dr Johnson another—who seem to defy Yeats's rather portentous assertion that

> The intellect of man is forced to choose
> Perfection of the life or of the work.

None of the three were perfect in any ordinary sense of the word, but they all made of their lives something almost as interesting as their work. In Johnson's case, one has to admit, while admiring him this side idolatry, that nothing in the work ever quite matches the greatness of the life. In the case of Byron, the work becomes a sort of parody of his own egotism, the Byron of the letters being curiously less real than the narrator of *Don Juan*. In Scott's case, one feels that the marriage of 'real' and 'artistic' self is held much more coolly in check.

In this study, I shall be examining the way in which his own highly developed imagination and fantasy-life grew into art, how his vision of himself as an old border minstrel produced the poetry, and how his

desire to be a soldier and a man of action created his novels of
adventure. Similarly, other self-portraits or self-images are fed into
the fiction: himself as a disappointed lover; himself in pursuit of his
ancestors; himself as an eighteenth-century rationalist, as an Episcopalian, as King Lear, as a medieval baron, as a Stoic.

At the same time, I am well aware of how dangerous it is to make
these leaps between Scott's life and work. Unlike Byron, he had none
of the 'self-awareness' which we esteem so highly. He was not
interested in self-exploration. On the contrary, he had ideals of
behaviour, and tried to make his own life match up to them. In so far
as he recognized the self-fantasizing streak in his nature, he mocked at
it, and disregarded it. No one was less of an egotist. His fictions are not
about himself. They bubble over with a selfless interest in the world
outside him: its past, its landscape, and the fulness of human oddity.
He is, as Virginia Woolf wrote, 'the last great novelist to practise the
great, the Shakespearean art of making people reveal themselves in
speech'.[4] But also, surely, he was the first. Where else, in the fiction of
our language, is there such an astonishing range of human types, set
so intelligently against so wide a variety of historical and geographical
backgrounds?

Today, for some reason, Scott is the least read of our great writers,
and not least by those professionally engaged in the study of literature. It is rather a mercy in a way. It will be sad when he comes in for
the kind of treatment that has submerged E. M. Forster, D. H.
Lawrence and Virginia Woolf: a 'case-book' on *The Surgeon's Daughter*,
seminars on *The Fair Maid of Perth*, learned journals teeming with
critical assessments of *The Talisman*. Like the Victorians, we have
made a religion out of literature. But, unlike them, we are more
interested in exegesis of the sacred texts than in manufacturing
objects of piety about them. How much more helpful than the industry of critics would be a Mrs Dalloway teapot stand and paperweights
in the shape of that lighthouse, or E. M. Forster toby-jugs and
oleographs of views from his Italian fiction. Such was the tribute paid
to Scott by his idolaters. But, while we can be glad that he has escaped
the A-level syllabus and the campus bookstore, it is sad that so many
literate, English-speaking readers should deprive themselves of such
a deep fund of possible enjoyment. For it is the art of enjoyment which
has been lost: just as our actors are no longer bold enough to perform
convincingly florid productions of Shakespeare, so the size and colour
and energy of Scott's work, its unique combination of intellectual

depth with total lack of pretension, is critically disconcerting. Even for a generation which drank port by the pint, had Tasso and *Lalla Rookh* on their bedside tables, saw Kean's Shylock or Kemble's Iago (or perused his nephew's new edition of *Beowulf*), the poetry and fiction of Scott were a heady dissipation. Written at the gallop, they are intended to be read at the gallop, quaffed in long draughts, and, if necessary, read lightly (Scott himself refers (in *Redgauntlet*) to 'the laudable practice of *skipping*'). Virginia Woolf again was right when she wrote that 'either Scott the novelist is swallowed whole and becomes part of the body and brain, or he is rejected entirely'.[5]

Scott purists do not often follow this line. In an attempt to recommend the Great Unknown to a wider public, they often dismiss the majority of what he wrote. 'What trash are his works, taken all together', Pope waspishly declared of Ben Jonson; and Scott apologists will start by saying that Scott wrote only for money (who but a fool ever did otherwise, as Johnson observed), and that he is best appreciated in a very few novels. For the most part, they will maintain, he is shamefully careless, prodigal in his fecundity, too prolific to be taken 'whole'.

Yet although all his novels have flaws, they all have great scenes, memorable characters, high rhetoric, intense pathos, carefully constructed comedy. They were all written fast. They all made a lot of money; but this seems a peculiar reason for not believing them to be great. He was a genius in the popular sense of the word. Works which one can see to be deeply thought and—what is not often conceded—carefully constructed, flowed out of him as fast as his pen could write. It is said that he squandered his gifts, just as he squandered his money. Of course he did. Extravagance was fundamental to him. Without it, we would not have the Waverley Novels. He is at his best when most slapdash, most expansive, most generous, most comprehensive.

Many of the attitudes which he struck in his life sound deeply eccentric now, and it may seem, as they are related, as if this book is satirizing him. Nothing could be further from its purpose. On the face of it, it does seem odd that a middle-class Edinburgh lawyer should devote all his energies to turning himself into a feudal landowner on a medieval scale. Yet, as the vast testimony of his friendships show, and as one can discern by reading his letters, his Journal, and his novelistic asides, no one was more normal. Fantasy and affectation, which grew into art, remained perpetually outside that well-balanced, cheerful, brave, but entirely orthodox personality. Those who have never visited Abbotsford think of it as a vast baronial castle. It is actually smaller than many of its suburban imitations, the dwelling not of a medieval baron, but of a successful bourgeois. The land about it, the trees, the men, the sheep, were what consumed Scott's fortune. Beneath whatever melodramatic exterior he sometimes adopted— and the plaid and the bright uniforms were much less usual wear for him than the plain black of the lawyer's office—lurked a man only extraordinary by the depth of his ordinariness. But it was an ordinariness infused with astonishing energy, which only hyperbole can describe.

CHAPTER TWO

The Border Minstrel: Scott's Poetry

To ransack every crypt and hallow'd spot,
And from oblivion rend the spoils they yield,
Restoring priestly chant and clang of knightly shield.

(Harold the Dauntless: Canto III. i)

'My great-great-great grandfather—it's a shame to the English
language that we have not a less clumsy way of expressing a
relationship of which we have occasion to think and speak so
frequently.'

The Antiquary

I

One of the most grotesque stories ever to appear in a newspaper must
be an item in the *Inverness Courier* on 1 April 1848, some sixteen years
after Scott's death. On the one hand, it can be seen as the final
melancholy consequence of Scott's obsession with the past, his desire
to cocoon himself in an artificial world of gothick battlements, tartans
and thumbscrews. But, viewed differently, it is a good example of the
way in which, as Wilde observed, Life holds up a mirror to Art.

We learn from a gentleman in Edinburgh, that among the latest victims of
the fever at present raging in that city was John Bruce, or 'John of Skye', for
some years the Highland piper at Abbotsford. In his best days, John was a
fine athletic man, and when dressed up in full costume, playing a pibroch, or
marching up to the dining-room at Abbotsford, to receive from the hands of
his illustrious master his Celtic *quaich* brimful of Glenlivet, he had a most
imposing and picturesque appearance. He imagined himself to be a descendant of the great Robert Bruce, and hinted at his pretensions to the throne,
which only his regard for 'the young lady queen' prevented him from asserting. He still wandered about, old and indigent, playing the pipes which he
had received from Sir Walter; but, like the minstrel of his great master's poem

His trembling hand had lost the ease,
Which marks security to please;
And scenes long past, of joy and pain,
Came wildering o'er his aged brain.

Though more than seventy years of age and subjected to much hardship and privation, John of Skye walked erect; and had a military air to the last. There was no relation to claim the poor piper's remains, and his body was sent to one of the dissecting rooms. A medical student purchased, for a trifle, the bagpipes which he was so proud to bear as a gift of the Great Magician, and with which he had once charmed 'high dames and mighty earls' in hall and greenwood.[1]

In the year of revolutions, the last minstrel lies under a student's scalpel. The paid inhabitant of an eighteenth-century folly has become a Victorian destitute. It is almost as if a character had wandered out of one of Scott's novels and was trying to find his way into one by Dickens: not too long a journey.

One knows that Scott, had he been alive, would never have allowed such a thing to happen to one of his retainers, and it reflects poorly on the surviving family not to have known about it. His daughters would have done something, but Anne had died in 1833, Sophia in 1837. But that apart, how differently Scott would have told the tale had he had the chance. The piper would have been both more absurdly eccentric and more dignified. The Waverley Novels, and the poems, are peopled in part by figures who have no place in the world because they have refused to change. On one level, they are obviously comic. For Lady Margaret Bellenden in *Old Mortality*, time has stood still since Charles II had breakfast at Tillietudlem Castle during the troubled 1650s, thirty years before, and for her no paragraph is complete without reference to his sacred majesty's disjune. And the Osbaldistones in *Rob Roy* have a similar dinosaur quality. Yet these rigid caricatures, who carry the past into the present simply by being themselves, are by no means always ridiculous. Old Mortality himself, who devotes his life to chiselling afresh the names of the Coven-anting martyrs on their gravestones, is viewed quite seriously. So too are many other 'dinosaurs'. Who, for instance, like Sir Henry Lee in *Woodstock*, would not pine for the company of Ben Jonson and memories of Shakespeare, when the contemporary world echoed to the mad farce of the Civil War and the ranting of crop-eared fanatics? And Scott's finest creation, Redgauntlet, achieves his finest moment when, after a lifetime of anachronistic devotion to the exiled Stuarts, he recognizes that his abortive attempt at rebellion is not regarded by the Hanoverians as even worth punishing. It is when he stands on the shore exclaiming 'Then is the cause lost forever!' that we feel him to be most fully heroic.

Scott recognized and understood the dinosaur mentality so well because, from an early age, he had it himself. So much of what he did and wrote formed the taste of the coming generation—and, indeed, was in tune with the Gothick of his own—that it is hard to realize how personal it all was. Indeed, when *The Lay of the Last Minstrel* first appeared in 1805, there were those who said that it was a plagiarism of Coleridge's *Christabel*. There are a number of similar lines, it is true. But, as Coleridge wrote in a noble defence of Scott,

No insect was ever more like in the colour of its skin and juices to the leaf it fed on, than Scott's muse is to Scott himself. Habitually conversant with the antiquities of his country, and of all Europe during the ruder periods of society, living, as it were, in whatever is found in them imposing either to the fancy or interesting to the feelings, passionately fond of natural scenery . . . how else, or what else could he have been expected to write? His poems are evidently the indigenous product of his mind and habits.[2]

The mind and habits grew out of two wholly different worlds: Georgian Edinburgh and the Borders. With its infinitely severe, neat squares and crescents, Robert Adam's Athenian University buildings, its pavements and its drains, Georgian Edinburgh put the past unmistakably behind it. It was a world of clubs and reviewers, of Hume and Adam Smith; a place where the hard, urbane lines of the Enlightenment seem more exactly set out than in any other European townscape. Above all, it was, and remains, a city of lawyers. Here, Scott's father worked as a Writer to the Signet (a Scotch solicitor). He was a first generation Georgian, leaving the sordid 'wynd' where his family had lived in the old city (and where six of his children had died) for a compact little house in George Square, which he built on the hard-earned, carefully-saved proceeds of his practice. Scott was three years old at the time. He had already contracted polio, and looked like going the way of the majority of his brothers and sisters. Instead, while the rest of the family settled down in the Athens of the North, he was sent off to his grandfather's farm in the Border Country to be nursed back to health in the fresh air.

Sandyknowe, the small hamlet where Robert Scott was a farmer, still feels deeply remote. It was worlds away from George Square. Old-fashioned remedies for lameness, such as wrapping his little legs in the bloody, newly-skinned hide of a sheep, were less effectual cures than time, and a visit to Bath; and Scott probably owed his life to the fact that the hamlet received such infrequent visits from any member

of the medical profession. Scott did not spend all that much time in
Sandyknowe, yet it was there that his imagination came to life. Above
the farm, on a rocky crag, stands Smailholm Tower, an old border
keep. It is an awe-inspiring building, rugged, lonely and violent. It
looks out across empty hills towards Bemersyde, seat of the Haigs,
and Dryburgh, in whose ruins Scott was to be buried. Here, for
hundreds of years, borderers had resisted siege when not out on
raiding parties besieging someone else. Their history, and the songs
they inspired, were to be Scott's chief obsession as a young man. His
early experience of the Borders (for a time he was at school in Kelso)
brought him deeply in touch with his ancestors—men who, as he
wrote later in life,

for three hundred years before the union of the kingdoms having murdered,
stolen and robbed like other Border gentlemen; and from James's reign to the
Revolution having held commissions in God's own parliamentary army,
canted, prayed, and so forth; persecuted others and been persecuted themselves during the reigns of the last Stuarts; hunted, drank claret, rebelled, and
fought duels down to the times of my father and my grandfather.[3]

It was this world which Scott's father was escaping to pursue a life of
modern middle-class religious rectitude in the city. But at Sandyknowe it was all near, clearly remembered, and alive. His aunt Janet
taught him the ballads; she told him of his ancestor Wat of Harden, of
his kinship with the Duke of Buccleuch, and of his own great-
grandfather's exploits in the Fifteen. Scott's intense and detailed
knowledge of the Borders and their history was to develop slowly,
beginning as an irrational, inescapable image, focussed on the dark
tower overshadowing the farm in which he first began to feel well and
to realize that he had escaped the clutches of death:

> Rude though they be, still with the chime
> Return the thoughts of early time;
> And feelings, rous'd in life's first day,
> Glow in the line, and prompt the lay.
> Then rise those crags, that mountain tower
> Which charm'd my fancy's wakening hour.

> (*Marmion*: Introduction to Canto III)

Yet it was in his father's Edinburgh house that he spent most of his
childhood. Walter Scott *père* is often made out to have been a religious

maniac who did everything possible to stifle the latent genius of his son. If so, we should be grateful to him. Yet although he was obviously austere and hard-working, there is no evidence that he was a monster, or that he brought up his children any more strictly than many other men of his class and type. Nor is there much evidence that Scott resented his upbringing. His father's portrait shows a tough, prudish face, but not a fanatical one. As a Writer to the Signet, he wanted his son to better himself by practising at the Bar. Kinship with the Duke of Buccleuch was, for him, not a poetical fancy, but a way of advancing his children in the world. They all turned out poorly, except the novelist; some of them total wastrel, not to say criminal, types. Scott published nothing during his father's lifetime: the idea of doing anything so frivolous would have horrified the old man, who had planned for 'Wattie' an existence which would eradicate forever the terrible insecurity of agriculture and enmity to the Crown, and for this, the boy was sent to the university, trained as a clerk in the office and pushed into becoming an advocate. Scott's father wanted the child to become an urban, Georgian, British gentleman, to learn the law and mix with lawyers, and spend his evenings in the civilized society which the clubs and assembly rooms of eighteenth-century Edinburgh provided. By all means visit relations in the country; by all means, have an interest in genealogy. But a gentleman's place is in the town, and at his desk.

And this is the pattern of life which, very largely, Walter Scott obediently followed, without any apparent resentment. From his youth until his ruin in 1826, he always maintained an Edinburgh establishment, and most of his friends, for at least half the year, were Edinburgh lawyers. He professed, in a letter to the tragedian Joanna Baillie, to despise Georgian architecture, 'the cat-lugged band-box with four rooms on a floor and two stories rising regularly above each other'.[4] But his own house in Castle Street, where nearly all his novels were written, is scarcely less of a band-box than his father's house in George Square. It was at a window of this house that those gentlemen, one of them Lockhart, saw the ceaseless hand at work:

Happening to pass through Edinburgh in June 1814, I dined one day with . . . William Menzies . . . whose residence was then in George Street, situated very near to, and at right angles with, North Castle Street. It was a party of very young persons, most of them, like Menzies and myself, destined for the Bar of Scotland, all gay and thoughtless, enjoying the first flush of manhood, with little remembrance of the yesterday, or care of the morrow. When my companion's worthy father and uncle, after seeing two or three bottles go round, left the juveniles to themselves, the weather being hot, we adjourned to the library which had one large window looking northwards. After carousing here for an hour or more, I observed that a shade had come over the aspect of my friend, who happened to be placed immediately opposite to myself, and said something that intimated a fear of his being unwell. 'No,' said he, 'I shall be well enough presently if you will only let me sit where you are, and take my chair; for there is a confounded hand in sight of me here, which has often bothered me before, and now it won't let me fill my glass with a good will.' I rose to change places with him accordingly, and he pointed out to me this hand which, like the writing on Belshazzar's wall, disturbed his hour of hilarity. 'Since we sat down,' he said, 'I have been watching it—it fascinates my eye—it never stops—page after page is finished and thrown on that heap of MS. and still it goes on unwearied—and so it will be until the candles are brought in, and God knows how long after that. It is the same every night—I can't stand a sight of it when I am not at my books'—'Some stupid, dogged, engrossing clerk, probably,' exclaimed myself, or some other giddy youth in our society. 'No, boys,' said our host, 'I know what hand it is—'tis Walter Scott's. . . .'[5]

The moving hand had learnt its fluency as an apprentice in his father's office. His father paid him piece-rates, and on one occasion Scott covered more than 120 pages without stopping for food or rest.

Presumably, had he been a great success as an advocate, Scott would have remained in Edinburgh until he died. His impatience with humdrum professional life is mythologized in many places in his fiction; one thinks of Frank Osbaldistone in *Rob Roy*, or Alan Fairford in *Redgauntlet*, both young men too brave and 'poetical' to be able to endure the routine of office work. But had his career as an advocate been a great financial success, Scott would certainly have had more sense than to give it up. Nor is there anything to show, before the age of thirty, for all his prodigious memory for other people's poetry and fiction, that he had any literary talent of his own. More than half his life was spent in desultory antiquarian research, reading bad novels, and indulging his chief genius as a young man: that of friendship.

By pulling strings with grand friends and relations, he managed to secure two jobs which put his knowledge of the law to use without the necessity of practising at the Bar. He became Sheriff for the County of Selkirk, and a Clerk to the Court of Sessions in Edinburgh. This meant having two houses—one in the city, the other in the Borders.

After his marriage, he was always a man with two homes. At 39 Castle Street, the shadow of his dead father distorted his guilty desire to be industrious into the secret but voluminous practice of literature, while at his dinner-table, or the New Club, or the Speculative Society, he conversed with men whose history had been written, and whose minds had been fashioned, by Hume. As a border sheriff, he was never far from the dark, irrational tower of his infancy. His neighbours were farmers and aristocrats and peasants, whose history was recorded in ruins and unwritten ballads and legends; men and women who saw ghosts and fairies on dark nights, and who still remembered old feuds.

2

It is not surprising, then, that one of Scott's earliest published works, printed in Matthew Lewis's *Tales of Wonder* (1801), should recall the scenes of his early childhood. It is called 'The Eve of Saint John'.

The Baron of Smaylho'me leaves his tower, professedly to join 'the bold Buccleuch' at the battle of Ancram Moor against the English. But when he returns, covered in gore, it is because he has been settling a private quarrel with his wife's lover, Sir Richard Coldinghame. The theme of the poem owes a certain amount to the 'Ballad of the Daemon Lover', which Scott included in his *The Minstrelsy of the Scottish Border*, for when the baron returns, his page discloses that the lady has been entertaining her lover in his absence. How can this be, since at the moment of their reported love-making, the baron had killed the lover in combat?

With trepidation, he greets his lady, and they retire to bed:

> 'Now hail, now hail, thou lady bright!'
>   'Now hail, thou Baron true!
> What news, what news from Ancram fight?
>   What news from the bold Buccleuch?'
>
> 'The Ancram Moor is red with gore,
>   For many a southron fell;
> And Buccleuch has charged us evermore
>   To watch our beacons well.'
>
> The lady blush'd red, but nothing she said;
>   Nor added the Baron a word:

> Then she stepp'd down the stair to her chamber fair,
>   And so did her moody lord.

But as the baron sinks into a deeper sleep, the spectral lover returns to tell the lady that his adultery is being punished in purgatory, and that her husband must suffer the guilt and punishment of a murderer. With splendid economy, the poem ends

> There is a nun in Dryburgh bower,
>   Ne'er looks upon the sun;
> There is a monk in Melrose tower
>   He speaketh word to none.
>
> That nun who ne'er beholds the day,
>   That monk who speaks to none—
> That nun was Smaylho'me's Lady gay
>   That monk the bold Baron.

Perhaps there is little here to indicate that the author would one day be capable of writing *Marmion* or *The Heart of Midlothian*. The verbal confusion of *nun* and *none* is clumsy. And the reasons for his choosing to invent this macabre fantasy must be buried deeper than the tomb where he and Lady Scott now lie in the ruins of Dryburgh. The most striking aspect of the story is the sense, unwillingly recognized by the baron, that the past must be lived with; that the dead will not always be silent in their graves.

A similar fancy is present in the magical properties of Michael Scott's book, in *The Lay of the Last Minstrel*. Melrose Abbey, the picturesque ruins of which the narrator describes for the delight of his Regency audience in one of the poem's more famous anthology pieces, is a dangerous place in the Last Minstrel's story. Sir William Deloraine is commissioned to go there 'to win the treasure of the tomb'. The monk whom he asks to open the grave shakes with fear. Anticipating Flecker, he chides the knight for assuming too lightly that the past can be assaulted, pried upon and used:

> For threescore years, in penance spent,
>   My knees those flinty stones have worn;
> Yet all too little to atone
> For knowing what should ne'er be known.

(Canto II.v)

This sense that the past was awesome and alive was much more than a literary affectation. Lockhart's story of the discovery of the regalia of the Scotch royal house in Edinburgh Castle is well known:

His daughter tells me that her father's conversation had worked her feelings up to such a pitch that when the lid was removed she nearly fainted, and drew back from the circle. As she was retiring, she was startled by his voice, exclaiming in a tone of the deepest emotion, 'By G—, no!' One of the Commissioners, not quite entering into the solemnity with which Scott regarded the business, had, it seems, made a sort of motion as if he meant to put the crown on the head of one of the young ladies near him, but the voice and aspect of the Poet were more than sufficient to make the worthy gentleman understand his error.[6]

It was from such deeply held passions that his art was to grow. The people of the ballads which he collected in *The Minstrelsy of the Scottish Border* were quite real to him. Kinmont Willie and Dick o' the Cow and the others, are exactly like his own ancestors; many of them, of course, actually *were* his ancestors. Many other compilations of ballads had been made since the middle of the eighteenth century, and most of them were known to Scott. In terms of scholarship, Scott was noticeably inferior to Ritson; in terms of range, he surpassed Bishop Percy, but not in that nebulous, odd art which can make an anthology a companion for life. We still keep Percy's *Reliques*, not Scott's *Minstrelsy*, on the bedside table. Yet many of Scott's faults as an editor point the way to the stirrings of his creative imagination. His very desire to 'improve' and prettify the ballads, his inability to leave a good thing alone, were symptoms of his restlessness with the activity, his desire to realize the world of the ballads in other ways. The Borders inspired his most intensely felt poetry and fiction. *Marmion*, *The Abbot*, and *The Bride of Lammermoor* may not be technically the best of Scott, but there is an urgency and fulness about them not to be found even in more obviously magnificent works. All the names in the ballads—Elliotts, Scotts, Humes, and the like—have a peculiar meaning for us when we return to the *Minstrelsy* from Scott's mature work. The traditions he draws on in his early work are all almost within touching distance.

In the *Minstrelsy*, he records a ballad about the Battle of Pentland Hills, fought in 1666, which was 'copied verbatim from the recitation of an old woman'. The ballad reflects the world which was to be its own undoing:

> The Whigs, they, wi' their merry cracks,
> Gar'd the poor pedlars lay down their packs;
> But aye sinsyne they do repent
> The renewing o' their Covenant.

The Whigs and Covenanters, at least in Scott's Tory account of things, marked the beginning of the modern world's obliteration of its past; and the Last Minstrel, in Scott's first long poem, is a victim of this world:

> Old times were changed, old manners gone;
> A stranger fill'd the Stuarts' throne;
> The bigots of the iron time
> Had call'd his harmless art a crime.
> A wandering Harper, scorn'd and poor,
> He begg'd his bread from door to door,
> And tuned, to please a peasant's ear,
> The harp a king had loved to heard.

(Introduction)

There can be few more eloquent or economical descriptions of the passing of an heroic age. Covenanting times, far more than the Jacobite Rebellions, excited Scott's bitterest and most inconsistent feelings. But what makes *The Lay of the Last Minstrel* so distinctly, and indigenously, as Coleridge had it, a product of Scott's mind, is its double historical perspective. Not only the Minstrel is a repository of ancient things, despised by the present and fast vanishing away. The poem itself speaks from its own position at the beginning of the nineteenth century. Donald Davie puts it well, in a brilliant lecture on Scott's poetry, when he says that 'the distinction of the poem is precisely that its author, while not pretending to be other than he is, a man of the Regency, can nevertheless assimilate into that modern posture habits of thought and feeling from an older and very different age.'[7] The Minstrel, who tells his story to the Duchess of Buccleuch at the end of the seventeenth century in Branksome Tower, is himself observed by the sympathetic eye of his self-conscious successor, who dedicates his poem to the Duchess's descendant, the Earl of Dalkeith.

The Lay of the Last Minstrel is a very fine poem, and it made Scott's reputation. As Davie implies, its attitude to the past is something quite new, something much more subtle than any other picturesque reconstructions by that historically-minded generation of writers. A very young man could not have written it. It was published in 1802, when Scott was thirty-one: late to be embarking on a poetic career, particularly at the beginning of the nineteenth century. Yet it reflects, behind its entertaining colour and exuberance and movement, a serious and *clever* sense of the way that time and memory work. For all its similarity to *Christabel*, it represents, as Coleridge acknowledged, a new voice in poetry. Generations much richer in poetic talent and taste than our own have feasted on it; and it was a direct source, apart from other influences it may have had, for *The Eve of St. Agnes*.

For all that, it is un uneven poem, and the double time-scale is precarious. It is much better managed in *Marmion*, which was written largely at Ashiestiel, the nicest house he ever had (rented from a cousin), on the banks of the Tweed, just after taking up his duties as 'the Shirra' in Selkirkshire. The happy atmosphere of the place is reflected in the Introductions to each canto, dedicated in turn to six friends. In these epistles, love of place and family and friends is blended with his delicate sense of the past. It is as if the magic works best when he is within riding distance of his childhood haunts, and the homes of his ancestors. 'Beardie', the great-grandfather who went out in the Fifteen, and vowed never to shave until the Stuarts were restored to the throne, breathes a benign influence:

> And thus, my Christmas still I hold
> Where my great-grandsire came of old,
> With amber beard, and flaxen hair,
> And reverend apostolic air—
> The feast and holy-tide to share,
> And mix sobriety with wine,
> And honest mirth with thoughts divine:
> Small thought was his in after time,
> E'er to be hitch'd into a rime.
> The simple sire could only boast
> That he was loyal to his cost;
> The banish'd race of kings rever'd,
> And lost his land—but kept his beard.

> (Introduction to Canto VI)

Marmion has had a mixed reception, ranging from Jeffrey's famous condemnation in the *Edinburgh Review*,[8] which sees 'the whole story' turning 'upon a tissue of . . . incredible accidents', largely 'borrowed from the novels of Mrs Radcliffe and her imitators' to Ruskin's notion

that it was 'a consummate historical morality and truth', superior to
Chaucer.[9] Taste, and politics, partly account for these violently differing views; but they are also to be explained by Scott's choice of
narrative technique. By framing his story with six verse letters to his
friends, he seems to be deliberately making it harder for his reader to
concentrate on the historicity of the tale. Two voices seem to be
speaking: that of an eighteenth-century Tory rationalist, and that of a
timeless lover of romance, marvels and chivalry. The attitude to
chivalry is itself two-sided. Addressing his old friend William Rose in
the Introduction to Canto I, he laments the decline of chivalrous
values in national life, as well as in literature:

> While tyrants rul'd, and damsels wept,
> Thy Genius, Chivalry, hath slept:

And in his Essay on Chivalry, composed ten years later for the
Encyclopaedia Britannica, Scott describes the process more clearly:

As the progress of knowledge advanced, men learned to despise its fantastic
refinements; the really enlightened undervaluing them, as belonging to a
system inapplicable to the modern state of the world, the licentious, fierce and
subtle, desiring their abrogation, as throwing the barriers of affected punc-
tilio betwixt them and the safe, ready and unceremonious gratification of
their lust or their vengeance.

The system of chivalry, as we have seen, had its peculiar advantages during
the Middle Ages. Its duties were not, and indeed could not, always be
performed in perfection, but they had a strong influence on public opinion . . .
We can now only look back on it as a beautiful and fantastic piece of
frostwork, which has dissolved in the beams of the sun![10]

Yet for all his evident fondness for the trappings of chivalry, Scott's
attitude in the Essay is firmly modern; indeed, with one side of his
character, he too despises chivalry's 'fantastic refinements': 'the religion of the knights, like that of the times, was debased by superstition',
while courtly love was 'of a nature so extravagant and unbounded as
to approach a sort of idolatry', and 'the gross license which was
practised during the Middle Ages may be well estimated by the
vulgar and obscene language that was currently used in tales and
fictions addressed to the young and noble of both sexes'.

So although Scott promises Will Rose that he has a story to tell of

Honour, with his spotless shield;
Attention, with fix'd eye; and Fear,
That loves the tale she shrinks to hear;
And gentle Courtesy; and Faith,
Unchanged by sufferings, time or death;

he does not warn us that the behaviour of his protagonist will belie all
these glowing conceptions. Marmion is Scott's most outrageous hero.

His forehead, by his casque worn bare,
His thick mustache, and curly hair

(Canto I.v)

should warn us that he is a villain. But in fact, as a good-looking
Englishman, he engages our sympathies at once, and his complete
absence of morals is not viewed with any of the primness which marks
The Essay on Chivalry. In the second canto, which really does read like
Mrs Radcliffe, Marmion's discarded mistress is walled up in the
convent on Lindisfarne. Our fascination with the hero only increases,
and, although our view of his character is changed, our sympathy has
become more deeply engaged. We are in the hands of a poet who 'has
as much delight in creating a Iago as an Imogen'. The shrieks of poor
Constance die away. The great monastery bell tolls out, as for a lost
soul, echoing across the sea in a splendid passage, in which similar
thoughts to Auden's contemplating Breughel are implied:

Slow o'er the midnight wave it swung,
Northumbrian rocks in answer rung;
To Warkworth cell the echoes roll'd,
His beads the wakeful hermit told,
The Bamborough peasant rais'd his head,
But slept ere half a prayer he said;
So far was heard the mighty knell,
The stag sprung up on Cheviot Fell,
Spread his broad nostril to the wind,
Listed before, aside, behind,
Then couch'd him down beside the hind,
And quak'd among the mountain fern,
To hear that sound so dull and stern.

(Canto II.xxxiii)

The human and the natural world can only react to private calamity with ignorance and fear; the perspective of the artist is to be distinguished by its comprehensive sympathies.

Marmion has other wickedness to perform before the tale is done. Yet Ruskin thought that Scott should be considered different from Byron, 'in whose eyes mere courage with strong affections, are enough for admiration', because Marmion was 'meant only to be pitied—not honoured'.[11] This is largely true, at least in relation to early Byronic heroes such as the Giaour. For all his 'Byronic' energy, Marmion is eventually reduced, in his dying state, to a position in which the woman he has wronged can treat him as if he were as hopelessly ineffectual as Edward Waverley or Nigel Oliphaunt. Out of context, the famous lines are doubtless difficult enough to appreciate nowadays. It might be thought that the proper thing for Clare to have done in the circumstances would have been to take some revenge. But springing as they do from the deep wells of sympathy in Scott's nature, one sees how wedded his art was to his sunny, Christian pessimism. The pathetic scene is achieved without tastelessness. The affinities with Byron are nowhere more marked than in *Marmion*, yet nowhere is the difference of temper between the two poets more visible:

> O Woman! in our hours of ease,
> Uncertain, coy, and hard to please,
> And variable as the shade
> By the light quivering aspen made;
> When pain and anguish wring the brow,
> A ministering angel thou!
> Scarce were the piteous accents said,
> When, with the Baron's casque, the maid
>   To the nigh streamlet ran:
> Forgot were hatred, wrongs and fears;
> The plaintive voice alone she hears,
>   Sees but the dying man.
>
> (Canto VI.xxx)

In *Marmion* we find many of the elements which make Scott's fiction so successful: above all, a self-confident narrative technique. The plot—that of the disguised stranger, whose identity is only revealed at a fairly late stage of the story, is to become a relentlessly repeated device which we will meet in *Guy Mannering*, *Rob Roy*, *Ivanhoe*, *St. Ronan's Well* and *Redgauntlet*. So, too, the supposedly supernatural elements are treated as they will be in his novels. Apart from a few exceptions, such as *The Tapestried Chamber* and the apparitions of the White Lady in *The Monastery*, nearly all the supernatural manifestations in the novels turn out to have a rational explanation; yet we feel them to be supernatural because they have changed the lives of those who have experienced them. So, in the poem, Marmion is deceived into believing that his fight with Wilton was combat with a ghost. And he confesses that

> I have seen, since past the Tweed
> What much has chang'd my sceptic creed.

With the typical irony that these situations excite in Scott, we think the better of him for it. The meaning he attributes to the experience was more important than the experience itself.

But such clever mechanics of the plot would not in themselves make us read the poem more than once. It is the quality of the verse, now limpid, now fast, now gay, now sad, which makes us turn back to it again and again with renewed refreshment and pleasure. Scott was not merely an antiquary who doodled with verse until the whim took him to write a novel. He is one of our great narrative poets.

1808, the year of the poem, was also the year in which he finished editing Dryden, and it is in the tradition of Swift and Butler and Gower that Scott wields the octosyllabic couplet in *Marmion*. Its advantage, as in the great poems of our language in which it is used—*The Book of the Duchess*, *Confessio Amantis*, *Hudibras*—is its speed: its danger is monotony. Scott recognized this, and the monotone of the discourses to his friends is varied in the course of the narrative by other verse forms. But he shows what resources it has. There is the quiet sadness of his lament for Nelson:

> Now is the stately column broke,
> The beacon-light is quench'd in smoke,
> The trumpet's silver sound is still,
> The warder silent on the hill!

> (Introduction to Canto I)

There is the magnificence of the Scottish army arrayed for battle before Flodden, which Ruskin considered the finest description of a battle in the literature of the world. And there is the most delightful passage in the poem, the letter to William Erskine introducing Canto III, describing Scott's inspiration to poetry in the Borderlands of his infancy:

> It was a barren scene, and wild,
> Where naked cliffs were rudely pil'd;
> But ever and anon between
> Lay velvet tufts of loveliest green;

Marmion is a great entertainment: high light verse. But what makes it more than this, what justifies Ruskin's judgement of 'consummate historical truth', is Scott's highly informed and surprising temporal perspective. As in *The Lay of the Last Minstrel*, double time can seem merely quaint, as when we are told of Crichtoun Castle that

> The towers in different ages rose;
> Their various architecture shows
> The builders' various hands;

> (Canto IV.x)

This is the mindless sort of comment one would expect to hear on a guided tour of Lothian by a man who was bored with showing visitors the sights. But in other passages, when he juxtaposes specific moments in time, the double perspective works—and the oddest and most striking example, perhaps, is the passage just before the wood-man's song in Canto III. Within the narrative framework, the lyric is full of foreboding, since it turns out to be literally true that lovers will rest 'where early violets die', and that Marmion's body will be buried in an unmarked grave:

> Where shall the traitor rest,
>   He, the deceiver,
> Who could win maiden's breast,
>   Ruin, and leave her?
> In the lost battle,
>   Borne down by the flying,
> Where mingles war's rattle
>   With groans of the dying.

> (Canto III.xi)

It is one of Scott's finest lyrics. But its generalized sadness at the

separation caused by death, at our lying in our graves alone, 'with-
outen any companye', is emphasized by Scott's aside before the song
begins, in which he imagines exiles from the Forty-five, hearing the
song in America:

> And thought how sad would be such sound
> On Susquehana's swampy ground,
> Kentucky's wood-encumber'd brake
> Or wild Ontario's boundless lake,
> Where heart-sick exiles, in the strain,
> Recall'd fair Scotland's hills again.
>
> (Canto III.ix)

Here, the very arbitrary broadening of the historical perspective is
haunting, emphasizing the powerful sense, present in the best of
Scott, that history to the defeated may say Alas, but cannot help or
pardon.

As the body is laid to rest in Lichfield Cathedral at the end of the
poem, we look forward to the fate of that building at the hands of the
Parliamentarian iconoclasts in the seventeenth century. And there is
a final anti-heroic twist: the body is not Marmion's at all. An Ettrick
peasant has been carried south and buried in the tomb by mistake.

> The spoilers stripp'd and gash'd the slain,
> And thus their corpses were mista'en;
> And thus, in the proud Baron's tomb,
> The lowly woodsman took the room.
>
> (Canto VI.xxxvi)

One is reminded of death's sombre jokes; that

> in charnel at chirche. cherles ben yuel to knowe
> Or a knighte fram a knaue there   . knowe this in thin
> herte.

Hardy, too, would have liked the irony. Yet, for Hardy—despite his
obvious 'feeling for the past'—history is inescapably distant. The
Elgin marbles echoed the voice of Paul: but it is a voice the poet
cannot hear. And, at the end of his finest fantasy of past and present,
'the D'Urbeville knights and dames slept on in their tombs unknowing'. They are unknowing, of course, because the disastrous anti-

quarianism of Parson Tringham, even if accurate, was meaningless.
That old John Durbeyfield was rightfully Sir John D'Urbeville
counted for nothing. Simon Stoke, who 'had made his fortune as an
honest merchant (some said moneylender) in the North' had taken
over the name of D'Urbeville 'from a book': it had become inexorably
his. The past, for all its power to excite fantasy, is of no practical
importance to Tess's family. How different this is from anything to be
met with in Scott. The difference is partly chronological, Hardy being
born into the age of agricultural machinery and church restoration
whereas Scott was still in touch with the oral traditions of a heroic
past. But also, more profoundly, it is a national difference. For
Scotsmen of that generation, the figures of the past had an urgent,
believable, pristine reality. They were still alive. As Scott wrote in *The
Lady of the Lake*,

> Yet live there still who can remember well,
> How, when a mountain chief his bugle blew,
> Both field and forest, dingle, cliff, and dell
> And solitary heath, the signal knew;
> And fast the faithful clan around him drew,
> What time the warring note was keenly wound,
> What time aloft their kindred banner flew,
> While clamourous war-pipes yell'd the gathering sound,
> And while the Fiery Cross glanc'd, like a meteor round.
>
> (Canto III.i)

This seemed no more distant to Scott than 'the Troubles' would to an
elderly Irishman today. Scott's antiquarianism was always aware of
the latent violence in his nation's history, and in the Scotch temper.
There is a refusal in *Marmion* either to sentimentalize or prettify the
past. For all the magnificence of the Scotch army arrayed before
Flodden, and for all the heroism on both sides, we are left, not with a
fake glow of olden tymes so much as with a pathetic sense of human
lives caught up in history's meaningless events.

3

With his habitual casualness, he gave as his reason for abandoning
poetry that 'Byron beat me'. He pronounced the word *beat* in a
manner so Scotch that even Lockhart thought that he had said 'Byron

bet me'.[12] Whether wager or defeat was the cause, Byron's ascendancy meant an inevitable decline in Scott's popularity, and also in his powers as a poet. There is a closeness between the two great imaginations of the age which makes one feel them to be like two sides of the same coin.

When *The Lord of the Isles* was published in 1815, James Ballantyne, the printer, called on Scott and found him hard at work on the last volume of *Guy Mannering*. The poem was selling all right, but Scott could tell from Ballantyne's manner that something was wrong.

> 'Well, James,' he said, 'I have given you a week—what are people saying about Lord of the Isles?' I hesitated a little, after the fashion of Gil Blas, but he speedily brought the matter to a point—'Come,' he said, 'speak out, my good fellow; what has put it into your head to be on so much ceremony *with me* all of a sudden? But I see how it is, the result is given in one word—*Disappointment.*'[13]

The conversation switched to other things.

Later that week, Ballantyne noticed that Scott had on his table a copy of *The Giaour*. He picked it up, and found that it was inscribed, by the author, *To the Monarch of Parnassus, from one of his subjects*. But Scott was not deceived: 'James, Byron hits the mark, where I don't even pretend to fledge my arrow.' He lent the book to Ballantyne, and turned back to writing his second novel.

There, for lesser men, would have been the end of the matter. But Scott wrote to Byron, and when he next visited London the two poets met. In 'English Bards and Scotch Reviewers' Byron had been savage about Scott:

> Thus Lays of Minstrels—may they be the last!
> On half-strung harps whine mournful to the blast.
>
> And thinkst thou, Scott! by vain conceit perchance
> On public taste to foist thy stale romance. . . .

He had accused Scott of being one who would

> forego the poet's sacred name,
> Who rack their brains for lucre not for fame . . .
>
> And thus we spurn Apollo's venal son,
> And bid a long good-night to Marmion.

Scott had not bothered to retaliate; indeed, there is no evidence that he felt sufficiently hurt to *want* to retaliate. Byron had, after all, provided him with some wonderful advertisement by saying that Scott was the most popular poet of the age:

> While Milton, Dryden, Pope alike forgot,
> Resign their hallow'd bays to Walter Scott.

It is noticeable, of course, that Byron's choice of great poets would be precisely Scott's own, though Scott would have added Swift to the catalogue—as would Byron, had scansion allowed. Byron's very abuse showed him to be in the same camp as Scott himself. Besides, Scott did not believe in replying to public criticisms, more than once advising Maturin, for instance, against it. He bore no grudge against Byron, and quickly came to see him as a kindred spirit. For all his sense of the proprieties, he never entered into the chorus of condemnation of Byron's private life, and his letters contain a number of refusals to gossip about it. When Byron died, Scott wrote in the *Edinburgh Weekly Journal* that 'we feel almost as if the great luminary of Heaven had suddenly disappeared from the sky'. Nor was that the end of the matter, as J. L. Adolphus discovered; for when he visited Abbotsford after Byron's death, Scott pointed out the spot in the hall where 'the deception of sight' made him 'imagine the figure of Lord Byron' standing there.

What had happened between 1809, when Byron accused Scott of being 'Apollo's venal son', and 1813, when he saluted him as 'The Monarch of Parnassus'? The simplest answer is that, in 1812, Byron had published the first two cantos of *Childe Harold's Pilgrimage*, and had suddenly learnt what it was like to be a popular bestseller. As Scott wrote on another occasion, 'At last *Die wolken laufen zusammen*.'[14] What is so striking about the friendship is that once Byron's debt to Scott had been recognized, they came to live in each other's work. Byron outgrew the self that had produced *The Giaour* (in imitation of Scott's early manner), and he became addicted to Scott's novels. He knew many passages of them by heart, and Charles Mackay, in his account of Byron's last voyage, says that 'he never travelled without copies of them, and *Quentin Durward* was one of the last books he read.'[15] Scott, on the other hand, once the great luminary had appeared in the sky, not infrequently took to rumbustious pastiche of Byron in lighter mood. His verse letter from Orkney to the Duke of Buccleuch describes the northern boatmen in pursuit of the whale. His original fancy is too mild for Byron, and closer to Moore:

> Had your order related to nightcaps or hose,
> Or mittens of worsted, there's plenty of those.
> Or would you be pleased but to fancy a whale?
> And direct me to send it—by sea or by mail?
> The season, I'm told, is nigh over, but still
> I could get you one fit for the lake at Bowhill.

But his travelling companion has no wish to witness the whale hunt, and insists on pressing on for port. There can be no doubt about the Byronic tone of what follows:

> To see this huge marvel full fain would we go,
> But Wilson, the wind, and the current, said no.
> We have not got to Kirkwall, and needs I must stare
> When I think that in verse I have once call'd it *fair*;
> 'Tis a base little borough, both dirty and mean.
> There is nothing to hear, and there's nought to be seen,
> Save a church, where, of old times, a prelate harangued,
> And a palace that's built by an earl that was hang'd.

In fact, this was written before *The Lord of the Isles*, but it reads as though Scott was saying farewell to his early manner. He loved the story of Byron and Moore in Venice: 'While they stood at the window of Byron's palazzo . . . looking at a beautiful sunset, Moore was naturally led to say something of its beauty when Byron answered in a tone that I can easily conceive, "Oh come, d— me, Tom, don't be poetical."'[16]

Scott, of course, could not always help being 'poetical', but, as the editor of Swift and Dryden, he recognized its absurdity. This was not to say that he meant his poetry to receive no serious attention, but was based, rather, on his conviction, expressed in a letter to Miss Seward, that 'the immortality of poetry is not so firm a point of my creed as the immortality of the soul.'

Visitors to Abbotsford frequently wanted to 'view fair Melrose' and were always surprised that the author of *The Lay of the Last Minstrel* had never taken his own counsel or seen it by the pale moonlight.

In calling back the sins of my youth I was surprised into confessing, what I might as well have kept to myself, that I had been guilty of sending persons a bat-hunting to see the ruins of Melrose by moonlight, which I never saw myself. The fact is rather curious, for as I often slept nights at Melrose (when I did not reside so near the place) it is singular that I had not seen it by moonlight on some chance occasion. However, it so happens that I never did, and must (unless I get cold by going on purpose) be contented with supposing that these ruins look very like other Gothick buildings which I have seen by the wan light of the moon.[17]

This shows the novelist's touch more than the Romantic poet's. It would deeply matter, somehow, had Wordsworth disclosed in a throwaway line, that he had never been near Tintern Abbey. But there are ways and ways of perceiving the truth. Henry James once said that a young woman could compose a whole novel about army life having done no more than pause by the door of an officers' mess.

4

Scott carried over the use of verse into his career as a novelist. He describes his first essay in fiction in the preface to *Waverley*. In the year 1807–8 (the year in which, on top of his professional duties, he edited Dryden, saw *Marmion* through the press and, having severed his connections with the *Edinburgh Review*, began to get involved with the *Quarterly*) Scott was approached by John Murray, Byron's publisher, with a literary project. He was asked 'to arrange for publication some posthumous productions of the late Mr Joseph Strutt, distinguished as an artist and as an antiquary, amongst which was an unfinished romance entitled "Queenhoo Hall".'[18]

Strutt deserves mention in any survey of historical fiction as the first antiquary of the eighteenth century to fully appreciate that the clothes people wore in the past were different from those worn in his own day: the first step towards Scott's realistic reconstructions of past ages. Strutt was a patient scholar, quite a learned philologist (he knew Anglo-Saxon, a fairly unusual accomplishment at that date) and a very skilled line engraver.

It is astonishing, nevertheless, that Scott consented to take on this thankless labour, given how much he had on hand already. Nothing illustrates his generosity of temper more clearly than his description of Strutt as a 'distinguished artist', unless he was thinking of the plates which illustrate his exquisite *Manners of the English*.[19] *Queenhoo Hall* is sad stuff. One gets a fairly strong taste early on when

The baron's fair daughter turning to the chamberlain, who stood behind her, said with a smile, 'I thought our May-games were concluded.'

'By our holy dam, my lady,' said Oswald, bowing. 'I weened they were: but I trow the varlets have contrived some new knackeries. . . .'

and so on.

Those who have a harsh opinion of Scott's medieval fiction should take a look at some of the drivel that preceded it. Yet, cruelly, *Queenhoo Hall* reads at times like a terribly bad parody of Scott's feebler work. A strange knight turns up at the jousting, on his surcoat the device of a heart transfixed with an arrow, surrounded with the motto *'True to Her I Love'*. Another stranger is introduced—a damsel in distress who faints away when she sees the armour of the anonymous champion, claiming that he is 'Darcy's murderer'. Darcy turns out to have been her brother, and it takes three volumes to sort out their identities. In fact, Darcy is still alive, and, like innumerable Scott heroes, is coming back to reclaim his rightful heritage from a villainous crook called Gaston St. Clere. Everything is cleared up when he explains to the company that he, not Gaston, is the rightful heir to Gay Bowers: 'The cause respecting our mother's jointure is upon the eve of determination; and your presence, my dear Emma, will be of much service. This, as well as those that preceded it, my counsel assures me cannot fail of being decided in our favour.'

Darcy, it will be noted, speaks exactly like an eighteenth-century gentleman. It is left to the minor characters to converse in the peculiar olde tyme diction that Strutt thought appropriate for men and women of the reign of Henry VI.

The whole novel is written from a self-consciously 'modern' point of view. There is a rationalistic explanation, for example, of how the 'weird woman' (Vol. I, Sect. iv. Ch. 1) became a witch: 'She was the daughter of a gentleman of fortune, who resided at Waltham Holy Cross. Nature had been exceedingly unkind to her, for she was very ill-featured, and deformed from her birth.' Rather as with the Black Dwarf, there is in fact nothing 'supernatural' about her; and her background interestingly matches that of Blind Alice in *The Bride of Lammermoor*. She is unlike the Black Dwarf or Blind Alice in that Scott

makes us feel not only that they might, after all, be in touch with
something we do not understand; but, more importantly, we see why
the characters in the book are afraid of them. But Strutt's witch has a
wholly improbable pedigree. Brought up by a Voltairean, faithless
father, she falls into a number of matrimonial misadventures. Without the consolations of hope in the benignity of the Supreme Gover-
nor, she loses all her money, and retreats far from human habitations:

in order to impress the minds of those who waited upon her with stronger
notions of her sagacity, she procured two or three mutilated old manuscripts—of a large size, and filled the margins with various characters,
perfectly unintelligible, and as uncouth as any of those which the reader may
find abounding in the four books of Occult Philosophy, by the celebrated
necromancer Henry Cornelius Agrippa; and as all old witches are supposed
to have a great partiality for cats (which, by the bye, the learned have asserted
are not real grimalkins, but familiar sights) Dame Sad kept several, and
among them three remarkably large ones, as black as a sloe. . . .

It is not a very convincing picture of how anyone would become a
witch in the fifteenth, or any other, century. Worse, though, is the
constant presence of the tedious old antiquary Strutt himself, as
comical a figure as Monkbarns or Jedediah Cleishbotham, but not
consciously so. Scott probably loved him, but he had the sense, when
letting his own antiquarian passions run riot all over the page, to put
his reflections into the mouths of those who might believably be
expected to say such things. And there is nearly always some figure in
the dialogue who can staunch the flow with a 'Lat be thin olde
ensaumples, I thee preye!'

But how was Scott to finish off *Queenhoo Hall*? The sad story of
Darcy and Gaston St. Clere had been more or less concluded; there
could be no doubt that all the right young people would be paired off,
or that the villain would get his just reward. Alas, there had also been
a disastrously overloaded comic sub-plot, too tedious to catalogue,
concerning Gregory the Jester, Ralph the Tasker and Robin Toss-
pot. Scott picks up his pen:

The next morning the bugles were sounded by day-break in the court of Lord
Boteler's mansion to call the inhabitants from their slumbers, to assist in a
splendid chase.

It is hard not to feel a sense of wonder at Scott's first published sentence of prose fiction. What wells of light, and movement, and of sheer *goodness* are one day to be tapped! Scribbling this task for Murray at his writing-table in Ashiestiel, Scott cannot have known the gift he was about to bestow on the world, or what ruinous consequences it would have in his own life. Indeed, when a little later he started to doodle with *Waverley*, he lost the manuscript and only found it among some fishing-tackle in the attic when he was about to move house.

There was no way in which *Queenhoo Hall* could be transformed into a great novel, but Scott's conclusion does introduce an element of life and motion into the story which it had almost entirely lacked until this point. Strutt's way of telling an exciting story, when he had one to tell, was to have characters sitting about recounting their adventures in digressions which take up whole volumes. In Scott's continuation, we see them in action. The plot is given a new twist; it is rather too late in the day for it to be entirely acceptable, but it holds our attention. Henry and Emma are set upon during the hunt; Henry is left for dead and Emma wounded. The wicked Gaston has been up to his tricks again, but he is eventually foiled, captured, and imprisoned, and hangs himself in his cell. The comic sub-plot is wound up, characteristically, by stock Shakespearean devices. Gregory the Jester, who has fled at the hour of danger, exposes his cowardice by boasting of his courage, in the manner of Parolles to Bertram, or Falstaff after the Gadshill escapade. Gregory, incidentally, becomes a much better jester under Scott's pen. This is doubtless partly because Scott uses authentic jokes. There is a splendid mock sermon, with a typically Scott footnote: 'This tirade of gibberish is literally taken or selected from a mock discourse pronounced by a professed Jester in an ancient manuscript in the Advocate's Library.'

The whole book is wound up hastily, carelessly, and with almost outrageous untidiness:

Here the manuscript, from which we have painfully transcribed, and frequently, as it were, translated this tale, for the reader's edification, is so indistinct and defaced, that, excepting certain howbeits, nathlesses, lo ye's etc., we can pick out little that is intelligible.

Scott marries off the major characters, and brings the story to an end.

One obvious feature of the continuation of *Queenhoo Hall* is the way in which Scott conveys a change of mood, even a change of action, by

the use of verse. Once the vigorous idea of the hunt has been introduced, Scott follows up with the famous hunting song, which sounds,
bright and clear as the bugle of the opening sentence, to awaken the
slumber of any reader who has managed to struggle through three-
and-a-half volumes of Strutt's turgid prose:

> Waken, lords and ladies gay,
> The mist has left the mountain grey,
> Springlets in the dawn are steaming,
> Diamonds on the brake are gleaming:
> And foresters have busy been
> To track the buck in thicket green;
> Now we come to chant our lay,
> 'Waken lords and ladies gay.'
>
> Waken lords and ladies gay,
> To the greenwood haste away. . . .

The use of song to indicate, in a compressed or oblique form, the
content of the story which the straight narrative cannot fully reveal
was something which Scott learnt to develop while composing his
great narrative poems.

We see this powerfully at work in *The Lady of the Lake*, Scott's third
great poem, although the double time scale used in *The Lay of the Last
Minstrel* and *Marmion* does not always succeed. The anonymous
hunter sees magnificent Highland scenery of the kind which inspired
Shelley to write 'Mont Blanc':

> mountains, that like giants stand,
> To sentinel enchanted land.
> High on the south, huge Benvenue
> Down to the lake in masses threw
> Crags, knolls, and mounds, confusedly hurl'd,
> The fragments of an earlier world;

(Canto I.xiv)

But the thoughts which this sixteenth-century wanderer—James V
incognito—has about the scenes he encounters are more fitted to a
Regency tourist. The mountain-tops and clouds seem to remind him
of the Brighton pavilion:

> The rocky summits, split and rent,
> Form'd turret, dome, or battlement,

> Or seem'd fantastically set
> With cupola or minaret,
> Wild crests as pagod ever deck'd
> Or mosque of Eastern architect.

(Canto I.xi)

And not content to admire their solitary splendour, he thinks how much more impressive they would be if they were populated by figures from the romances of Horace Walpole or Matt Lewis:

> And, 'What a scene were here,' he cried,
> For princely pomp or churchman's pride!
> On this bold brow, a lordly tower;
> In that soft vale, a lady's bower;
> On yonder meadow, far away,
> The turrets of a cloister grey;

(Canto I.xv)

One can almost see the architecture of Balmoral springing up before one's eyes.

The final absurdity occurs when he arrives in sight of the Lady of the Lake's house:

> Due westward, fronting to the green
> A rural portico was seen,

(Canto I.xxvi)

Byron records in his journal on 18 September 1816, 'I remember at Chamouni, in the very eyes of Mont Blanc, hearing a . . . woman exclaim to her party, "Did you ever see anything more *rural*?" "*Rural!*" quotha!—Rocks, pines, torrents, Glaciers, Clouds, and Summits of eternal snow far above them and—"*Rural!*" '[20]

No doubt the tourist—whom Byron admits was 'a very good kind of woman'—had enjoyed *The Lady of the Lake* when it appeared eight years earlier. Scott's descriptions of landscape are unashamedly those of a tourist, and of a patriot who wants to encourage southern visitors to admire the beauty of the Highlands for themselves. Wordsworth might conceivably have gone to see the Highlands had it not been for Scott; Keats, never. Scott was delighted and amused when he heard that local innkeepers were cashing in by showing scenes from *The Lady*

of the Lake to tourists from London. He had none of the Romantic
desire to hug experience to himself and then show off about it.

Nevertheless, in *The Lady of the Lake* Scott's attitudes to the landscape are a little odd. In his fiction, he can get round some of these
difficulties more easily:

> The scene could neither be strictly termed sublime nor beautiful and
> scarcely even picturesque or striking. But its extreme solitude pressed on the
> heart; the traveller felt that uncertainty whither he was going, or in what so
> wild a path was to terminate which, at times, strikes more on the imagination
> than the grand features of a show scene, when you know the exact distance of
> the inn where your dinner is bespoke and at the moment preparing. These are
> ideas, however, of a far later age, for at the time we treat of, the picturesque,
> the beautiful, the sublime, and all their intermediate shades, were ideas
> absolutely unknown to the inhabitants and occasional visitors to Glendearg.

(The Monastery, Chapter V)

The distance of the narrative voice in prose is sufficiently variable to
enable Scott to get away with these transitions. He wants us to enjoy
the solitude of Glendearg, even though he knows that his characters—in *The Monastery*, as in *The Lady of the Lake*, from the early
sixteenth century—are unable to appreciate 'nature' in the modern
way. If one does not examine it too scrupulously, the *effect* of *The Lady
of the Lake* is exactly the same; only when one pauses to analyse it does
the discrepancy disturb. With Gower and Dryden, Scott shares the
narrative poet's most necessary gift of speeding over technical
difficulties. When we read the poem continuously, with one half of our
minds we follow the fortunes of the lonely traveller, while with the
other we simply long to pack our bags and be in the Highlands.

Yet, as the careful distinctions in that passage from *The Monastery*
show, Scott was aware of the jarring tones this double perspective
could produce. He resolves it by a complete change of tone, introduced by the element of song. James V has no sooner crossed the rural
portico than Ellen has welcomed him. Questions of anachronism are
resolved in the timeless, inexplicably poignant quality of her lyric:

> 'Soldier rest! thy warfare o'er,
>   Sleep the sleep that knows not breaking;
> Dream of battled fields no more,
>   Days of danger, nights of waking.
> In our isle's enchanted hall,

> Hands unseen thy couch are strewing,
> Fairy strains of music fall,
> Every sense in slumber dewing.

(Canto I.xxxi)

The Lady of the Lake is the last long poem in which Scott's narrative gifts seem fully engaged; but it is a flowering of his lyric genius. The use of lyrics was, in future, greatly to enrich his prose manner; in particular, he was able, as with Madge Wildfire's famous song in *Heart of Midlothian*, to change the tone and mood of a passage, describing movements of the inner life of his characters which his prose was too diffident or energetic, or simply too rational, to describe. It may be thought a deficiency that Scott, who so hated displays of emotion in life, was often unable to describe them fully even in art. Yet there is a sort of realism about this. Very often we cannot admit that we are feeling religious, or in love, or patriotic, even to ourselves; the irrational powers of song can express feelings too deep for utterance. In this category too must be placed Lucy Ashton's song in *The Bride of Lammermoor*, which hints so fully at the combination of submissiveness and high passion in her nature, and the exquisite lyrics of the White Lady in *The Monastery*, which draw back the rather detached Augustan mind that is describing the religious changes of the sixteenth century into the heart and nature of religious experience. The lyrics in the novels are much more than props for his fiction. They are among the best things he wrote.

CHAPTER THREE

The Man of Action
Waverley and *Rob Roy*

The privilege of free action belongs to no mortal.

Redgauntlet

'But I hae dream'd a dreary dream
Beyond the Isle of Sky;
I saw a dead man win a fight,
And I think that man was I.'

'The Battle of Otterbourne'

In 1815, Scott was forty-four. Like many others, he took the first opportunity of visiting the Continent after the defeat of Napoleon. He visited Waterloo, wrote his worst poem on the subject, and arrived in Paris in time to witness the magnificent Season which took place that year around what was, in effect, the Duke of Wellington's court. Scott went everywhere and met everyone. He was invited to dine at the British Embassy, and it was there that he met the Tsar.

For the occasion Scott wore the blue and red uniform of the Edinburgh Light Horse, an equestrian Home Guard which he and his friends had started during an invasion threat in 1797. He never saw action, except to do riot duty. He helped to take a few shots at some rebellious miners at Cross Causeway, and threatened some mill workers with the sabre at Moredun Mill.

When Scott was presented to the Tsar, Nicholas I noticed his limp and asked him, in French, during which engagement he had been wounded.

It was potentially a highly embarrassing moment. Byron, in similar circumstances, would no doubt have been mortified. But Scott merely tried to reply, in his appalling French, that it was a natural impediment. He failed to make himself understood, and the Emperor persisted. Where had he been wounded? Seeing that he would not be satisfied until supplied with an answer, Scott replied, with complete gravity, that he had been 'engaged . . . in some slight actions . . . the battle of Cross Causeway and the affair of Moredun Mill'.

The whole episode is characteristic. Why was Scott wearing uniform at all? Because he loved it. Like Kipling in this respect, he was a man of action *manqué*. He had thrown himself into the role of cavalryman with almost passionate enthusiasm, rather to the embarrassment of his fellows. Many of them complained that he had entered into it all a little too zealously. He even referred to his family, at this stage, as 'infantry', and all the details of his domestic life were transposed into military metaphor. At the same time, of course, he would not really have been fit for active service, even had the Edinburgh Light Horse been called upon to see it. He was made quartermaster, and nicknamed 'Earl Walter'. As he charged about on an old horse, giving orders to Skene, the Duke of Buccleuch and others, his actual function was to supervise the stores. It was while so engaged on the sands of Musselburgh in 1807 that he had conceived of the battle scenes in *Marmion*.

Yet, the element of pure fantasy and self-dramatization in all this was perfectly good-humoured. He knew perfectly well that he was not a soldier, even though he admitted to Southey years later, when his elder son Walter got his first commission, that this choice of career 'would have been my own had lameness permitted'.[1] He wrote in similar vein to his mother: 'Walter pronounces so anxiously for the army that I shall not cross him, for although it is not the line I would have *wished* him to have chosen, yet it is that which, but for circumstances, I would have preferred myself.'[2]

His son must often have had cause to regret his choice of career, even though he did quite well for himself, rising to the rank of lieutenant-colonel, for it set off in Scott an almost manic vicarious interest in his military career. Scott used to bombard him with information about how a young officer in the 18th Hussars should conduct himself:

I beg you to mind your handwriting a little as it gets worse and worse, like the pigs as they grow up, and remember what I have been so often telling you about languages. Assuredly to have French and German at your finger-ends is of great consequence in your profession; as also the use of the pencil in habitually sketching from nature, and accustoming yourself to observe the surface of the ground, and the advantages which it offers for military operation . . . Next to a good stout heart and a sound judgement, a good *eye* is of the greatest consequence for an officer of light troops, and that it can only be acquired by practice.[3]

The Duke of Wellington scarcely wrote more confidently about the military life than did Scott when contemplating the hussar he had sired. 'It is upon discipline . . . that the utility of an army must always depend, and there was never more reason for keeping officers in mind of their duty than at present, when the troops of other countries are setting the example of mutiny. . . .'[4] The advice poured out. In the event, Scott, though an affectionate father to all his children, was disappointed in Walter: he grew into the puppyish young hussar that his father had been pressing him to become for years, and Sir Walter did not like what he had made. Hogg tells us, quite plausibly, that Scott used to mock his son's dandified ways, and make allusions to his false moustachioes.[5] Certainly if the portrait which dominates the library at Abbotsford is anything to go by, Colonel Scott, the second baronet, looked quite ridiculous.

It is not entirely true, though, to describe Scott's military fantasy-life as purely vicarious as he sank into middle age. The French had been beaten—partly thanks, no doubt, to 'Earl Walter' and the Edinburgh Light Horse—but the enemy, in the form of radicals, artisans, mobs, and revolutionaries, was still at the gate. In December 1819, Scott wrote to Morritt,

They have in Glasgow about three thousand steady Volunteers to keep ten times the number of radicals in order, and the Volunteer regiment here are designed to garrison the castle, as it is momently expected that all the military may be sent to the west. Meanwhile, the Loyalists are arming fast. The Edinburgh regiment is getting strong and is very efficient, and they are raising sharp-shooters and cavalry. A fine troop of the latter, all handsome youths and well-mounted, made me wish myself twenty years younger, that I might join them again.[6]

A month later, he was writing to Lady Abercorn,

In consequence of the bad disposition upon the English frontier, we have determined to levy men, and, as in the circumstances of my family distress, I could not attend myself, I ordered my Piper to play our Gathering through the neighbouring hamlets, and I had within twenty-four hours the offer of a hundred as handsome young fellows as are to be seen anywhere, and I assure you I was not a little flattered by their personal attachment to myself. We propose that they should wear green jackets and trousers, with their own grey plaids, which they wear very gracefully, and the Scottish blue bonnet.[7]

It is a striking response to a national emergency. It makes one feel that the Tsar's question was a good one, perhaps a good one to ask of any novelist: where had he been wounded? For it is usually from wounds, rather than from whole parts of the imagination, that fictions grow. Although Scott suffered more illness in his life than most people, his novels are not those of a diseased imagination: indeed, there is no great writer who is more obviously wholesome. Yet if one considers his life, the most obvious area of real damage was in his financial affairs. His natural recklessness with money should have made him avoid involvement with business enterprises altogether. But since, as he once wrote, 'trade has all the fascination of gambling without its moral guilt',[8] he would probably have been drawn to it even if he had not been to school for a while in Kelso and formed a lifelong friendship with the Ballantyne brothers, James and John.

In 1802, Scott had provided James Ballantyne with some capital to set up as a printer in Edinburgh, and by 1805 had bought a third share in the firm. It was the greatest mistake of his life. In time they joined forces with Constable, the brilliant, grandiose, self-made publisher of the *Edinburgh Review*. They brought out Scott's editions of Dryden and Swift, his *Lives of the Novelists*, and other money-spinners. All these business connections, for a number of reasons both professional and private, Scott kept secret. He was young (thirty-one in 1802); he had a wife and a growing family; he wanted to establish himself. The income from the printing firm seemed at this stage of life a welcome source of money. Unfortunately, neither Scott, nor the Ballantynes, nor Constable, had sufficient acumen to run a business, still less to run one on the huge scale that soon became necessary. There is nothing more disastrous for those who are incapable of handling money than to be given plenty of it. *The Lay of the Last Minstrel* was an instant best-seller; and in 1810 *The Lady of the Lake* made them a fortune. From then on, the firm was always in financial difficulties of one sort or another; sometimes minor, increasingly, major. None of the partners were sufficiently aware of what was going on to be able to predict the final collapse, which came about after a general crisis on the stock market at the end of 1825. But there were many minor disaster before then.

An expanding business needs increased production, and this was Scott's special contribution to the partnership. That ceaseless pen which Lockhart and his friends observed in 1814 was the firm's most precious asset. In 1810 *The Lady of the Lake* rescued them from near ruin, and it was in that year that they promised to the public an

anonymous novel called *Waverley: or, Tis Sixty Years Since*. Only a little
of it can have been written. James Ballantyne liked it as far as it went;
but although he thought it 'spirited', he thought it too carelessly
written to be worth promoting. With typical publisher's percipience,
he saw that there was no future in such a book. Scott put it away in a
trunk, where it lay in his attic at Ashiestiel for the next three years. He
forgot all about it, and only discovered it when searching for some
fishing-tackle and sorting through his things before the move to
Clarty Hole, the farm which he renamed Abbotsford.

   By 1814, the firm was in worse trouble than ever, and the partners,
if not actually quarrelling, were in a state of tension. '*Don Roderick*
helped to damn him—& the failure of *Rokeby* completed it,' Constable
complained of Scott.[9] The public were no longer rushing to buy
Scott's latest poems. The magic had vanished from them. Byron had
appeared on the scene.

   It was at this stage that Scott came across his old manuscript,
scarcely begun and quite forgotten, and resurrected the romance of
Waverley. He finished the second and third volumes in three weeks. It
was rushed through the press on 7 July, and published anonymously.
It was not a good time of the year for selling books, but it was only two
days before the small first edition of a thousand copies had sold out. It
was the first best-selling novel in the modern sense of the word. By the
end of the year it had gone through four impressions.

   As Scott went about his work as a Clerk to the Court of Sessions in
Edinburgh, he must have heard much to satisfy him during the
second half of 1814. Even though his business interests were secret,
people must have noticed that he was becoming a man of substance.
And he must often have heard enthusiastic talk of his novel, which
was ascribed to various hands and, that most enviable combination,
was universally acclaimed as a work of genius which everyone wanted
to read and to buy. It tells us a lot about the citizens of Edinburgh at
that date. To look at their houses, their carefully planned gardens and
streets, their University, and their clubs, you would think that they
were all reading Cicero, Johnson's *London*, or Addison. But behind
those austere classical facades the lamps burned far into the night
while they read of the adventures of that ineffectual young man,
Edward Waverley, an officer in the Hanoverian army, sent north to
help check the Jacobite rising of Forty-five. They read of his
encounter with Baron Bradwardine, that Jacobite eccentric on the
edge of the Highlands; then, before many pages were past, with the

desperate zealot Fergus MacIvor, and his beautiful sister Flora; and, at length, with the Chevalier himself. Scott's early readers were gazing on something new. *Waverley* was an adventure story and a romance; but a romance peopled not with the half-real oddities of Mrs Radcliffe's fiction, but with real people, whose accent and appearance and substance rivalled the characters in Shakespeare. No wonder that the citizens of Edinburgh read on, their minds swimming not with the carefully measured sentences of Augustan prose, but with swirling, intense descriptions of Highland scenery, the haunt of wild clansmen and the scene of heroism as rugged as that of Homer. For them the story must have had unique appeal. In Edward Waverley's defection to the Jacobite side they must have joyfully relived their own secret prejudices; in his return to an acceptance of the Hanoverian dynasty, they could safely enjoy a spiritual compromise which was their own. But it was not a uniquely Scotch pleasure. The citizens of London were lapping it up also.

For forty years, Scott had been meditating on his theme. As a boy and as a young man, he had met men and women with memories of the Jacobite risings. As we have already noticed, his mind was a magnificent hybrid; rooted in all moral aspects in the universe of Hume, yet emotionally belonging to the feuds and poetry of the Heroic Age. 1745 was the year in which the Heroic Age came to an end. Scott had an acute and highly intelligent sense of the way in which, perhaps uniquely at that moment in history, quite different aeons momentarily touch one another. Sometimes the result is comic, as when Baron Bradwardine tries to perform the ancient ceremonial of removing the Chevalier's boot; sometimes tragic, as at Preston Pans. Yet, even more subtly, Scott can show us encounters between people who effectually inhabit different eras of history, in which nothing *happens*. Writer and reader share the *frisson* of a moment of which the actual participants in the scene are unaware.

A good example of this occurs during the very brief interlude when Edward Waverley is being delivered by Major Melville into the hands of the Hanoverian authorities. He is soon to be intercepted by his new-found Highland friends and taken to safety in the castle of Doune. His guard on the march is a man called Gifted Gilfillan.

Gifted Gilfillan's character is so fully realized, and comes before us so strongly, that it almost obscures the point of the narrative, providing something in the order of an epic digression. Like the digressions in *Beowulf*, it elaborates the complexities of the hero's position in history, showing us how time, moving on from feud to feud, places those characters who merely stay the same in strange positions. The seventeeth-century past has already been evoked by Flora MacIvor's song, comparing Waverley to Captain Wogan, who changed sides to the royalists after the execution of Charles I; and in Gilfillan, we hear an echo of Covenanting times. Yet he is initially represented as a more nebulous figure from *the past*, before it is specified from which period he might have accidentally drifted:

> The spiritual pride which in mine Host of the Candlestick mantled in a sort of supercilious hypocrisy, was in this man's face elevated and yet darkened by genuine and undoubting fanaticism. It was impossible to behold him without imagination placing him in some strange crisis, where religious zeal was the ruling principle. A martyr at the stake, a soldier in the field, a lonely and banished wanderer consoled by the intensity and supposed purity of his faith under every earthly privation; perhaps a prosecuting inquisitor, as terrific in power as unyielding in adversity; any of these seemed congenial characters to this personage.

> (Chapter XXXV)

The Chaucerian fullness of character which emerges in the next few pages reinforces these complex and ironical reflections. Though so distinctively himself, he is a 'type' who crops up frequently in Scott's pages. His fanaticism is analogous to that of Douce Davie Deans, which, in 1736, produced a religious recluse; to that of the Templar Knight, which brought with it power in the reign of Richard I; to the Covenanting 'martyrs' in *Old Mortality*, now on the verge of possessing power, now driven into the hills to re-emerge as 'establishment' figures in the times of William III.

Much of this Covenanting episode in *Waverley*—involving a blacksmith called Mucklewrath, a moderate Presbyterian called Morton, the ludicrous yet moving rant of Gilfillan—seems to anticipate the themes of *Old Mortality*. And, anyway, Scott could never resist Covenanters. Despite having very different religious sensibilities himself, he longed to have a Cameronian minister as his domestic chaplain at Abbotsford. And for that reason, Gilfillan crops up in *Waverley*, as startling a reminder of the past as a ruin in an Anglo-Saxon poem, that seems like the work of giants: 'While I live, I am and will be called Habbakuk Gilfillan, who will stand up for the standards of doctrine agreed on by the ance-famous Kirk of Scotland before she trafficked with the accursed Achan, while he has a plack in his purse, or a drap o' bluid in his body.' Of course, in all fundamental ways, Scott is not on Gilfillan's 'side'. Apart from anything else, the aged fanatic does not like dogs. When the pedlar stops and begins to whistle for his animal, Gilfillan

> signified gruffly, that he could not waste his time in waiting for a useless cur.
> 'But if your honour would consider the case of Tobit—'
> 'Tobit!' exclaimed Gilfillan with great heat. 'Tobit and his dog baith are altogether heathenish and apocryphal, and none but the prelatist or a papist would draw them into question. I doubt I hae been mistaken in you, friend.'

> (Chapter XXXVI)

He has: for when the pedlar whistles again, six or eight stout High-landmen emerge from the undergrowth waving claymores, and carry off Waverley to the comparative safety of the Castle of Doune.

It is on a superficial level, as much as an atavistic one, that we 'take sides' over historical questions. Few issues in the past have more romantic appeal than the Jacobite rebellion. Scott's treatment of the theme has, of course, determined everything that has been said since, in prose or rhyme, about the affair of Forty-five. But even attempts at the heroic manner which might have been delightful enough in child-hood—D. K. Broster's books, for instance—betray a desire to take sides in a way which distorts their vision and which, in a curious way, Scott lacks. Consider the figure of Cameron of Lochiel. He seems to be asking to be put into an historical romance, following his prince though his reason sits in the wind against him. But for Scott he is merely a figure on the edge of the canvas, an echo reminding us of the size of the heroic sacrifice which far less worthy men could accomplish later at Carlisle. What Scott discovers (in both senses of the word) in his novels is that if we respect the past, it is impossible to take sides. Time changes sides, as we see in the fortunes of the Covenanters; the issues of the present are determined by the past. As he grew older, however, we find that Scott developed an increasing sense, correct surely, that the nineteenth century was horrible in quite unique ways. The old adversaries of the past were infinitely closer to each other than they were to the modern world.

Pervaded with these thoughts about the workings of time, *Waverley* achieves its great power over the mind, however, by its unerring, epic sense of adventure. It is necessary in an adventure story to be able to identify with the hero, though how we do so will differ. That is why although *Treasure Island* never fails to be terrifyingly exciting (and, perhaps, the best *constructed* novel in the language) it loses something as soon as we reach the age when we can no longer imagine that Jim Hawkins was really capable of swimming across the bay, dragging the *Hispaniola* behind him. The hero in old literature is attractive because he differs from us. Breca's swimming-match with Beowulf is impressive because we could not have done it; Jim Hawkins's swimming feat is impressive because (if we are caught at the right age) we believe that we could.

In spite of the distressing spread of childish 'adult fantasy', few modern readers, even today, go on seriously expecting to identify with Biggles or Boy Wonder in—to echo Virginia Woolf's portentous phrase—books designed for grown-up persons.[10]

Does this mean that we have lost the ability to appreciate *heroic* literature? In many individual cases, it probably does. For every undergraduate who is inexpressibly moved by the great speeches at Maldon, there are twenty who find it at best foolish bombast, at worst a sinister idolatry, a cult of violence. *The Battle of Maldon* and *Waverley* have this in common: in the final resort, on the field of battle, you become what you are by a recognition of who you are. Waverley's self-condemnation on the field of Preston Pans, the feelings of guilt and treachery which sweep over him as a result of being caught up in the victorious rebellion is the sort of moment we find in Malory. Rather as Malory's knights stave off chaos and ignominy recollecting the high honour of belonging to the Round Table, and the men at Maldon are inspired by the memory of their families, at Preston Pans the opposing armies come so close that

Waverley could plainly recognize the standard of the troop he had formerly commanded, and hear the trumpets and kettle-drums sound the signal of advance, which he had so often obeyed. He could hear, too, the well-known word given in the English dialect, by the equally well-distinguished voice of the commanding officer, for whom he had once felt so much respect. It was at that instant, that, looking around him, he saw the wild dress and appearance of his Highland associates, heard their whispers in an uncouth and unknown language, looked upon his own dress, so unlike that which he had worn from his infancy, and wished to awake from what seemed at that moment a dream, strange, horrible and unnatural. 'Good God!' he muttered, 'am I then a traitor to my country, a renegade to my standard and a foe . . . to my native England?'

(Chapter XLVI)

Waverley experiences the Maldon-style tug of national loyalty *after* he has admired all the virtues, actually joined the ranks, of the enemy. It is the kind of morally complex trap which so frequently ensnares the hero of Scott's novels. This feeling is intensified when Waverley is obliged to supervise an English prisoner, Colonel Talbot, who turns out to be an old friend of his father's.

This fundamentally heroic position is placed in very nice tension by Scott. Edward Waverley is an effective hero precisely because it is necessary that we should identify with him; he is more or less neutral in every sense of the word. Why so many of the Scott heroes have this passive, dithering quality—whether they conform to some Tory notion of obedience to be met in the pages of Burke[11]—can perhaps never be established with certainty. But in the case of Edward Waverley, it has two magical effects. He is obviously not of the present day; he is living 'sixty years since'. But by being so colourless and feeble, he acts as a carrier of our own exploration into his adventures. He does not fall in love with Flora so much as we do. When he dresses up in the tartan, we do so too; we have got out the fancy-dress box and are going to enjoy ourselves. There is nothing wrong with this, and one scarcely ever reads Scott without this element being present: it is the kind of thing one enjoys in a debased form in 'costume' dramas and films. Yet at the end of the book, one puts away the fancy dress with all kinds of disturbing thoughts. We have experienced something much more than a charabanc tour of the Highlands, or Mrs Skewton's visit to Warwick Castle.

The passive hero-as-victim doubtless reflects a 'view of history'; yet he discovers, in spite of all this, that he has loyalties too. The fact that we have entered so fully into Waverley's romantic attachment to the Highlands—to the lyrics of Flora, to the tartans, to the hunt—means that we will enter even more fully into the awakening of his conscience in the encounter with Colonel Talbot. By then the noise of the pibroch has become comic, like Baron Bradwardine's obsession with removing the Chevalier's boot; and the hard-bitten worldliness of Fergus MacIvor is shown up in a less happy light than the fine qualities of Talbot. We begin to long for home. Even Flora's nobility of temper starts to seem like the fanaticism of Maud Gonne. Our emotions have been skilfully manipulated almost in a full circle; and it is then that we are ready for the heroism of the Jacobites at Carlisle. This happens again and again in Scott: it is one of his great contributions to our understanding of what heroic literature is, the skilful irony with which he makes us find valour, loyalty and enterprise most moving in characters who have become unsympathetic. The immoral crusader in *Ivanhoe*; the ranting fanatics of *Old Mortality*; the stubborn little woman who cannot bring herself to tell a single untruth in order to save her sister's life in *The Heart of Midlothian*: these are the figures in Scott who not only move us most deeply, but who trouble the mind with questions too complex for the historians to answer and which can only be explored through the broader sympathies of art. It is this which makes Scott so important, making him not only great, but the cause of greatness in others, blossoming out into all manner of improbable influences in the century to follow. Yet, to begin with, *Waverley* is little more than a highly intelligent adventure story.

Intelligence certainly distinguishes the book, intelligence in the fullest sense. Its splendidly well-organized plot, and the richness of its characters, are all woven in with the highly delicate sense of time, and of the processes of history, which informs the whole. Not since Shakespeare had such a huge variety of human character been presented in a single work; never, perhaps, had they been presented in a book so carefully thought. Yet no book is less 'intellectual'. Apart from so much else, it is the prototype of all boys' adventure stories which have been written since. It is as an adventure story that the plot moves on, and it is these elements which make one most aware of the personality of Scott himself behind the book. Few writers were less egotistical. Until he wrote *Redgauntlet*, Scott never directly or knowingly 'put himself into' one of his novels. But the character of the hero *manqué*, the man of action who is always hampered from action, always put upon by others, corresponds, obviously enough, with the highly uniformed figure who, a year after *Waverley*, limped up to be presented to the Tsar, and tried to explain that he had never seen action.

All Scott's novels have adventurous elements, but the next to have adventure as its *raison d'être* in the manner of *Waverley* was *Rob Roy* (1818). Although it is set in 1715, historical awareness is much less important to this book than to *Waverley*. In *Waverley*, the whole novel is full of the sense that in 1745 something violent, old, and beautiful, never to be seen again, was stamped out finally. But in *Rob Roy* the Fifteen is simply another adventure, happening almost on the margins of the story. The key to the book is much closer to the heart of Scott's life: the conflict between adventure and commerce. It concerns another young Englishman, like Edward Waverley, who goes

north and becomes involved, through a series of rather arbitrary
chances, with Jacobites, papists and Highlanders. But Frank Osbaldistone is much more obviously a part of Scott himself than Waverley
had been. When he feels constrained to tell his father that, because of
poetical inclinations, he cannot continue in the family firm, Frank
quotes

> A clerk condemn'd his father's soul to cross,
> Who penned a stanza when he should engross,

—the very couplet Scott himself quotes in his autobiographical fragment to explain the difference between his father's temperament and
his own.[12]

In the course of his adventures Frank Osbaldistone learns the
lessons which were coming home to Scott as he became entangled in
business with Constable and the Ballantyne brothers. He thinks that
he can live in the world quite independently of any interest in money.
He leaves his father's counting house, goes north—and learns his
mistake. His uncle, Sir Hildebrand Osbaldistone, maintains an
antique, eighteenth-century establishment in Northumberland. The
only interests of his large family (apart from the villainous Rashleigh)
are field sports; when Frank first glimpses them they are chasing a fox
across their estates, and when he goes inside Osbaldistone Hall, he
finds

> huge antlers of deer, which might have been trophies of the hunting of Chevy
> Chace . . . ranged around the walls, interspersed with the stuffed skins of
> badgers, otters, martens, and other animals of the chase. Amidst some
> remnants of old armour, which had, perhaps, served against the Scotch, hung
> the more valued weapons of silvan war, crossbows, guns of various device and
> constriction nets, fishing-rods, otter-spears, hunting-poles, with many other
> singular devices and engines for taking or killing game.
>
> (Chapter V)

It is almost like P. G. Wodehouse's Bludleigh Court, and these
opening impressions of the Osbaldistones are extremely funny, showing us Scott in his most relaxed comic vein. The rather cavalier
manner in which they are all killed off at the end of the book in order to
provide the satisfactory conclusion of Frank inheriting the estate and
marrying Diana Vernon might be criticized if the book were being

read by the wrong canons of taste; yet that too is delightful. What is
made perfectly clear is that had they not died, they would all have
been ruined without the capital of Frank's capitalist father to keep
them going.

These stern economic lessons seem implicit even in the most absurd
element of the plot, the villainies of Rashleigh, who is held partly
responsible for the Fifteen. The over-populated Highlands cannot
subsist on agriculture alone, and, in order to prevent their thieving
and plundering, or, worse, being levied into a military force against
the government, London merchants pay the Highlanders what is, in
effect, danegeld or protection money. It is therefore in Rashleigh's
impenetrably evil interests to ruin a firm which helps to supply the
Highlanders with their blackmail. One can reject Rashleigh's villainy
as melodramatic and improbable, as it is: but it is melodramatic in an
austerely monetary way.

Once Frank Osbaldistone has crossed the border, he encounters
Rob Roy again (they had met before, on the road north), but not
through the medium of a Jacobite sympathizer, as Waverley had met
MacIvor through Baron Bradwardine. On the contrary, Frank's
guide in the Highlands—a remote cousin of Rob Roy's who delights
in the ludicrous niceties of Scotch genealogy—could not be more
opposed to the free-booting, dishonest and inevitably papistical ways
of the Highlanders. This is the Bailie Nicol Jarvie.

The Bailie takes over the book as soon as he appears. He is one of
the richest, funniest characters that Scott ever drew, and he rightly
steals the show, not only because he is such a distinctive character,
but because, by the book's inner logic, he should. *Waverley* had been
concerned with the Highlands and with Edinburgh, a Romantic
Scotland. The Scotland of *Rob Roy* is the no less beautiful territory
between Glasgow and Argyllshire. Glasgow is the mercantile capital
of Scotland, as Edinburgh is the legislative capital, and the Bailie is a
thoroughly mercantile, bourgeois man, conceited, rich, Presbyterian,
law-abiding, dogged and courageous. It is not only his money which
triumphs in the end, by saving the Osbaldistones' firm from financial
collapse: it is his whole system of values. One sees this most clearly,
perhaps, in the most exciting scene in the book, when he and Frank
have been taken prisoner by Rob Roy's wife, Helen Macgregor. The
Bailie on home territory is a punctiliously fussy bourgeois. At home,
mealtimes are exact, and his Mattie fusses if he sets out on his journey
without his muffler. But confronted with physical danger, he is bold

and enterprising: when they are set upon by Highlanders in the inn, the Bailie saves the day by setting one of their plaids on fire. But when confronted by Helen Macgregor, he is horrified by her savagery. There is nothing he can do; he can only speak.

One of Rashleigh's more villainous underlings, a man called Morris, a spy and a turncoat, has also been captured, and Helen is determined to administer rough justice to him:

'I could have bid you live,' she said, 'had life been to you the same weary and wasting burden that it is to me—that it is to every noble and generous mind. But you—wretch! You could creep through the world unaffected by its various disgraces, its ineffable miseries, its constantly accumulating masses of crime and sorrow: you could live and enjoy yourself, while the noble-minded are betrayed—while nameless and birthless villains tread on the neck of the brave and the long-descended: you could enjoy yourself, like a butcher's dog in the shambles, battening on garbage, while the slaughter of the oldest and the best went on around you! This enjoyment you shall not live to partake of; you shall die, base dog, and that before yon cloud has passed over the sun.'

She gave a brief command in Gaelic to her attendants, two of whom seized the prostrate suppliant, and hurried him to the brink of a cliff which overhung the flood. He set up the most piercing and dreadful cries that fear ever uttered—I may well term them dreadful, for they haunted my sleep for years afterwards. As the murderers, or executioners, call them as you will, dragged him along, he recognized me, even in that moment of horror, and exclaimed, in the last articulate words I ever heard him utter, 'O, Mr Osbaldistone, save me!—save me!'

I was so much moved by this horrid spectacle, that, although in momentary expectation of sharing his fate, I did attempt to speak in his behalf, but as might have been expected, my interference was sternly disregarded. The victim was held fast by some, while others, binding a large heavy stone in a plaid, tied it round his neck, and others again eagerly stripped him of some part of his dress. Half-naked and thus manacled, they hurled him into the lake, there about twelve feet deep, with a loud halloo of vindictive triumph, above which, however, his last death shriek, the yell of mortal agony, was distinctly heard. The heavy burden splashed in the dark blue waters, and the Highlanders, with their pole-axes and swords, watched an instant, to guard lest, extricating himself from the lead to which he was attached, the victim might have struggled to regain the shore. But the knot had been securely bound; the wretched man sunk without effort; the waters, which his fall had disturbed, settled calmly over him, and the unit of that life for which he had pleaded so strongly was for ever withdrawn from the sum of human existence.

(Chapter XXXI)

One of the things which makes the scene so terrifying is Helen's certainty that her own self-absorbing sufferings entitle her to behave like an unacknowledged legislator. Frank Osbaldistone had had the (anachronistic) ambition of becoming a Romantic poet. There is no state of mind more despicable to the Romantic than the neutral, deadened, unnoticing mind, the sort which Helen ascribes (probably rightly) to Morris. But here, in Scott's scene, we see the life of sensation rather than of thought applied to the world of action, and the results are hideous. It is one of the many moments in Scott where we face naked, mad violence. All at once, the last vestiges of sympathy which we have entertained for the Highland brigands are gone. We see them as mere savages, divested of their heroic and romantic colouring—or, rather, we see the direction in which Heroism and Romance can lead.

There is only one voice that can break the silence after the execution of Morris, and it is of course the Bailie's.

> I looked at my companion Mr Jarvie, whose face reflected the feelings that were painted in mine. Indeed, he could not so suppress his horror, but that the words escaped him in a low and broken whisper—
> 'I take up my protest against this deed, as a bloody and cruel murder—it is a cursed deed, and God will avenge it in his due way and time.'
>
> (Chapter XXXII)

The Bailie's courage in the scene which ensues confirms forever the sense with which the book is full, that the bourgeois mercantile values of the Bailie are not merely powerful: they are good. Those for whom the term 'middle-class' is opprobrious should meditate upon the character of the Bailie.

When the story is done, we realize that there have been two types of men in *Rob Roy*. The distinction is not merely one between Jacobites and Hanoverians; it is rather between differing attitudes towards money. We see the Jacobites at their best in Rob Roy himself, and in Diana Vernon. Indeed, the romance of the book would be destroyed if we failed to retain our excitement in their presence to the end. But we also learn that the common-sense acceptance of hard work, the Protestant succession, and regular habits of life lead to a much sounder system of virtue than the rough old ways of pre-Georgian Scotland. Only a clever writer could avoid making this dull. But it was the truth as Scott saw it. It is the essence of his genius that he always managed to make the truth exciting.

How much of Scott's personal drama there is in *Rob Roy* is obvious. The desire to escape his father's office and to write poetry; the discovery of the Highlands, the intoxication with their beauty and the horror at their savagery, were all parts of his own experience. *Rob Roy* is evidence of his arrival in middle age. He might still fantasize about himself as a man of action; yet he knew that the mainspring of his working life was dependent not on poetry, but on the size of his bank balance.

The formula of the adventure story which he worked out in *Waverley* and *Rob Roy* was successful, and he could rely on it in the future. He rings the changes in it in various ways. In later novels his young hero would be a Scotsman more often than an Englishman. But nearly always he is a young man in an alien environment; and in two of his best adventure stories, *The Fortunes of Nigel* (1822) and *Quentin Durward* (1823) the young Scotsman is away from home.

In *The Fortunes of Nigel*, one of the finest of the later novels, the ineffectiveness of the hero is articulated more clearly than anywhere else in Scott's fiction. What Nigel says of himself could be said of Waverley, Frank Osbaldistone, and a dozen others:

I have been, through my whole life, one who leant upon others for that assistance which it is more truly noble to derive from my own exertions. . . . Live or die, sink or swim, Nigel Olifaunt from this moment, shall owe his safety, success and honour, to his own exertions, or shall fall with the credit of having at least exerted his own free agency. . . .

By the time of *The Fortunes of Nigel*, this self-image, which was never conceived in the least neurotically, is happily placed against a rich comic backcloth. Even Nigel's family piety is not allowed to be taken seriously, for he was one of those who 'had not escaped the predominant weakness in his country, an overweening sense of the pride of birth, and a disposition to value the worth and consequence of others according to the number and fame of their deceased ancestry'.

Nigel's slightly improbable adventures are set against some of the richest humorous realism Scott ever conceived. The movement, the look, the very smell of Jacobean London come to life in its pages, from the absurd king's court in which we observe the extraordinary mixture of pedantry and tomfoolery in the character of James VI (I), to the criminal underworld of Whitefriars and the Dickensian lairs of 'Alsatia'. There is not much chance for the priggish egotism of Nigel to flourish here. Scott's desire to be heroic, like his obsession with his own ancestors, could have been merely tiresome. In the Waverley Novels, he wrote it into self-parody and laughed it out of existence. The true heroism of his nature was to be shown not on the field of battle, but when he met his creditors in January 1826. But before then there were many novels to be written, many facets of his genius to be unfolded.

CHAPTER FOUR

Love and Friendship
Guy Mannering, *The Antiquary*, *St. Ronan's Well*, *The Surgeon's Daughter* and *Redgauntlet*

> But still the heart doth need a language, still
> Doth the old instinct bring back the old names.
>
> Coleridge: Wallenstein

I

Lockhart has a good account of the surprises in store for those unfamiliar with the dining-room at Abbotsford:

In sitting down to table, in Autumn, no one observed that in each of the three chandeliers (one of them being of very great dimensions) there lurked a tiny bead of red light. Dinner passed off, and the sun went down, and suddenly, at the turning of a screw, the room was filled with a gush of splendour worthy of the palace of Aladdin; but as in the case of Aladdin, the old lamp would have been better in the upshot. Jewelry sparkled, but cheeks and lips looked cold and wan in this fierce illumination; and the eye was wearied and the brow ached if the sitting was at all protracted.[1]

Scott was a major shareholder in the Edinburgh Oil Gas Company, and he was one of the first private householders to fit out his establishment with the new invention. Having no sense of smell (a fact he concealed when talking about gas) he had none of Lockhart's old-fashioned reservations on the subject. Indeed, there are few surer indications of what a fantasy-world Abbotsford became, than his conviction that gas, with its highly elaborate system of pipes obtruding into every corner of the house, was cheaper than candles. It needed the employment of a labourer for five hours every day to keep it operative, and it was always breaking down and plunging the house into darkness. 'In our new mansion we should have been ruined with spermaceti oil and wax-candles,' he boasts unrealistically in a letter; claiming, to the same correspondent, that 'there is no smell whatever, unless a valve is left open, and the gas escapes unconsumed, in which case the scent occasions its being instantly discovered.'[2]

Lockhart's point, that the gaslight actually distorted the look of things, seems emblematic of Scott's vision of modernity. His unerring sense of the past played him false when he came to contemplate the contemporary world. In fact, with a large part of himself, he was scarcely willing to exist in the modern world at all. No man was more clubbable; few, in the early decades of the nineteenth century, can have had more friends; and it was a great age of friendship. Moreover, all those friends remarked his conversational easiness, his lack of affectation. 'To hear him converse,' Mrs Hughes confided to her diary, 'is like swallowing large draughts of champagne without being intoxicated.'[3]

Yet, although Abbotsford is architecturally unpretentious by the standards of the age—little more than *cottage ornée*—it was in more senses than one a folly. The gaslight caught the jewels of soldiers' wives and duchesses; but it also transformed the coarse complexions of gentry families into cheeks and lips that looked as cold and wan as Emily in *The Mysteries of Udolpho*. Behind the table laden with hideous Coalport china, champagne glasses and newly bought cutlery, lurked the armoury. The fantastic light perhaps fell on a rusty thumbscrew, a battered targe, a dirk recovered from the field of Killiecrankie.

The contrast between the gas at Abbotsford and what it illuminated has struck everyone who ever meditated upon Scott's life. For some, it will confirm the idea that his attitude to the past was essentially uninvolved; that his fiction is, for the most part, frivolous, because the past can be enjoyed in it so safely, so amusingly wrapped up in its beautiful ancient trappings. For others, it will remain a paradox, but one which shows Scott's abundant common sense; the light at the dinner-table embodying Sydney Smith's famous injunction to shun dark rooms.

There is certainly something odd about Scott's attitude to the present day. Gas was not the only modern invention he patronized. There was an extraordinarily elaborate system of air-bells at Abbotsford. 'By pressing down a piston into this upper and wider cylinder,' he proses to a correspondent, 'the air through the tube, to the distance of a hundred feet if necessary, is suddenly compressed, which compression throws out the light piece of wood, which strikes the bell.' He adds, with what can only be an enthusiast's conviction, 'it never fails, indeed *cannot*. It may be called the *ne plus ultra* of bell-ringing—the pea-gun principle, as one may say.'[4]

Similar delight was derived from the railways, which he rightly saw would revolutionize the nation's eating habits, enabling Londoners to taste fresh Scotch turbot. He had none of the old Tory landowners' horror of the new contraptions puffing their way over his estates; even though, in the event, the 'Scott country' was curiously sparse territory for the railway companies, as it remains to this day.

Water closets, too, were important to him, and one of the grave disadvantages of Continental travel, to his mind, was the primitive arrangements made by the foreigners in that regard.

And yet, politically, it would have been hard to be more reactionary. He had a horror of revolutions, and applauded the Peterloo 'massacre'. As he became involved with politics, the popularity of 'the Shirra' declined very steeply. In Jedburgh, in 1830, he made a speech opposing reform which was howled down by mobs of angry labourers and artisans. 'And these unwashed artificers', he exclaimed through the noise, 'are from henceforth to select our legislators.'[5] The allusion to Shakespeare would have been lost on them. Making his way back to the carriage, he bowed to the mob, with the gladiatorial salutation 'Moriturus vos saluto'. He could not have known how true the words were to be.

In the following year he again made his way to Jedburgh to make an election speech in favour of the Tory candidate, his cousin Henry Scott. The streets were crowded with weavers from Hawick, who shouted insults at anyone who was not wearing the reform colours. Even allowing for the noisier political atmosphere of these days, their attacks on Scott were particularly fierce. His carriage was pelted with stones, and they shouted 'Burke Sir Walter!'* The words went home, if the missiles did not. In his delirium in the months that followed, he kept muttering, 'Burke Sir Walter! Burke Sir Walter!'

It must have been unthinkable to Scott that someone with his intense love of the Borderers should be so harshly treated by the very people whose heritage he had done so much to restore and to popularize. Moreover, he had been a kind and generous magistrate and landlord. Tom Purdie, the poacher brought before the bench in Scott's early days at Selkirk, was offered employment that same evening as a shepherd and gamekeeper at Ashiestiel, and then at

---

* Burke was a murderer who smothered his victims: 'burke' became synonymous with 'squash' as a verb of violence.

Abbotsford. He was probably Scott's closest friend. After Purdie's death, much of his affection was turned towards William Laidlaw, the Abbotsford factotum, whom he greeted on his return from Italy in 1832 with more warmth than he expended on his family. There was nothing *lofty* about Scott, and it was not snobbery which made him a Tory; rather, it was an Augustan fear of chaos, a countryman's fundamental loathing of egalitarianism and industrialization. He had no sense of what industrial life was like or of the world which it was bringing into being. He could see enough from a distance to discern that it was horrible. Near at hand, he saw only the mob. The old world that they were destroying was all that he stood for. His last parting from Hogg, the Ettrick Shepherd, is sadly believable:

> Turning half round, leaning on his crutch, and fixing his eyes on the ground for a long space, he said, 'You have written a great deal which might be made available, Hogg, with proper attention, and I am sure that one day or other, it will be made available to you or your family, but in my opinion this is not the proper season. I wish you could drive off the experiment until the affairs of the nation are in better keeping, for at present all things, and literature in particular, are going downhill to destruction and ruin.' And then he mumbled something to himself, which I took to be an inward curse. I say again, and I am certain of it, that the democratic ascendancy, and the grievious and shameful insults that he received from the populous of his own country, broke the heart of and killed the greatest man that country ever contained.[6]

Ruskin was surely right to make the exaggerated claim that Scott's Toryism was the Toryism of Homer. It bore no very particular relationship to the political issues of the day, even if, as Hogg's account shows, it eventually came to cloud his mind to such a degree that he felt that writers should abandon their craft in favour of the Struggle. It was a Toryism which protested against the erosion of the romance, above all the distinctiveness, of rural life.

'Everyone will own', he once wrote, 'that the subject is of the most momentous interest to this country.'[7] His words have been proved both sane and true: yet he was speaking not of universal male suffrage or Catholic emancipation or parliamentary reform, but of tree-planting. Radicalism (*pace* Cobbett) had no real interest in rural life. Memory and poetry themselves were to be wiped out by it. The bigots of that time lapped up his harmless art, but they thought the odd views of life which had helped to produce it were a crime. Hazlitt's essay on Scott reflects this paradox, exclaiming against what he took to be Scott's kowtowing Toryism, which 'supported the worst abuses of authority in the worst spirit', while having to recognize in Scott's novels a range of creations which 'taken together are almost like a new edition of human nature.'[8]

These paradoxes seem close to Abbotsford. Buried too deep for analysis, some obsession created Abbotsford, extending it, cultivating it, rebuilding the house and knocking it down again, filling the estates with tame gillies and shepherds and gamekeepers. The *cottage ornée* swelled in his mind into a castle of Gothic romance into which all his fortunes were poured. No bit of bog on its borders could come on the market without his wanting to buy it. No historical fake or relic of Scotland's past could appear in the salerooms but Scott would want it for the library. No modern invention was too costly or too elaborate for this palace of art.

One can never explain the consuming passion some men feel for their houses. Scott was not unique in wanting to live handsomely or establish an estate. Nor is the house grandiose. But his obsessive devotion to Abbotsford seems at times to contrast with his common sense and his fundamental decency. When it came to his estates and his house, he was like a gambler held to the tables by an inescapable addiction.

A tendency to shut off the most important and painful areas of experience was habitual to Scott. Indeed, in the year that the lease expired on Ashiestiel and he first bought Clarty Hole, the marshy swamp that was to become Abbotsford, another area of his life was sealed into the private world of fantasy. Lady Forbes died. She was his first, perhaps his only, love.

It is hard to say whether there was any connection between Williamina and the building of Abbotsford; but, in a peculiar way, there might have been.

It is important to realize that Scott's common sense—which made him such an amiable companion for so many people—was precisely what contributed to the private intensity of his passions. Although he felt things deeply, he hated displays of emotion. Post-Victorian taste would think him dangerously bottled up, but this would be an anachronism. He would have shared Bishop Butler's view that in order to lead a virtuous life, it was necessary to be dispassionate: 'I hate red eyes and blowing of noses. *Agere et pati Romanum est.* Of all schools commend me to the Stoicks. We cannot, indeed, overcome our affections, nor ought if we could, but we may repress them within due bounds and avoid coaxing them to make fools of those who should be their masters.'[9]

'Affections' is a Bishop Butler word. For Butler, the affections were neutral things which, if governed by 'cool self-love', could be harnessed for private and public good.

> Men have various appetites, passions, and particular affections, quite distinct both from self-love and from benevolence: all of these have a tendency to promote both public and private good, and may be considered as respecting others and ourselves especially and in common: but some of them seem most immediately to respect others, or tend to public good; others of them most immediately to respect self, or tend to private good.[10]

Butler believed that 'cool self-love' would lead both to private and to public well-being: 'The thing to be lamented, is not that men have so great regard to their own good or interest in the present world, for they have not enough; but that they have so little to the good of others.' This is an emphasis we find again in the moral philosophy of Hume.

I mention these matters because Scott quite consciously moulded himself into the embodiment of Augustan virtue which Butler drew as an ideal in his *Fifteen Sermons*. Indeed, after Doctor Johnson, Scott is the great embodiment, if not saint, of Augustan values. Passion of any kind was hideously likely to become man's master. When poor Richard Heber, Scott's friend of early days—they had paced the Borders together collecting ballads—became involved, much later in life, in a sexual scandal which brought an end to his parliamentary career, Scott was horrified. His was not the humbugging horror which Victorians expressed over Vaughan of Harrow or over Wilde, but that of Augustan man, a rational being, appalled that a fellow-creature has become a victim of the passions. 'Here is learning, wit, gaiety of temper, high station in society and compleat [*sic*] reception every where all at once debased and lost by such degrading bestiality. Our passions are wild beasts. God grant us power to muzzle them.'[11] One can be sure that Scott never felt the temptations which ruined Heber. But he sees the issue as a more general one: any passion, if allowed to get out of control, could be equally ruinous.

The nature of Scott's stoicism will be examined in the chapter on his Journal. But we ought to look at it briefly now in relation to his love for Williamina Forbes.[12]

She was the daughter of Sir John Wishart Belsches-Stuart, and grand-daughter, on her mother's side, of an earl—Lord Leven and Melville. Scott met her, so the story goes, when she was only fourteen, five years his junior, one wet Sunday morning coming out of Greyfriars' Church in Edinburgh. She looked infinitely fragile: small, with very pale, almost translucent skin, and a face framed with very dark brown hair. Since he had an umbrella, the opportunity seemed a perfect one. Knowing his intense feelings of boredom whenever he went to church, one can imagine that his eye had already fallen upon her during the sermon. He walked her home, and continued to do so, on and off, on subsequent Sundays for the next three years. They went on jaunts together, too, into the country. The two families knew each other slightly already, and it was doubtless thought harmless enough that the two young people should be thrown together. We do not have much record of how she responded to Scott's attentions, nor of what they talked about. But by the time of his twenty-fifth birthday, he was earning enough money as an advocate to marry on, but scarcely enough to support a woman of Williamina's breeding. In January 1797, she was married to William Forbes, a banker; so far as is known, she had no more communications with Scott.

On one level, Scott survived the blow well enough. He threw himself into his work, he saw a lot of his friends, and he got married: all usual enough remedies to heal a broken heart. And, in subsequent years, he got along perfectly well with William Forbes. They were in the Edinburgh Light Horse together; they belonged to many of the same clubs; later still, Forbes was able to help Scott in his financial difficulties.

But the wound went deep. He had too much natural wisdom, and too much benevolence, to allow himself to be embittered by it. Still less would he want to make any immediate or obvious parade of his grief in public. 'If I were either greedy or jealous of poetic fame,' he wrote much later to Lady Purgstall, '—and both are strangers to my nature—I might comfort myself with the thought that I would hesitate to strip myself to the contest so fearlessly as Byron does, or to command the wonder and terror of the public by exhibiting in my own person the sublime attitude of the dying gladiator.'[13]

The 'cool self-love' of the reader of Bishop Butler, or of Hume's *Treatise on Human Nature*, is as far removed as possible from the self-consuming egotism of the Byronic hero. Yet 'we cannot overcome our affections, nor ought if we could'. He never 'got over' Williamina.

In 1811, the year after her early death, and the year in which he acquired Clarty Hole, he wrote *Rokeby*. Although it was Doctor Pusey's favourite among Scott's works, most readers think of it as a failure. The story is set in Yorkshire during the Civil War, and bears no very obvious relationship to Scott's own love story. But tradition has associated Matilda, the pathetic heroine, with Williamina. She is forced into the position of having to marry someone in order to prevent her father from being beheaded. *Faute de mieux*, she chooses Wilfrid, the delicate, poetical youth who has been in love with her from the beginning of the poem. But he will not consent to a match that is forced on her so unwillingly.

> But now bear witness, earth and heaven,
> That ne'er was hope to mortal given,
> So twisted with the strings of life,
> As this—to call Matilda wife.

With this sad speech, overcome by extremes of passion, he dies; luckily, Redmond O'Neale, the honest page, turns out to be the villain's son, and is able to marry her instead. It is a poem which repays re-reading, but it is not vintage Scott. What it reveals very clearly is how he viewed his own love story. We will probably never know the truth of his relations with Williamina. Though richer, William Forbes was not *so* much grander than Scott, who was, after all, the cousin of a duke. Perhaps the sad fact was that she simply preferred the other man. But, as it is repeated in his art, it is always the story of a young girl forced into matrimony against her will by overbearing parents.

Scott frequently admitted that he was not at his best when writing about love: it always has a whiff of fantasy about it, even in the novels. But this does not mean that he did not know about, still less that he did not care about, the subject. On the contrary, he cared about it so much that it was the one area of life about which he was unable to think straight.

He continued to love Williamina for the rest of his life; but the love remained buried and hidden and it in no way affected either the happiness of his marriage, or the easiness of his social encounters. Were it not for his Journal, begun towards the end of 1825, we should know nothing of it. The intensity of griefs and calamities which came upon him after 1826 began to wear him down: he was ruined; his wife had died; illness had begun to overtake him. In this new and vulnerable phase of life, he began to confide his private thoughts to the Journal. We see how well-balanced they were with his earlier social manner in the entry for 16 July 1827, when a party of friends took him to St. Andrews. He had been there with Williamina in 1793:

> This day we went off in a body to St. Andrews . . . The ruins . . . have been lately cleard out. They had been chiefly magnificent from their size not their extent of ornament. I did not go up to Saint Rule's tower as on former occasions; this is a falling off for when before did I remain sitting below when there was a steeple to be ascended? But the Rheumatism has begun to change that vein for some time past though I think this is the first decided sign of acquiescence in my lot. I sate down on a gravestone and recollected the first visit I made to St. Andrews now 34 years ago. What changes in my feeling and my fortune have since taken place, some for the better, many for the worse. I rememberd the name I then carved in runic charcters on the turf beside the castle gate and I askd why it should still agitate my heart. But my friends came down from their tower and the foolish idea was chased away.[14]

Even at this stage, he did not name Williamina, and there was no divorce between the cheerful self who greeted his friends and the honest private tone of the Journal. But, that autumn, he began to correspond with Lady Jane Stuart, Williamina's mother. Lady Jane had been going through Williamina's things, and had offered Scott her commonplace book. On 25 October, he records,

> When I came home a surprize amounting nearly to a shock reachd me in another letter from L.J.S. Methinks this explains the gloom which hung about me yesterday. I own that the recurrence to these matters seems like a summons from the grave. It fascinates me. I ought perhaps to have stopd it at once but I have not the heart to do so. Alas—Alas—but why Alas?[15]

It shows how well he had himself under control, that he scarcely knew, or would admit to knowing, why he had felt gloomy the previous day. Over thirty years after the event, he was still fighting to keep it from his mind. But Lady Jane invited him to see her, and the visits became habitual. 'I went to make another visit', he wrote on 7 November,

> and fairly softend myself like an old fool with recalling old stories till I was fit for nothing but shedding tears and repeating verses for the whole night. This is sad work. The very grave gives up its dead and time rolls back thirty years

to add to my perplexities.—I don't care—I begin to grow over-hardened and like a stag turning at bay, my natural good temper grows fierce and dangerous. Yet what a romance to tell and told I fear it will one day be. And then my three years of dreaming and my two years of wakening will be chronicled doubtless. But the dead will feel no pain.[16]

The angry, disgruntled side of his nature was to burst in what he himself referred to as *hysterico passio*. This is the miserable figure depicted by Hogg; an angry figure, old at fifty-seven, shaking his stick at the weavers of Hawick. But for the greater part of his artistic career, it lay quite buried. As he planted, and bought and planned the fantasy at Clarty Hole, no one can know how often he thought of the light hazel eyes and the pale cheeks, and the very dark hair that he would never see again. The shy lame boy who was not quite up to marrying the grand-daughter of an earl, established, in the most exaggerated way, his pedigree with Wat of Harden and the Duke of Buccleuch by building his folly in the heart of the country of his ancestors. Duchesses begged to be invited to stay. There is nothing like a building for proving a point. But Scott had far too much goodness of nature, and far too little awareness of himself, to have been conscious of the point it made.

2

Scott's reputation as an historical novelist rests on his commonsense realism. The Waverley Novels are distinguished from everything that went before, either in fiction or in straight historical writing, by his recognition of what people in the past were really like. Movements, ideas and historical processes become intelligible to us in his pages not because of his analytical capabilities but because of his Shakespearean instincts and insights into the nature of character. There is, for instance, no more acute analysis of the political and religious issues dividing Scotland towards the end of the seventeenth century than in Scott's portraits of the fanatics in *Old Mortality*.

But Scott did not only write historical fiction; and when we turn to the novels which cover the period of his own lifetime, or the times in his immediate memory, we discover features and oddities which, if not unique to these books, are more marked here than anywhere else in his art. Such novels include *Guy Mannering* (1815), which is set in the late 1770s; *The Antiquary* (1816), *St. Ronan's Well* (1823) and *The Surgeon's Daughter* (1827), which are set at the time of the French revolutionary wars; and *Redgauntlet* (1824), which happens shortly before Scott's birth.

All these novels are, in their way, excellent; but three in particular—*The Antiquary*, *St. Ronan's Well* and *Redgauntlet*—are great novels by any canon of taste. Yet all these novels have flaws in common; they are all oddly disjointed, and disjointed in the same way. Most strikingly, they all have roughly the same plot: a young man, whose birth is a mystery, and whose true identity is hidden from the reader at the beginning of the story, turns out to be the heir to an inheritance which changes the whole pattern of his life; and the plot involves the discovery of what his true identity is, and why it has been concealed. He is also in love with a beautiful young woman who cannot marry him, either because it is assumed that he is illegitimate, or because there is some insuperable family obstacle preventing the match. In the happier books, this obstacle is removed. In the later novels, the plot is darkened, and, for one reason or another, the lovers are not united.

So, in *Guy Mannering*, Bertram can marry Julia Mannering as soon as he discovers that his name is not Brown. 'Henry Bertram', says Colonel Mannering, 'heir of Ellangowan, whether possessed of the property of his ancestors or not, is a very different person from Vanbeest Brown, the son of nobody at all.'[17] In *The Antiquary*, similarly, there are no objections to Lovel marrying the daughter of Sir Arthur Wardour when it turns out that he is really the heir of Lord Glenallan. But in *St. Ronan's Well* Francis Tyrrel can never marry Clara Mowbray, because she has already been tricked into marrying his evil half-brother who, bafflingly, has the same name; anyway, by the end of the book she has lost her wits and died. In *Redgauntlet*, when Darsie Latimer discovers that he is really the son of Sir Harry Redgauntlet, it also follows that the girl he loves is his sister; and in *The Surgeon's Daughter* 'it might be thought the natural conclusion of the history of Menie Gray, that she should have married Hartley, to whom she stood much indebted for his heroic interference on her behalf. But her feelings were too much and too painfully agitated, her health too much shattered, to permit her to entertain thoughts of a matrimonial connection.'[18]

But it is only in *Redgauntlet* that the plot is of the slightest importance to the central themes and characters of the novel. Here, it really matters who Darsie Latimer is: the whole story hangs on his, and our, shock at discovering his connection with that violent old Jacobite family. His, and our, views of politics, life, and the past, are fundamentally bound up in the story. This, among other qualities, sets *Redgauntlet* apart, and I shall discuss it separately. But in the other novels the hero's inheritance, and his love affair with the heroine, always seem, in retrospect, to have been of only peripheral importance. When we remember *St. Ronan's Well*, we do not think chiefly of Francis Tyrrel and Clara Mowbray, but of the wonderfully powerful figure of Meg Dods, keeping her inn in the old style, and resisting all the new-fangled nonsense that has grown up around the fashionable watering-place down the road, 'the new Spaaw-Well', as she contemptuously calls it; or of her much-travelled, highly particular guest, Mr Touchwood, rather a Thackeravian figure, and of his friendship with Josiah Cargill, the minister of the parish, so absent-minded that he sets out for dinner at the inn in his night-shirt. And when we think of what makes *The Antiquary* great, we remember the astounding range and depth of its comic portraits: the women in the Post Office examining the letters before they are delivered ('Me, opened!' answered the spouse of the chief baker of Fairport; 'ye ken yourself, madam, it just cam open o' free will in my hand—what could I help it?—folk suld seal with better wax'); the funeral in Mucklebackit's cottage; the ludicrous vanities of Sir Arthur Wardour; the strangely moving (though so stagey) wisdom of Edie Ochiltree, the wandering mendicant; and, above all, the household and conversation of the Antiquary himself. Few novelists could match this achievement, presenting baronets, lairds, fishermen and postmistresses in equally realistic tones. So, too, in *Guy Mannering*, characters and, especially in that book, landscapes stay in our mind: Julia Mannering's description of the frozen lake and the game of curling, which has all the brightly defined beauty of a snowscape by Breughel; Dominie Sampson, the shy, awkward private tutor, with his habitual exclamation, 'Prodigious!'; Dandie Dinmont, that hard-spoken, totally honest, hunting man, one of the best examples of Scott's great ability to portray sheer goodness with no trace of sentimentality; and Meg Merrilies and the gypsies. These are the passages we return to, and love, and remember; and they would all exist quite happily if the young men never inherited the local estates or married the girl of their dreams.

Scott was fond of quoting, 'What the devil does the plot signify, except to bring in fine things?'[19] But this, like so many of his cavalier comments on his own work, leaves the question in the air. It is true that, for the most part, the plot of *Guy Mannering* is perfectly workable, even if it leads to the occasional fairly creaking piece of coincidence. But what can explain the total divorce of the plot from the life of the book?

The reasons are, I suspect, much more literary than the opening section of this chapter would suggest. On one level, of course, it is obvious why Scott used this story so often. He was the young man who, in building Abbotsford, returned to a sort of lost inheritance which he had dreamed about ever since his Aunt Janet told him of Wat of Harden and the generations of Scotts and Rutherfords from whom he traced his descent. Moreover, in establishing his pseudo-ancestral home, from which he could mix on more or less equal terms with his noble kinsman and neighbour the Duke of Buccleuch at Bowhill, he showed that he would have been more than worthy of marrying the daughter of Sir John Wishart Belsches-Stuart. Williamina, of course, is the bright, animated young Julia Mannering. But she is also the timid Isabella Wardour, child of a foolish baronet who wants her to marry someone with more to his name than the mysterious young Lovel; and she is also the pathetic Clara Mowbray, one of Scott's few really morbid creations, falling into an early death through love-melancholy. When someone challenged the sadness of this ending, Scott was quite firm about it—quite unlike his usual self, for he was usually content to agree with any hostile criticism of his work: 'I could not save her, poor thing . . . but of all the murders I have committed in that way, and few men have been guilty of more, there is none that went to my heart as the poor Bride of Lammermoor; but it could not be helped; it is all true.'[20]

All this suggests that these fantastic and sad tales had an inner truth which only he recognized. And they are often balanced by other, less dramatic depictions of the pangs of despised love. The young men must be satisfied, either by marrying their girls, or by an operatically tragic moment; but the old men who have had similar experiences in their youth must carry their sorrows through life. Jonathan Oldbuck's contempt for 'womankind' goes back to his early disappointment with Lovel's mother, Eveline Neville, and the papers dating from his career as a magistrate have inscribed upon them, in a small hand, *Eheu Evelina!* But his disappointment has not embittered him. He and Edie Ochiltree are the only two truly feeling people in the book. The jokes about 'the womankind' are superficial. He shows his true nature when he weeps in the fisherman's cottage and carries young Steenie Mucklebackit's coffin to the grave.

In *St. Ronan's Well* there is a similar case of blighted love growing into warm eccentricity in the figure of Josiah Cargill. Just as Oldbuck, since his disappointment, had plunged himself into antiquarian research, so Cargill 'sought relief not in society, but in solitary study'. But in spite of the chaotic domestic arrangements at Cargill's manse and his Spoonerish absent-mindedness—when Touchwood arrives to remind Cargill of their dinner engagement at the inn, the minister assumes that he had himself invited Touchwood to dine at the manse, and offers him a bowl of bread and milk—he has not abandoned that fundamentally Augustan good sense without which the virtuous life was impossible. His sordid lair, full of folios and unwashed linen, has an almost Johnsonian quality:

Do not let my fair readers do Josiah more than justice or suppose that, like Beltenebros in the desert, he remained for years the victim of an unfortunate and misplaced passion. No—to the shame of the male sex be it spoken, that no degree of hopeless love, however desperate and sincere, can ever continue for years to imbitter life. There must be hope—there must be uncertainty—there must be reciprococity, to enable the tyrant of the soul to secure dominion of very long duration over a manly and well-constituted mind, which is itself desirous to *will* its freedom. The memory of Augusta had long faded from Josiah's thoughts, or was remembered only as a pleasing, but melancholy and unsubstantial dream, while he was straining forward in pursuit of a yet nobler and coyer mistress, in a word, of Knowledge herself.

(Chapter XVI)

I often think that Josiah Cargill contributed to Browning's conception of the Grammarian. Both he and Oldbuck balance the rather wild passions of the young people in the stories they inhabit by a devotion to this cerebral pursuit. Both are fairly unmistakeable portraits of men whom Scott actually knew, but they embody an ideal to which, as the compiler of the Minstrelsy and the editor and collector of old folios, Scott himself aspired. The scene in *The Antiquary* in which old Elspeth sings a ballad describing the history of the Glenallans bears more relation to Scott's own passions than those of George Constable, the 'original' of Monkbarns.

'The herring loves the merry moonlight,
  The mackerel loves the wind,

> But the oyster loves the dredging sang
>   For they come of a gentle kind.'

A diligent collector of these scraps of ancient poetry, his foot refused to cross the threshold when his ear was thus arrested, and his hand instinctively took pencil and memorandum book. From time to time the old woman spoke as if to the children—'Oh, ay, hinnies, whisht! whisht! and I'll begin a bonnier ane than that—

> Now haud your tongue, baith wife and carle,
>   And listen great and sma',
> And I will sing of Glenallan's Earl
>   That fought on the red Harlaw.
>
> The cronach's cried on Bennachie,
>   And doun the Don and a',
> The hieland and lawland may mournfu' be
>   For the sair field of Harlaw.

I dinna mind the neist verse weel—my memory's failed, and there's unco thoughts come ower me—God keep us frae temptation!'

Here her voice sunk in indistinct muttering.

'It's a historical ballad,' said Oldbuck eagerly, 'a genuine and undoubted fragment of minstrelsy! Percy would admire its simplicity—Ritson could not impugn its authenticity.'

'Ay, but it's a sad thing,' said Ochiltree, 'to see human nature sae overtaen as to be skirling at auld sangs on the back of a loss like hers [The loss of her grandson].'

'Hush! hush!' said the Antiquary—'she has gotten the thread of the story again.' And as he spoke, she sung—

> They saddled a hundred milk-white steeds,
>   They hae bridled a hundred black,
> With a chafron of steel on each horse's head,
>   And a good knight upon his back—'

'Chafron!' exclaimed the Antiquary—'equivalent, perhaps, to *cheveron*; the word's worth a dollar'—and down it went in his red book.

(Chapter XL)

Oldbuck's rather absurd pursuit of his enthusiasm shows how clearly Scott perceived his own identical pastimes. Well could he have exclaimed with Oldbuck, 'My great-great-great grandfather—it's a shame to the English language that we have not a less clumsy way of expressing a relationship of which we have occasion to think and speak so frequently.' But this side of Scott's own nature is always viewed comically. Oldbuck's conviction that the earthworks on his

estate are an ancient Roman fortification is destroyed by Edie Ochiltree's commonsense disclosure that it was a ditch, dug for agricultural
purposes only a few decades before—'I mind the bigging o't.' Antiquarian research is an amusing enough obsession to carry a disappointed man through life. But Oldbuck's stature as a man is measured by the depth of his sympathies, by his Christian charity.

There can be no doubt that *The Antiquary* is a great work of art. The
dramas of the storm, or the duel which is interrupted by Edie Ochiltree are what those imperfectly acquainted with Scott might expect of
him; but there are also moments of high comedy, such as the Dickensian brilliance of the description of Griselda Oldbuck's arms, which
were 'terminated at the elbows by triple blond ruffles, and being
folded saltire ways in front of her person, and decorated with long
gloves of a bright vermilion colour, presented no bad resemblance to a
pair of gigantic lobsters'.

But when we recall the experience of reading *The Antiquary*—perhaps some weeks later—it is as though we are looking back
on two different books: an entirely convincing picture of provincial life
during the French revolutionary wars, in which Scott's rather 'poetical' feelings about the past have been humanized in the figures of
Monkbarns and Edie Ochiltree; and a Gothic Romance by Mrs
Radcliffe, in which Lady Glenallan has offered Elspeth a golden
bodkin with which to murder Lord Glenallan's heir, Eveline has been
driven to a desperate death on the cliffs because she believes herself to
have committed incest, and Lord Glenallan has lived a life of pious
gloom analagous to Philip II's solitude in the Escorial, a piety which
is not merely wholly unconvincing, but completely divorced from any
of the community surrounding him. 'Lord deliver me from this Gothic
generation', exclaimed the Antiquary—'A monument of a knight
templar on each side of a Grecian porch, and a Madonna on top of
it—*O crimini!*'

The novel itself is such a monster. When Lovel believes that he has
received a preternatural visitation in his sleep, Oldbuck tries to
dissuade him: 'Excuse me, my young friend,—but it is we silly
mortals deceive ourselves and look out of doors for motives which
originate in our own wilful will.' Yet the whole Glenallan plot suggests the opposite. E. M. Forster's comments on *The Antiquary* in
Aspects of the Novel must have been imbibed by many who have never
read a word of Scott. Forster, it will be remembered, thought Scott
had 'a trivial mind and a heavy style'. People (the lecture was

delivered in 1927) only thought Scott was a great writer because they remembered having him read aloud during childhood. 'Is he really more than a reminder of early happiness?' Forster asks, while conceding that 'he could tell a story'. He then tells us the story of *The Antiquary*, making it seem as slapdash, perfunctory, and above all 'passionless' as possible: '*The Antiquary* is a book in which the life in time is celebrated by the novelist, and this must lead to a slackening of emotion and shallowness of judgement, and in particular to that idiotic use of marriage as a finale.'[21] No admirer of Scott would deny that the plot of *The Antiquary* is disjointed. It is a deliberately unfair choice as an example of Scott's ability to 'tell a story'. The plots of *Redgauntlet* or *The Heart of Midlothian* or *The Bride of Lammermoor* would stand up to analysis of this kind, which is presumably why Forster chose not to use them. But of course he fails to analyse why the plot seems disjointed, just as he fails to see that Lovel's marriage at the end, far from being a trivial afterthought to round the whole thing off, is actually integral to the book's theme.

Edgar Johnson defends the book against Forster by saying that the whole plot hangs together because of the coherence of its view of time.[22] Because the fake past, dreamt up by Dousterswivel, is exposed by a vision of the real past, half discerned by the Antiquary himself, and naturally understood by Edie Ochiltree, it is a book which resolves itself naturally into truth. This is gallant, and it is certainly the sort of process which we have seen at work in Scott's poetry. But it does not get round the fact that the story of Lady Glenallan's wickedness is incredible. Superb as the effect of her funeral in the ruins of St. Ruth's may be, we think of it, following all the practical jokes that have taken place there, as yet another piece of tomfoolery by 'this Gothic generation'; and, in a sense, our instincts are right.

E. M. Forster does not do the book justice: but nor, in an odd way, does Edgar Johnson. It lacks coherence, and we should *allow* it to lack coherence. 'What the devil does the plot signify except to bring in fine things?'—Scott's attitude to plot is more dismissive than Forster's own. The title of the book is *The Antiquary*, and it is the Antiquary that the book concerns; it is about him, and his way of life, and the life of the community at Fairport, a Scottish coastal town, during the French revolutionary wars. Why, then, is Lovel, the hero, important? Well, it turns out at a late stage that he is the son of the girl that Oldbuck had loved in his youth, and the Antiquary reveals that his fascination with the young man springs from the fact that he calls up the lovely April of his mother's prime. But what matters more to the Antiquary than the stirrings of old passion is having someone to talk to, having a friend:

To have lost a friend by death while your mutual regard was warm and unchilled, while the tear can drop unembittered by any painful recollection of coldness or distrust or treachery, is perhaps an escape from a more heavy dispensation. Look round you—how few do you see grow old in the affections of those with whom their early friendships were formed! Our sources of common pleasure gradually dry up as we journey on through the vale of Bacha, and we hew out to ourselves other reservoirs, from which the first companions of our pilgrimage are excluded. . . .

(Chapter XVI)

As soon as Lovel and Oldbuck find themselves waiting at the Queens-ferry for the diligence at the beginning of the book, the Antiquary knows that he has found himself a friend. On the comic level, he has found someone he can bore with his antiquarian prosing: but, the asides, the Johnsonian fear that friendship cannot last, the sense in all his conversation that 'man was not born for happiness', show it to be more important than that. So to be satisfying the book must have a plot which enables the young man to settle down respectably in Fairport, never getting very far with his long poem *The Caledoniad* and having plenty of time for talks and walks with Oldbuck. This, really, is the *logic* of the book, its inner motive, the 'fine thing' brought in by the plot.

How odd, this being so clearly the case, that E. M. Forster, who celebrates friendship so enthusiastically in his own novels, should not have noticed it here. It would be flattering to think that this revealed a psychologically interesting fact about Forster as a critic, but it is only one of many indications that he was in point of fact rather unintelligent. He suggests that our admiration of Scott is no more than the happy memory of the intense pleasure he gave us in childhood: but it would be a sage child who could appreciate *The Antiquary*. Most of Forster's comments are little more than cheap jokes designed to get a laugh out of his Cambridge audience. One can make any novel absurd by 'paraphrasing' plots.

It is *talk* which this book celebrates, and talk which makes it live—the gossip of the women in the post office, the oratory of Ochiltree, the Peacockian magic of Oldbuck's own conversations and fantasies. The book does not really suggest that we learn from age. Elspeth dies unconsoled for her guilt, Sir Arthur Wardour becomes more and more foolish, and Oldbuck is not so immune to tears and passion as he could pretend at the beginning of the story. But good dinners, old books, a comfortable house, and a view of the sea; the kind of talk which beguiled the first forty years of Scott's life before he wrote fiction: that is why Oldbuck is fighting the revolutionaries (there is a threat of invasion, to remind us of this, at the end of the book). The wise men in the story do not believe in revolutionary 'freedom'. Ochiltree, the sage wanderer, does not believe in freedom any more than Oldbuck; in his youth, as a soldier, he had helped to subdue an Irish rising. But, conversely, Oldbuck does not share Sir Arthur Wardour's panicky reflections on the French revolution. All they want is a quiet life: that is the path to virtue, and contentment.

Of course, this represents a very important strand of Scott's mentality; and the ways in which the Gothic plot threatens to destroy the realistic fabric of this book are shown, in his life, to be more than an artistic flaw. Like the Antiquary, he learnt to balance the passions of his youth against the delights of friendship and of the mind. Had Scott had better luck, and more good sense, he would have lived and died the Antiquary: instead he became Sir Arthur Wardour, duped by hare-brained financial schemes and *folie de grandeur*. There are moments when, in his ludicrous vanity, and in the way that he tries to subdue his daughter to his own egotism, Sir Arthur Wardour puts us in mind of Sir Walter Elliot. But when, at the end of the book, his fortunes mend a little and 'he talked of buying contiguous estates, that would have led him from one side of the island to another', he seems to resemble another Sir Walter. Scott's baronetcy was two years away when he was writing *The Antiquary*: he could hardly have known how much of his own history was going into the book, nor how much his life was to hold up a mirror to his art.

Yet while the disjointedness of his plots can be explained in terms of his own psychology, this can be only part of the truth. The love interest in his books is so fantastic precisely because it was so real to him. But biographical criticism can only deal in hints and echoes. Nothing can ever be certain, and much is bound to be distorted; and this is especially true with the greatest imaginative powers, which are always the least egotistical. The novel at its best is as far removed from direct autobiography as possible, and in Scott's novels this is unquestionably the case. They are the product of his insatiable delight in characters other than himself. If the story of the young man in love and done out of an inheritance is a piece of Scott's 'personal myth', it is fantastic because it was pushed to the furthest borders of his consciousness.

Much more important than any early aspirations as a lover or a landowner was Scott's passion for reading. Only fifteen years of his life were devoted to writing novels; but well over fifty years were spent reading them. More than once he misquotes Gray, 'that to lie upon a couch and read new novels was no bad idea of Paradise'.[23] He had read all the novels that there were to read. His *Lives of the Novelists* is not an uncritical account of eighteenth-century fiction, but it reflects such a profound enjoyment of reading that he can never be critical for long. His chief objects of censure are not implausibility, nor even incompetence, so much as errors of taste. Of the author of *Hermsprong*—whom, on the whole, he likes very well—he only complains that Bage's women are licentious and his men malign.[24] In his life of the *doyenne* of the Gothic novel, he conceded that, 'it may be true that Mrs Radcliffe rather walks in fairy-land than in the region of realities',[25] but he likes her none the worse for it: 'She has taken the lead in a line of composition, appealing to those powerful and general sources of interest, a latent sense of supernatural awe, and curiosity concerning whatever is hidden and mysterious.'

In the most famous of his reviews, that of Jane Austen's *Emma*—it appeared in the *Quarterly* in 1815—Scott recognizes the excellence of the new order of fiction:

A style of novel has arisen, within the last fifteen or twenty years, differing from the former in points upon which interest hinges; neither alarming our credulity nor amusing our imagination by wild variety of incident, or by those pictures of romantic affection and sensibility, which were formerly as certain attributes of fictitious characters as they are of rare occurence among those who actually live and die. The substitute for these excitements, which have lost much of their poignancy by the repeated and injudicious use of them, was the art of copying from nature as she really exists in the common walks of life, and presenting to the reader, instead of the splendid scenes of an imaginary world, a correct and striking representation of that which is daily taking place around him.[26]

His praise for Jane Austen is almost unqualified, and the distinction which he makes between her work and his own in the Journal is well known:

That young lady had a talent for describing the involvements and feelings and characters of ordinary life which is to me the most wonderful I ever met with. The Big Bow wow strain I can do myself like any now going, but the exquisite touch which renders ordinary common-place things and characters interesting from the truth of the description and the sentiment is denied to me.[27]

It has already emerged, in our discussion of Scott's own novels of contemporary life, that this is not, strictly speaking, true. Although in a completely different mode from Jane Austen, he does manage, 'the exquisite touch which renders ordinary common-place things and characters interesting'. But he does so in the oddest possible way. It did not need any tradition of fiction, the example of Maria Edgeworth or of Henry Mackenzie, to call it into being. Dandie Dinmont, Jonathan Oldbuck and Meg Dods are a new order of things altogether, closely observed provincial types who are completely lifelike. What distinguishes Scott's fiction in this respect from Jane Austen's is the extraordinary social range of his canvas. As he rather snobbishly observes in another passage in the Journal, her characters 'do not . . . get above the middle classes of society'. It is a telling phrase. Scott, of course, does get above those classes, not always with the happiest effects. But when he sinks below them to describe peasants and farmers and gypsies and fishermen, he never fails to sparkle. They are the liveliest beings in literature outside Shakespeare—as are his parsons, his innkeepers, his village idiots, and his soldiers. But they are all obliged to inhabit the Gothic castle of a melodramatic plot.

Scott was the happy prisoner of the literary traditions of his times, and drew on them all indiscriminately. He was quite right, of course, to have exciting plots. Novels do not live without them; or at least, the ones which do are exceptional. *The Waves*, *Afternoon Men* and *On Grand Central Station I sat down and wept* are all very well; but what do we read novels for, if not to find out what happens next? Scott's novels remain obstinately novels. By accepting the improbable conventions of Gothic fiction, he could let in fine things. The result sometimes seems clumsy. Even the ladies at the tea-table in *St. Ronan's Well* remark that Clara Mowbray looks as if she has stepped out of another mode of fiction—'Many people think her handsome—but she looks so like something from another world, that she makes me always think of Mat Lewis's Spectre Lady.' But the convention serves. Scott could draw on all levels of experience except his own when he chose to write realistic fiction. Then only the conventions of romance could speak of matters which lay buried until the arrival by post of a package from Lady Jane Stuart which broke a silence of thirty-five years.

But there is one exception, one book in which his 'personal myth' and his debt to the conventions of fiction seem perfectly married. It is one of his most magnificent achievements, and we must look at it in more detail.

3

Redgauntlet is a difficult novel to classify. It is not quite a novel of contemporary life; nor, really, can it be called an historical novel. The period in which it is set is rather before Scott's birth, yet much of it depends on his own personal memories, and Lockhart tells us that this book 'contains . . . more of the author's personal experiences than any other' of the Waverley novels. These personal experiences are moulded into the most exciting Jacobite adventure story ever written. But at the same time it is the book in which we are most aware of Scott as a *novelist*, experimenting with a variety of novel forms, stretching its limits, and drawing on the fictional preoccupations of his contemporaries. Nor was it without influence. *Wuthering Heights* and Lermontov's *Hero of Our Time* owe much to its fluid yet carefully controlled structure. No 'straight' English novel before it has quite such boldness or untidiness of technique (one discounts *Tristram Shandy*), nor is, at first sight, a better example of the Romantic formlessness of nineteenth-century fiction. It begins as an epistolary tale, like a novel by Richardson, with digressions and stories within the story in the manner of Fielding and the picaresque tradition. It continues as a double narrative, chronicling the adventures of its two heroes, Alan Fairford and Darsie Latimer; and part of this narrative is told in the form of Darsie Latimer's journal. Yet although, since its first reviews, there have been purists who have objected to this stylistic floppiness, to Scott's inability to make up his mind how it was to be written, this is actually one of its strengths. For, without this multiple structure, Scott could never have brought about the very clever manipulations of viewpoint which make the book not only a great novel, but a monument in the history of ideas.

We have already noticed that when Scott is writing about Williamina, the story moves into the realms of conventional fantastic fiction: she is transformed into the pallid, persecuted maiden of Gothic romance, the hero into the eighteenth-century fictional hero in search of his identity and heritage—like, in different ways, Theodore in *The Castle of Otranto* or Tom Jones. *Redgauntlet* has two young heroes, rather than one. Tradition generally recognizes that they are based on Scott himself and on his student friend William Clerk. Yet, in another way, they are both obviously two sides of the same character: Alan Fairford, anxious to do well at the law to please his strict old father, and vicariously delighting in Darsie Latimer's wild adventures and contact with the heroic past. Alan Fairford is Scott's Edinburgh self; Darsie Latimer his Border self. So, when the heroine appears, wearing the same green mantle which had veiled the face of Williamina when Scott first saw her in the rain outside Greyfriars' Church, it is hardly surprising that they both fall in love with her. When it emerges that she is Darsie Latimer's sister, there are no disturbing fears that his feelings will persist; no hint, as in nearly all Fielding's novels, of incest. He can become immediately detached: 'She held out her hand to her brother, who grasped it with a fondness of pressure very different from the manner in which they first clasped hands that morning.' This could not be acceptable in a novel with only one hero. But it is accommodated perfectly easily here, because we know that it leaves her free for the solid, pleasant Alan Fairford.

In terms of Scott's own attitude to Williamina the story makes very good sense. The passions which he felt for her belonged more properly to Romance than to Life. They were not the stuff of which solid domestic happiness is made. Doctor Johnson was of the opinion that 'marriages would in general be as happy, and often more so, if they were all made by the Lord Chancellor, upon a due consideration of characters and circumstances, without the parties having any choice in the matter.'[28] And Scott would have agreed. He was devoted to his wife, but, as he admitted to Lady Abercorn,

Mrs Scott's match and mine was of our own making, and proceeded from the most sincere affection on both sides, which was rather increased than diminished during twelve years marriage. But it is something short of love in all its forms, which I suspect people only feel once in their lives: folk who have been nearly drowned in bathing rarely venturing a second time out of their depth.[29]

He is at pains to emphasize this point of view in the novel:

Let not those . . . who enter into a union for life without those embarrassments which delight a Darsie Latimer, or a Lydia Languish, and which are perhaps necessary to excite an enthusiastic passion in breasts more firm than theirs, augur worse of their future happiness, because their own alliance is formed under calmer auspices. Mutual esteem, an intimate knowledge of each other's character, seen, as in their case, undisguised by the mists of too partial passion—a suitable proportion of parties in rank and fortune, in taste and pursuits—are more frequently found in a marriage of reason than in a union of romantic attachment where the imagination, which probably created the virtues and accomplishments with which it invested the beloved object, is frequently afterwards employed in magnifying the mortifying consequences of its own delusion, and exasperating all the stings of disappointment. Those who follow the banners of Reason are like the well-disciplined battallion, which, wearing a more sober uniform, and making a less dazzling show than the light troops commanded by Imagination, enjoy more safety, and even more honour, in the conflicts of human life. All this, however, is foreign to our present purpose. . . .

(Chapter Seventeenth)

Like so many of Scott's asides, of course, it is very far from foreign to the purposes of the book, which is, among other things, a debate between common sense and the irrational. Anyone who could write a paragraph like the one just quoted could make out a good enough case for reason, cool self-love and detachment. Perhaps only Scott, placed between the two worlds of the violent Jacobite past and the serenely ordered intellectual world of Hume; between the superstitions and fears of his rural inheritance and the bland decency of his clubs; between the humdrum existence of a professional lawyer and the mad worlds of contemporary fiction, could have achieved the balance which makes *Redgauntlet* so remarkable. The book is powerful because Scott accepts the irreconcilable nature of all these opposites. When he stage-managed the visit of George IV to Edinburgh in 1822, parading the ludicrously obese monarch in the kilt, there could have been no more public declaration in his belief that the Hanoverian cause had won, and that the Jacobites were, in Redgauntlet's phrase, 'lost forever'. Nor is there any hypocrisy in Scott's veneration of George IV, both as a man and a monarch. Yet who, contemplating that royal belly which nearly reached the ground, or the flabby pink legs swathed in stockings and skein-dhu which protruded beneath the tartan, can for a moment have believed that the new order was nobler than the old?

The plot of *Redgauntlet* is so familiar that there is no need to rehearse
it here. But it might be helpful to examine the ways in which it works.
Alan Fairford is pursuing his legal studies in Edinburgh under the
strict surveillance of his father. In every respect, this section of the
book is generally admitted to reflect Scott's personal experience; Mr
Fairford having all the piety, parsimony, honesty and diligence of
Walter Scott *père*. But his young friend Darsie Latimer, having come
into some money, decides to wander a little on the east coast of
Scotland in pursuit of adventure.

A mysterious, rather sinister figure by the name of Herries has been
calling at the office; so has a beautiful young woman in a green
mantle: and both of them seem to be interested in pursuing Darsie
Latimer. The girl wants to warn Darsie of something. But the old
man's intentions seem less clear, and the dark mutterings which are
overheard between him and the older Mr Fairford begin to give cause
for alarm. Darsie Latimer has already reached the Solway Firth: here
he nearly gets swallowed up in the quicksands, but is rescued by a
rough though noble figure whom he takes to be a fisherman:

His features were high and prominent in such a degree that one knew not
whether to term them harsh or handsome. In either case, the sparkling grey
eye, aquiline nose and well-formed mouth, combined to render his physiog-
nomy noble and expressive. An air of sadness, or severity, or both, seemed to
indicate a melancholy and at the same time a haughty temper. I could not
help running mentally over ancient heroes, to whom I might assimilate the
noble form and countenance before me.

(Letter Fourth)

Yet all is not well. As Darsie is put to bed in the fisherman's cottage,
worn out and sick, the 'fisherman' paces the floor, while a storm rages
outside.

'An odd amusement, this,' I thought, 'for one who had been engaged at
least part of the preceding day in violent exercise, and who talked of rising by
the peep of dawn on the ensuing morning.'
Meantime I heard the storm, which had been brewing during the evening,
begin to descend with vengeance sounds as of distant thunder (the noise of
more distant waves, doubtless, on the shore), mingled with the roaring of the
neighbouring torrent, and with the crashing, groaning, and even screaming of
the trees in the glen, whose boughs were tormented by the gale. . . .

(Letter Fourth)

By morning, Darsie is afraid: '*Alan, there is something terrible about this man.*'

These rather flattering visions of Mr Herries are contradicted in the next chapter, which is a letter from Alan Fairford describing Herries's visit to the household in Edinburgh:

I can only say I thought him eminently disagreeable and ill-bred. No *ill-bred* is not the proper word on the contrary, he appeared to know the rules of good breeding perfectly, and only to think that the rank of the company did not require that he should attend to them—a view of the matter infinitely more offensive than if his whole behaviour had been that of uneducated and proper rudeness. While my father said grace, the Laird did all but whistle aloud; and when I, at my father's desire, returned thanks, he used his toothpick, as if he had waited that moment for its exercise.

So much for Kirk—with King, matters went even worse. My father, thou knowest, is particularly full of deference to his guests; and in the present case he seemed more than usually desirous to escape every cause of dispute. He so far compromised his loyalty as to announce merely, 'the King' as his first toast after dinner, instead of the emphatic 'King George', which is his usual formula. Our guest made a motion with his glass, so as to pass it over the water-decanter which stood beside him, and added, 'Over the water'.

(Letter Fifth)

It has not actually been spelt out at this stage, of course, that the mysterious fisherman and the ill-mannered laird are the same person, but no hardened novel reader could be in much doubt of the matter. Both expressions of slightly priggish fear and disgust do much to increase the stranger's fascination over us. The whole climate of the adventure story makes us want to escape the dull world of Alan's father; but the irrational fears of Darsie Latimer seem to draw on a different *genre* altogether.

'The plot thickens, dear Alan.' Darsie falls in with a benign old Quaker called Joshua Geddes whose house is on the edge of the Solway Firth, while Alan meets the Lady of the Green Mantle and falls in love. Darsie's sojourn with the Quaker appears to contain two scarcely relevant digressions, but they are both integral parts of the plot. First, he meets a blind old fiddler called Willie Steenson (Stevenson) who tells him a horrifying story of diabolism. His father was the tenant of an old Jacobite laird called Sir Robert Redgauntlet, 'who lived in these parts before the dear years . . . Far and wide was Sir Robert hated and feared. Men thought he had a direct compact with

Satan—that he was proof against steel.' Steenie Steenson came to pay
his annual rent to his Laird. He had put his purse down on the table
before the terrifying old man, but as he did so, Sir Robert was seized
with apoplexy: 'Terribly the Laird roared for cauld water to his feet,
and wine to cool his throat; and Hell, hell, hell, and its flames, was aye
the word in his mouth. They brought him water; and when they
plunged his feet into the tub, he cried out it was burning; and folk say
that it *did* bubble and sparkle like a seething caldron.' (Letter
Eleventh.) Sir Robert died, needless to say, and his heir, Sir John
Redgauntlet, again summoned Steenson to ask for his rent. Steenie
says that he has already paid for it, and Sir John asked him for the
receipt to prove it. He could not produce it; nor could he afford to pay
the rent over again. As he came disconsolately away, he fell in with a
stranger, who offered to get him a receipt from the old Laird. They
rode together into the thickest part of a neighbouring wood, where
they came to a house which seemed exactly like Redgauntlet Castle,
but which Steenson realized was the gate of hell. There he found the
old Laird, sitting at a drunken rout surrounded by the villains of
Scotch history.

> There was the Bluidy Advocate MacKenzie who, for his worldly wit and
> wisdom had been to the rest as a god. And there was Claverhouse, as beautiful
> as when he lived, with his long, dark, curled locks, streaming down over his
> laced buff-coat, and his left hand always on his right spule blade, to hide the
> wound that the silver bullet had made.
>
> (Letter Eleventh)

Sir Robert Redgauntlet roared at Steenie through the noise to come
and collect his receipt, and told him that he would find his money in
the 'Cat's Cradle'. When Steenie returned to Sir John Redgauntlet
with the receipt, his story was of course not believed, particularly
since the receipt had been dated after the old Laird's death; but when
they searched for the money they found it in the place that the fiend
had indicated.

We are not asked by Scott to take this story entirely at face value. As
John Buchan pointed out, it is very cleverly told, so that we can see,
even within Wandering Willie's narrative itself, inconsistencies and
confusions which allow us to provide quite rational explanations of
how the money came to be recovered.[30] But the effect of the tale is to
associate the name of Redgauntlet with the very deepest feelings of

terror. Above all, perhaps, we remember that 'he had a way of bending his brows, that men saw the visible mark of a horse-shoe in his forehead, deep-dinted as if it had been stamped there.'

The next digression, equally essential to the plot, is the controversy surrounding Joshua Geddes's fisheries. The locals object to the Quaker's habit of netting fish at the mouth of the firth and a riot develops in consequence. In the midst of the fighting Darsie Latimer is kidnapped, and finds himself face to face with his old pursuer, Mr Herries. The older man appears to have rescued Darsie once more, but it soon becomes clear that he has taken him captive. Darsie finds himself borne off to the north of England. Upon no very good charge, he is brought before a magistrate who seems to be in collusion with Herries, and it is during these rather alarming discussions that Latimer first notices the old man's brow:

The furrows of the brow above the eyes became livid and almost black, and were bent into a semicircular, or rather elliptical form, above the junction of the eyebrows. I had heard such a look described in an old tale of *diablerie*, which it was my chance to be entertained with not long since; when this deep and gloomy contortion of the frontal muscles was not inaptly described as forming the representation of a small horse-shoe.

(Chapter Sixth)

But there are worse shocks in store. Darsie Latimer has not been imprisoned in the Herries household long before something in the looking-glass has caught his attention. It has already become clear that 'Mr Herries' is a Jacobite and up to no good.

He had claimed over me the rights of a guardian; he had more than hinted that I was in a state of mind which could not dispense with the authority of such a person. Was this man so sternly desperate in his purpose—he who seemed willing to take on his own shoulders the entire support of a cause which had been ruinous to thousands—was he the person that had the power of deciding on my fate? Was it from him these dangers flowed, to secure me against which I had been educated under circumstances of such secrecy and precaution?

And if this was so, of what nature was the claim he asserted? Was it that of propinquity? And did I share the blood, perhaps the features, of this singular being?—Strange as it may seem, a thrill of awe, which shot across my mind at that instant was not unmingled with a wild and mysterious feeling of wonder, almost amounting to pleasure. I remembered the reflection of my own face in the mirror, at one striking moment during the singular interview of the day, and I hastened to the outward apartment to consult a glass which hung there, whether it were possible for my countenance to be again contorted into the peculiar frown which so much resembled the terrific look of Herries.

(Chapter Eighth)

'Mr Herries' is, of course, Edward Redgauntlet; Darsie Latimer is his nephew, the son of Sir Henry Redgauntlet, a Jacobite hero who had been captured at Culloden and escaped the English troops.

The way in which their consanguinity is established has more in common with the *doppelganger* themes of Romantic fiction, than with any realistic procedures. And it is noticeable that the mere establishment of the hero's identity is only part of the plot; not, as in *Guy Mannering*, *The Antiquary*, or *St. Ronan's Well* the whole of it. Darsie Latimer's identity is only the first stage of his involvement with the abortive attempt to restore the Stuart line to the throne.

Apart from the very obvious remarks already made about Scott's uses of conventional forms of fiction to describe matters which were personally near to him, there is no discernible reason for the *doppelganger* motive to crop up in this Jacobite adventure story. But remembering the date of the novel—1824—it might be helpful to consider one or two other literary developments of the time.

Six years earlier, Scott had reviewed Mary Shelley's *Frankenstein* for the *Quarterly*. He distinguished her use of the supernatural from that of her forerunners in horror literature, by comparing books which delighted in fantasy for its own sake, and those, like *Frankenstein*, in 'which the laws of nature are represented as altered, not for the purpose of pampering the imagination with wonders, but in order to show the probable effect which the supposed miracles would produce in those who witnessed them'.[31] This is what explains the essential seriousness of Mary Shelley's book. But it would apply, equally, to Wandering Willie's Tale, which we see not only as an example of superstition working on the mind of a peasant, but of the disturbing effects of supernatural reflections on the romantic sensibility of Darsie Latimer.

Yet perhaps the most striking feature of Mary Shelley's romance is the sympathetic quality of the monster. Frankenstein himself persists in telling everyone that his creation is 'as hellish as his form, full of treachery and fiend-like malice'.[32] But in fact, for all his murderous instincts, for all the horror of his shadow falling on the snow at the

beginning of the book, we come to see things largely from the monster's point of view. The awakening of his love of nature, and his
perusal of *Paradise Lost* and the *Sorrows of Werter* establish him as a
wholly reputable Romantic hero, so that by the end of the book we feel
far more anger with his creator than with the monster himself. Indeed, the confusion among the minds of cinema-goers, the almost
general belief that Frankenstein is the name of the monster, has a sort
of justice about it. Creator and creature are emanations of the same
romantic energy.

Even more do we feel this to be the case in *Melmoth the Wanderer*,
written by that peculiar Irish parson Charles Maturin and published
in 1820. Scott had quite a lot to do with Maturin, reviewing several of
his books favourably, lending him money, and encouraging him in his
literary career. The novel by which he is best known is a Pandora's
box, with endless stories within stories, many of them lifted directly
from other books, most notably the fiction of Diderot. But if it has a
main story, *Melmoth the Wanderer* concerns a young man inheriting his
fortune from an uncle, and discovering that he is related to a man who
has sold his soul to the devil in exchange for a protracted existence in
the world—when the story opens, the Wanderer is some two hundred
years old. Melmoth is perhaps less sympathetic than Frankenstein's
monster, and there is much more in this book of what Scott would
have seen as a morbid delight in the fantastic for its own sake. But the
details of the story overlap quite strikingly with *Redgauntlet*. A young
man, with an uncle whose evil heritage goes back several centuries, is
inextricably tied up with the evil fortunes of his birthright. Like
Melmoth, Darsie Latimer finds that he has the same name as his
pursuer. They even, as the young man in Maturin's book discovers
when contemplating with horror the portrait of his wicked ancestor,
look alike. But, like all these emanations, the Wanderer is attractive.
When the end comes, and he is finally summoned to his hellish
reward, he has a dream in which he remembers all the victims whom
he has helped to suck into his own ruinous schemes. Then, 'The
burning waves boomed over his sinking head, and the clock of eter-
nity rung out its awful chime—"Room for the soul of the Wanderer!"—and the waves of the burning ocean answered, as they lashed
the adamantine rock—"There is room for more! . . ."'[33] In the next
chapter, his nephew and the Spaniard watch as the body of the lost
soul begins to age: 'The fearful lustre of his eyes had been deadened
before their late interview, but now the lines of extreme age were

visible in every feature. His hairs were as white as snow, his mouth had fallen in, the muscles of his face were relaxed and withered.'[34] He asks them to leave him alone, and when they return to the room he has disintegrated entirely.

It would be far-fetched to compare all this with Redgauntlet's final farewell to his nephew on the shore: 'Bless you, young man! If I have dealt harshly with you, forgive me. I have set my whole desires on one point—God knows, with no selfish purpose; and I am justly punished by this final termination of my views, for having been too little scrupulous in the means by which I pursued them. . . .' (Chapter Twenty-third.) There is nothing devilish about him here, even though, with his departure, the Jacobite cause seems to evaporate with all the terrifying swiftness of the mortal frame of Melmoth the Wanderer.

Of course, if we were looking for a direct experiment with the *doppelganger* theme in Scotch Literature, we should examine Hogg's *Confessions of a Justified Sinner*, which appeared in the same year as *Redgauntlet*; but both books, I think, owe much to Maturin. Hogg's story really writes itself, given the original conception of a man possessed by a wicked alter-ego or devil, who persuades him to stir up fights, murder members of his own family, and so on. Scott's use of the motif is altogether more oblique and subtle. It is only in the most skeletal form that the fantastic conventions of horror literature shape the story. Scott is concerned to show the powerful attraction, not of evil, but of nobility distorted into fanaticism.

Redgauntlet can thrill us in the first half of the book, but we do not exactly wish to be on his side. Then the emphasis of the story changes. Alan Fairford, just about to achieve some success in his first brief, breaks off the case on hearing that Latimer is in captivity. He comes south, and meets a man called Maxwell of Summertrees—'Pate-in-Peril'—whose memory of the Redgauntlets is very different from anything we have heard to date. Fairford rather snootily observes that since Sir Henry Redgauntlet had fled to England after Culloden he had made himself 'less of a Scottishman' than his brother. Pate-in-Peril knew the man, and he dismisses the sneer.

'Poor Harry was none of your bold-speaking, ranting reivers, that talk about what they did yesterday, or what they will do tomorrow; it was when something was to do at the moment that you should have looked at Harry Redgauntlet. I saw him at Culloden, when all was lost, doing more than twenty of these bleezing braggarts, till the very soldiers that took him cried out not to hurt him— . . . for he was the bravest fellow of them all. Weel, as I went up by the side of Harry, and felt him raise my hand up in the mist of the morning, as if he wished to wipe his eye—for he had not that freedom without my leave—my heart was like to break for him, poor fellow. . . .'

(Chapter Eleventh)

The image of two men, handcuffed together on the field of defeat and hiding their tears from one another, has a subdued poignancy which attracts our respect more than any of Edward Redgauntlet's bragging. Once we have heard it, our sympathies are engaged. Redgauntlet's fanatical refusal to recognize that the cause is lost is more palatable when we remember the nobility of the cause itself, and the heroism of the Jacobites in 1745.

This is a book which expounds the tragedy of Toryism. Bagehot said that Toryism was enjoyment. *Redgauntlet* puts us more in mind of Stanley Baldwin's assertion that the last ditch was his spiritual home. A conservative temperament always hovers on the brink which divides these positions. Scott analyzed it perfectly in his art—the habit of mind which, by holding on to good things for too long, distorts them and makes them ridiculous. But the book has a final twist: for its historical realism is not the final word. Of course, General Campbell is right when, at the end of the book, he tells Redgauntlet that 'It is now all over, and Jacobite will be henceforward no longer a party name.' Of course, Redgauntlet's cause has not been worth fighting for; and even he has become disillusioned by the coarseness and unreliability of the Chevalier. But Redgauntlet, like his brother at Culloden in the hour of defeat, leaves us feeling that victory is itself fragile, and that loyalty is more important than success.

'The fatal doom,' he said, with a melancholy smile, 'will, I trust, now depart from the House of Redgauntlet, since its present representative has adhered to the winning side. I am convinced he will not change it, should it in turn become the losing one.'

(Chapter Twenty-third)

As it happened, one fat Hanoverian monarch was to succeed the next in comfortable succession until the reign of Edward VII. But in 1824 no one was to know that. Scott's rage and horror at Reform can hardly be palatable to many readers today, but there can be no doubt of his courage in opposing it. *Redgauntlet* does not leave us with the comfortable and patronizing conviction that it is foolish to hold on to old ideas and old ways indefinitely. Instead, it poses the much more complicated question of how often we can yield to change on the grounds of expediency and common sense without sacrifice of principle.

There is one event above all in 1824 which should not go unmentioned, and that is the death of Lord Byron. Scott heard news of it when *Redgauntlet* was half finished, so that we can hardly claim that Byron's death is reflected in its pages. But Byron's gesture of going to fight in Greece had been on Scott's mind for a long time. He saw it, not as a political action, of which he would have stoutly disapproved, but as an atonement, through heroism, for his dissipated career. He believed that Byron was 'dying of homesickness ... He went to Greece in the hope of doing some gallant deed that would wipe out his disgrace and create for him such sympathy in the breasts of his countrymen, as would enable him to return—"his faults forgiven, and his sins forgot".'

It is a peculiar but beautiful notion. And the sense that the heroic deed can cancel out a catalogue of bad behaviour is part of the logic of *Redgauntlet*. There is something quite Byronic, in the early stages of this novel, about the hero's evil fascination. By the end, both Redgauntlet and Byron seem to say that a noble action is more important than the cause for which it is made.

CHAPTER FIVE

Scott's Religion
The Monastery and *The Abbot*

The enthusiasm of our Scottish ladies has now grown to such a
height that I am almost certain it will lead to some dangerous
revolution in the state.

Scott, quoted by Hogg.

I would if calld upon die a martyr for the Christian religion.

(Journal)

I

In the summer of 1828, four years after *Redgauntlet*, the Regius Professor of Hebrew elect at Oxford was travelling in the north on his
wedding journey. Since his bride was a friend of the Morritt family, to
whom Scott had dedicated *Rokeby*, and since the young couple had
read that poem in the uncertain days of their courtship as a story of
their own romance, John Morritt wrote a letter of introduction to the
Laird of Abbotsford.

My dear Morritt [Scott replied],
    Mr Pusey shall be welcome when he casts up. I suppose we shall probably
see him at Abbotsford and have only to hope that my dogs may be made to
comprehend that he spells his name with a single s, for as *Pussey* he would
meet a shrewish reception. This is Anne's wit, not mine. If we are here we can
only offer him the most slender of all hospitality a breakfast for I do not
believe we have knives and forks enough to dine above two people our
residence here at this session being so temporary. . . .[1]

The scarcely welcoming tone, and the weary joke, reflect much of
Scott's mood at this time. With his fortune in ruins and his wife in the
grave, he hardly felt equal to face the hordes of sight-seers who still
regarded a visit to Abbotsford as a necessary thing to say they had
done before journeying south. The exaggerated claim about knives
and forks can hardly have borne much relation to the truth since, in

the same letter, Scott urges Morritt to come himself, bringing all the children: 'Mrs Baillie I hope will also come with you baby and all. We have room for cavalry infantry bag and baggage if you have any. . . .'[2] Nevertheless, Pusey's visit went off well enough, although the learned Doctor fell in the Tweed and narrowly escaped drowning.[3]

When one contemplates this visit, one recognizes the wisdom of Scott's vision of change in *The Lay of the Last Minstrel* and *Redgauntlet*. Time goes backwards as well as forwards. Who, at that breakfast table, could have predicted the reversals of ecclesiastical affairs which were to be brought about when Pusey himself had become a widower, devoted to the foundation of ritualist churches and convents, spending his days reading the Fathers and writing to nuns about the value of hair-shirts and flagellation? Still less predictable, in that year before Catholic emancipation, would have been the fortunes of Pusey's colleague at Oriel, John Newman, who, while Scott lay dying, 'was saying prayers (whatever they were worth) for him continually, thinking of Keble's words: "Think on the minstrel as ye kneel".'[4] Only twenty-one years after Scott's death, his granddaughter had embraced the doctrines of Rome, and Newman, now a priest of that persuasion, was saying mass each day in the newly-built oratory while he awaited the result of his trial for libel. Only Scott's sense of how seemingly moribund historical issues can crop up and repeat themselves could explain the phenomenon. But a discussion of his place in the Tractarian mind belongs more properly to the chapter in which I shall be discussing the popularity of his medieval fiction. On the most obvious level, it is hard to avoid the conclusion that he would have been horrified to think of his descendants going over to Rome.

Hogg tells us that Scott

was no great favourer of sects, and seldom or never went to church . . . He dreaded religion as a machine by which the good government of the country might be deranged, if not uprooted. There was one evening when he and Morritt of Rokeby, some Fergusons and I, were sitting over our wine, that he said, 'There is nothing I dread so much as a very religious woman; she is not only a dangerous person, but a perfect shower-bath on all social conviviality. The enthusiasm of our Scottish ladies has now grown to such a height that I am almost certain it will lead to some dangerous revolution in the state.'[5]

There is another delightful story of his admiration for the master-builder at Abbotsford, a Galashiels man called Paterson. He told

Laidlaw, one of his most trusted servants, what a fine man Paterson was, and Laidlaw replied

'O he's a verra fine fellow. An extraordinar fine fellow, an' has a great deal o' comings and gangings in him. But dinna ye think, Mr Scott, that it's a great pity he should have been a preacher?'

'A preacher?' said Scott, staring at him, 'Good Lord! What do you mean?'

'Aha! it's a' ye ken about it!' said Laidlaw, 'I assure you he's a preacher, an' a capital preacher too. He's reckoned the best Baptist preacher in Galashiels, an' he preaches every Sunday to a great community o' low kind o' folks.'

On hearing this, Sir Walter (then Mr Scott) wheeled about and halted off with a swiftness Laidlaw had never seen him exercise before, exclaiming vehemently to himself, 'Preaches! D— him!' From that time forth, his delightful colloquies with Mr Paterson ceased.[6]

It would be easy, given the intellectual climate in Edinburgh after Hume, to get all this wrong, and to think of Scott as a sceptical empiricist and no more. In fact, and this is what makes the breakfast with Dr Pusey so haunting, he was a convert to the Episcopalian Church of Scotland. His distaste for Protestant ranting was not based on ignorance of it: one remembers the hours of sermonizing which he suffered every Sunday of his Presbyterian youth. He was much closer, once more, to Bishop Butler's position, who, during his interview with John Wesley in 1739, said soberly, 'Sir, the pretending to extraordinary revelations and gifts of the Holy Ghost is a horrid thing, a very horrid thing': that is, a thing which shocked and horrified. It was horrid, because for a believer in the Church, the Holy Ghost moves more indubitably through the agencies of reason and tradition than through the exciteable medium of enthusiastic utterance.

At first sight, it could be thought that Scott's Episcopalianism had no very pious motive. As we have seen, he worshipped quite regularly in Greyfriars' Presbyterian Church while he was courting Williamina. Then, when he knew himself to be rejected, he took the first chance of a holiday and travelled to the Lake District in the summer of 1797. There he met the young Frenchwoman, Charlotte Charpentier, to whom he almost immediately proposed marriage.

Although not so nobly born as Williamina, the future Lady Scott was the ward of Lord Downshire. It is hard to see why this peer, who lodged in the Charpentiers' house before the children were born, should have become their guardian when their mother died. Years later, when Lady Scott was dying, she was heard to murmur, 'Lord

Downshire, father . . .' and speculation inevitably leads to the possibility that she was the natural child of the Marquess. When Scott met
her, she was leading the sort of existence that was mapped out for
Harriet Smith in *Emma*, as the companion and confidante of Miss
Jane Nicholson, daughter of the Dean of Exeter and grand-daughter
of the Bishop of Carlisle; it was her connection with the Bishop which
explained the presence of the two young ladies in Cumberland. Scott
evidently found Charlotte very charming, and his letter of proposal to
Lord Downshire was accepted. He wrote to an aunt that there had
been some difficulty with his own father:

One main article was the uncertainty of her provision, which has been in part
removed by the safe arrival of her remittances for this year, with assurances of
their being regular and even larger in future, her brother's situation being
extremely lucrative. Another objection was her birth: 'Can any good thing
come out of Nazareth?' but as it was *birth merely and solely* this has been
abandoned. . . .[7]

'Nazareth' presumably means France, but difficulties about her
'birth' suggest, once more, illegitimacy. However, he adds, 'She is a
brunette;—her manners are lively, but, when necessary, she can be
very serious. She was baptized and educated a Protestant of the
Church of England.'[8] They were married in Carlisle Cathedral on
Christmas Eve 1797, and remained in happy union until her death
thirty years later.

After his marriage, Scott regarded himself as an Episcopalian. He
worshipped at the Episcopalian Church in Edinburgh—now a ware-
house for bathroom fittings—and, when at Abbotsford, read mattins
to the guests and servants from the Scottish Prayer Book, though
frequently sending his children off to the local Presbyterian church. It
would be quite wrong to think that he maintained a consistently
hostile attitude to the varieties of Scotch Protestantism, as Hogg's
stories would suggest. Although he once said that the only good thing
about going into a Presbyterian church was the knowledge that one
would come out of it again, he had a sentimental fondness for the
religion of his parents, and even for the more extreme sects which
flourish north of the Border. Among the other mascots and trophies
assembled at Abbotsford, he had hoped to include a domestic chaplain. The man he had in mind was not an Episcopalian, but an uncle
of his beloved Laidlaw, who was a Cameronian, an adherent of the

most rigid sort to the Solemn League and Covenant. This piece of fantasy—Richard Cameron, the founder of the sect, had been chaplain to one of Scott's ancestors—very nearly came off. He wrote to Laidlaw:

If, as the King of Prussia said to Rousseau, 'a little persecution is necessary to make his home entirely to his mind' he shall have it; and, what persecutors seldom promise, I will stop whenever he is tired of it. I have a pair of thumbikins also much at his service, if he requires their assistance to glorify God and Covenant. Seriously, I like enthusiasm of every kind so well, especially when united with worth of character, that I shall be delighted with this old gentleman.[9]

In the event, he did not come. It is typical of Scott to be delighted by religious enthusiasm which appealed to his antiquarian interests, but to stop speaking to his builder when he discovered he was a Baptist. Much of his religious observance was tied up with his feeling for the past. He was not unlike Pleydell, the lawyer in *Guy Mannering* who offered Colonel Mannering the choice of going to the Established or the Episcopalian Church on Sunday morning, and, after the service, spoke of the difference between Presbyterian sects:

'And you, Mr Pleydell, what do you think of their points of difference?'
    'Why, I hope, Colonel, a plain man may go to Heaven without thinking about them at all;—besides, *inter nos*, I am a member of the suffering and Episcopal Church of Scotland—the shadow of a shade now and fortunately so;—but I love to worship where my fathers prayed before me, without thinking the worse of the Presbyterian forms because they do not affect me with the same associations.'[10]

As in Pleydell's case, Scott's piety was quite real. It was not merely that the antiquity of episcopal forms appealed to his aesthetic and historical whims. As we have already noticed, he was a greater believer in the immortality of the soul than the immortality of poetry. Lockhart tells us that his father-in-law adhered to the Church, 'whose system of government and discipline he believed to be the fairest copy of the primitive polity, and whose litanies and collects he reverenced as having been transmitted to us from an age immediately succeeding that of the Apostles'.[11] Its historicity, in other words, was its truth.

During his last illness, Scott asked Lockhart to read to him; 'and when I asked from what book, he said,—"Need you ask? There is but one.'' Lockhart read from the fourteenth chapter of St. John.[12] As he sank into death, he muttered passages from the Bible,

or some of the magnificent hymns of the Romish ritual, in which he had always delighted . . . We very often heard distinctly the cadence of the *Dies Irae*; and I think the very last stanza that we could make out, was the first of a still greater favourite:

> Stabat mater dolorosa
> Juxta crucem lachrymosa,
> Dum pendebat Filius. . . .[13]

Everyone knows about Scott's last words, which Grierson dismissed as a 'pious myth—a concession to the censorious piety of the Evangelical age'.[14] A relation of Scott's wrote to Lockhart saying how frequently he had, in life, stressed the importance of being good, and of being religious. In Lockhart's account, three days before Scott actually died, he summoned him to the bedside and said, 'Lockhart, I may have but a minute to speak to you. My dear, be a good man, be virtuous—be religious—be a good man. Nothing else will give you any comfort when you come to lie here.'[15] I do not see why, if Scott had often said such things to his family, he should not have said them at the end; but many will agree with Grierson that this is a piece of pious fabrication. A quotation of a less contentious kind may be given from the Journal, and it expounds Scott's religious position more clearly: 'I would if calld upon die a martyr for the Christian religion, so completely is (in my poor opinion) its divine origin proved by its beneficial effects on the state of society.'[16] This is not the utterance of an 'enthusiastic' man, who has experienced the ecstasy of an evangelical conversion; it looks outwards, instead, to Christianity as a social force, capable of inspiring, at its best, unselfish and benevolent members of society. His religion was more like Butler's than Wesley's. That does not make it any less deep; the one sure anchor, in those last years, which saved him from despair. It was not the sort which was 'a perfect shower-bath on all social conviviality', but it guided and informed the profound interest he took, in his fiction, in the conflicting forces of religious fanaticism and cool, reasoning common sense.

2

The Monastery was published in March 1820, but he had been working at it before dictating *Ivanhoe* the previous year. In the three years that preceded it, he had, apart from *Ivanhoe*, produced *The Black Dwarf*, *Old Mortality*, *Rob Roy*, *The Heart of Midlothian*, *A Legend of Montrose*, and *The Bride of Lammermoor*. It is one of the most prodigious examples of artistic fertility and industry, comparable with Michelangelo's ceiling of the Sistine chapel or the symphonies of Mozart. It is the more remarkable when we remember that he wrote all these novels while exercising his duties as Sheriff of Selkirk and Clerk to the Court of Sessions at Edinburgh; that, throughout this period, he was suffering from crippling pain from gall-stones and rheumatism; that while writing essays and reviews, he was at the same time constantly expanding his estates at Abbotsford, and conversing with builders and gasmen.

So it is no surprise to find signs of haste and exhaustion in *The Monastery*. Father Philip, the sacristan, and Abbot Boniface, are crudely-realized gluttons, slapping their well-filled bellies with many a yo-ho-ho, Friar Tuckish figures like the monks in 'Tomorrow is Friday'. The details of their day-to-day existence in the cloister are not described, and the authenticity of liturgical and sartorial arrangements is questionable. We find an abbess wearing a dalmatic, a garment usually reserved for the use of deacons at high mass; at other times it also seems to be casually adopted instead of an overcoat.

The novel is set in the 1560s (at the latest) but Sir Piercie Shafton, the Elizabethan courtier, quotes freely from Lyly's *Euphues*—published in 1580—and from Sidney's *Arcadia* (1590). Yet, although the details of the book are extremely slapdash, it has some wonderful characters and some great scenes. Scott tells us in the Introduction—which, of course, happily admits the book's faults—that

the general plan of the story was, to conjoin two characters in that bustling and contentious age, who, thrown into situations which gave them different views on the subject of the Reformation, should, with the same sincerity and purity of intention, dedicate themselves, the one to the support of the sinking fabric of the Catholic Church, the other to the establishment of the reformed doctrines.[17]

Scott was not a religious novelist in the way that Charlotte M. Yonge or Cardinal Newman, both great admirers, could be so described. He would not have considered the private conversation of a human soul with its Maker as an appropriate subject for romance.

Yet, in spite of the many satirical portraits he has drawn of ranting fanaticism, he wrote from a position of commitment. He was horrified by the vandalism of the reformers. He wrote in *The Abbot* that

although in many instances, the destruction of Roman Catholic buildings . . . might be . . . an act of justice [or] an act of policy, there is no doubt that the humour of demolishing monuments of ancient piety and munificence, and that in a poor country like Scotland, where there was no chance of their being replaced, was both useless, mischievous and barbarous.

(Chapter VIII)

Yet there can be no doubt from *The Monastery* and its sequel that he believed the Reformation to be divinely inspired. And this conviction leads to the peculiar figure of the White Lady, a supernatural being who, unlike almost all other preternatural apparitions in Scott's fiction, admits of no 'rational' explanation. She flits across the moors near the Tower of Glendearg, as real as the widows and farmers and soldiers and priests who encounter her. She is a tutelary spirit to the family of Avenel, an aristocratic family fallen on bad times in the social upheaval of the world. Lady Avenel and her daughter Mary seek refuge in the Tower with the widow Glendinning and her two sons. It is hard to describe the White Lady to someone who has not read the book without making her sound absurd. When she first encounters Father Philip, the sacristan, one assumes that it will be revealed later that he was drunk, or that she was really Mary Avenel in disguise. But she appears to most of the major characters in turn, and she is quite real. Moreover, she is a Protestant. For when Lady Avenel, in her dying confession, reveals to the Sacristan that she inclines to the reformed religion, and the monk confiscates her Bible, the White Lady snatches it back, and returns it to the Glendinnings. All this sounds plain silly. But the level on which it happens and, above all, the sheer excellence of the writing, redeem it. When she returns the Bible to Halbert Glendinning amid the swirling mists of Glendearg, it is a compelling and completely moving account.

'If I have been a loiterer, Lady,' answered young Glendinning, 'thou shalt now find me willing to press forward with double speed. Other thoughts have filled my mind, other thoughts have engaged my heart, within a brief period—and, by Heaven, other occupations shall henceforward fill up my time. I have lived in this day the space of years—came hither as a boy—I will return a man—a man, such as may converse not only with his own kind, but

with whatever God permits to be visible to him. I will learn the contents of
that mysterious volume—I will learn why the Lady of Avenel loved it—why
the priests feared, and would have stolen it—why thou didst twice recover it
from their hands—What mystery is wrapt in it?—Speak, I conjure thee.'
The Lady assumed an air peculiarly sad and solemn, drooping her head, and
folding her arms on her bosom she replied:-

> Within that awful volume lies
> The mystery of mysteries!
> Happiest they of human race
> To whom God has granted grace
> To read, to fear, to hope, to pray,
> To lift the latch, and force the way;
> And better had they ne'er been born,
> Who read to doubt, or read to scorn. . . .

(Chapter XII)

People did not like the White Lady when the book was first published
and although, for me, she is one of the most powerful elements in the
novel, she may well be to few readers' taste.

The processes by which the Reformation happened are plotted
more realistically in the fortunes of the individual characters. We
know from the start that Halbert Glendinning, with his fondness for
soldierly pursuits, will make a way for himself in the world; and since
that world is presided over by the Regent Murray, and the Protestant
party is in the ascendant, it is inevitable that Halbert will be a
Protestant. It is equally inevitable that his brother Edward, quiet,
serious, contemplative and withdrawn, should feel called to the cloister when his brother wins the heart of Mary Avenel, with whom he
had himself been in love.

Religion, in Scott's pages, is more often a source of division and
pain than of solace and peace, and in *The Monastery* we see each
character inevitably lining up behind one faction or the other.
Perhaps the point comes home to us most strongly when the Sub-
Prior, Eustace, encounters the fanatical Protestant preacher Henry
Warden. It is a great triumph for the monastery to have captured this
dangerous heretic, and it is with a feeling of victorious satisfaction
that the Sub-Prior has the prisoner shown into his room:

As they gazed on each other, old recollections began to awake in either
bosom, at the sight of features long unseen and much altered, but not
forgotten. The brow of the Sub-Prior dismissed by degrees its frown of

command, the look of calm yet stern defiance gradually vanished from that of Warden, and both lost for an instant that of gloomy solemnity. They had been ancient and intimate friends at a foreign university, but had been long separated from each other; and the change of name, which the preacher had adopted for motives of safety, and the monk from the common custom of the convent, had prevented the possibility of their hitherto recognising each other in the opposite parts which they had been playing in the great polemical and political drama. But now the Sub-Prior exclaimed, 'Henry Wellwood!' and the preacher replied, 'William Allan!' and stirred by the old familiar names, and never-to-be-forgotten recollections of college studies and college intimacy, their hands were for a moment locked in each other.

(Chapter XXXI)

It is an excellent moment, and Scott does not spoil it by sentimentalizing their positions. After only a few sentences, they are quarrelling, leading to the monk's pregnant utterance 'We can no longer be friends. Our faith, our hope, our anchor on futurity is no longer the same.' That haunting phrase, *our anchor on futurity*, takes us to the heart of the novel's achievement. The narration has begun with a nineteenth-century antiquary standing among the ruins of Melrose with a Scottish Benedictine, now exiled from his Continental monastery because of the Napoleonic persecutions. We cannot know what futurity holds for the Sub-Prior when he utters the words from a position of power. He eventually becomes the Abbot; but his election is hugger-mugger, and the procession which follows it is less grand than pathetic:

The great gate of the Abbey was flung open, and the procession moved slowly forward from beneath its huge and richly adorned gateway. Cross and banner, pix and chalice, shrines containing relics, and censers streaming with incense, preceded and were intermingled with the long and solemn array of the brotherhood, in their long black gowns and scapularies hanging over them, the various officers of the convent each displaying his proper badge of office. In the centre of the procession came the Abbot, surrounded and supported by his chief assistants. He was dressed in his habit of high solemnity, and appeared as much unconcerned as if he were taking his usual part in some ordinary ceremony. After him came the inferior persons of the convent; the novices in their albs or white dresses, and the lay bretheren distinguished by their beards, which were seldom worn by the Fathers. Women and children, mixed with a few men, came in the rear, bewailing the apprehended desolation of their ancient sanctuary. . . .

(Chapter XXXVII)

Walking with the Abbot is a young novice called Edward Glendinning. Accompanying the Earl of Murray, who comes with a troop of soldiers to assert the victory of Protestant laymen over their former priestly masters, is his elder brother Halbert.

The sequel, *The Abbot* is a much finer novel. Whereas *The Monastery*, in its careless way, had been concerned with the party of new men who arose under the Regent Murray, with the awakening of the Protestant conscience, its political fortune, and its compelling truth, *The Abbot* concerns the losers in that conflict, and above all the figure of Mary Queen of Scots. It is hard to imagine an historical novel going very badly wrong with Queen Mary as one of its principal characters. She is one of the most endlessly puzzling and attractive figures in history, and Scott intensifies her interest and tragedy by concentrating on one very short incident in her life—her escape from the castle of Lochleven. With this historical 'background', he could have got away with almost anything. But his earlier carelessness is lain aside. He tells us in the Introduction that he has taken criticisms of *The Monastery* to heart. There is to be no more of the White Lady, and no more carelessly conceived characters like Sir Piercie Shafton. He makes us realize how brilliantly he understood the *shaping* of a novel.

But it is more than a very clever book. It takes up and develops the great theme of emerging Protestantism. In *The Monastery*, Scott had already established his commonsense view that religious opinions depend as much on character and environment as on the promptings of the intellect. In *The Abbot*, we see in the figure of its hero that the Reformation was a triumph of the human will. The papist, as a man who subordinates his will to the authority of the ages, has been (until our own age, when new and peculiar breeds of papist have arisen) in most important respects a passive man. And, in so far as he is passive, he would seem to be a poor figure to become the central intelligence of a novel. Perhaps this is why, in the last two centuries, there have been no great novelists who have also been practising Roman Catholics, those Protestant writers who have embraced the Roman faith almost always producing inferior novels in consequence. Evelyn Waugh, for example, described the theme of *Brideshead Revisited* as 'the operation of divine grace on a group of diverse but closely connected characters'. It is hard to imagine how anyone except a Roman Catholic of that date could have the temerity to trace so nebulous and sacred a thing in fiction. It cannot be done; it should not be done. If the attempt is made, as in all Waugh's later fiction, the characters cease to be free agents. But one is less aware of divine grace working upon them than of the intensely embarrassing sugary mind of the author who appeared, in *Brideshead*, and the books which followed, to have lost all the heady freedom and cleverness which distinguished his, admittedly slight, early novels.

The eighteenth-century Jesuit Jean Pierre de Caussade's *L'Abandon à la Providence divine*, counselling its readers to accept the will of Providence in all aspects of life, and to make no effort to change their destiny, is as far removed as possible from the imaginations which could conceive of Tom Jones or Pechorin or Quilp. And yet the intense conservatism of de Caussade's point of view would seem to fit, in a very striking way, the wispy central figures of so many of Scott's novels.

In his famous review of his own work in the *Quarterly*, he particularly singled out for censure the insipidity of his heroes:

His chief characters are never actors, but always acted upon by the spur of circumstances, and have their fates uniformly determined by the agency of subordinate persons . . . Every hero in poetry, in fictitious narrative, ought to come forth and do or say something or other which no other person could have done or said; make some sacrifice, surmount some difficulty, and become interesting to us otherwise than by his mere appearance on the scene, the passive tool of the other characters.[18]

When one thinks of the way in which Edward Waverley sets out to Scotland as a Hanoverian soldier and becomes involved in the Jacobite rebellion on the wrong side almost before he has had time to think about it, one sees the force of all this. Like many of his successors, he spends much of the novel either in prison or held in someone's house against his will. He is literally deprived of the ability to act. Much has been written about the essential conservatism which underlies this treatment of the hero in the Waverley Novels. A little has already been said in this book about the effect which the passivity of the heroes has on the general shape of Scott's fiction. The neutering of their wills could very well bear some half-hidden resemblance to de Caussade's position in *L'Abandon*. But the general effect of the novels is just the reverse, for they enable us to see the great movements and events which fill their pages with the necessary sympathy. *Waverley* would hardly be a better book if its hero had felt none of the attractions of Jacobitism; if he had not fallen in love with Flora MacIvor but, instead, had clapped her brother in prison at the first opportunity. Nor would we be better satisfied had Edward Waverley been found cheerfully on the victorious side at Culloden, rather than awkward and guilt-ridden, taking part in the infinitely more precarious Jacobite victory at Preston Pans.

'The privilege of free action belongs to no mortal,' Redgauntlet bitterly exclaims: and it seems to be the point in Scott's mind where the codes of heroic necessity meet the empiricist determinism of Hume. 'Liberty, when opposed to necessity, not to constraint, is the same thing with chance; which is universally allowed to have no existence.' But although the Waverley Novels perpetually hover on the edge of this view, the sheer liveliness of the characters always contradicts it. Meg Dods beating Captain MacTurk out of the Cleikum Inn with her broom defies Hume's assertion as violently as Doctor Johnson's shoe, kicking a stone, had refuted Bishop Berkeley.

When the hero of *The Abbot* is first presented to us—as a small boy—it seems that he is struck in the same passive mould as many of his predecessors in the Waverley Novels: he has been saved from drowning by a wolf-hound, and we meet him hanging from the animal's jaws.

The dog belongs to Mary Avenel, now the wife of Halbert Glendinning, and since they are childless, she leaps at the opportunity of taking the boy into her household. His parents are dead; his only living relation appears to be an itinerant, rather nunnish, grandmother; the arrangement seems to suit everyone.

But Roland Graeme is not like the other Scott heroes. He has the pertness and cheek which would better fit a hero in Stendhal or Lermontov. Certain of his superiority to the rest of the household, he is determined to get on in the world. Henry Warden, now the Protestant chaplain to the Glendinnings, excites Roland's contempt. So do all the other Glendinning servants and retainers. There are constant rows and, not long after his seventeenth birthday, he finds that he has taxed even Mary's patience too far and is thrust out to make his own way in the world.

The opening chapters tend to finish on a note, familiar to Scott readers, of the hero asserting his independence against the encroachment of events and of the will of others. For Roland is less of a free agent than he would like to believe. His grandmother, a fanatical adherent to the old religion, has been keeping a close watch on him, and catches up with him as soon as he has abandoned the courtly little world of Avenel. 'Have I relinquished the hawk and the hound,' he asks himself, 'to become the pupil of her pleasure as if I were still a child? . . . This may not, and must not be. I will be no reclaimed sparrow-hawk who is carried on a woman's wrist, and has his quarry only shown to him when his eyes are uncovered for his flight.' Yet by the end of the next chapter he has rejoined the service of Halbert Glendinning, and is going to seek his fortunes in Edinburgh, much less of a free agent than he supposed: 'Am I for ever to be devoured with the desire of independence and free agency and yet to be for ever led on, by circumstances, to follow the will of others?'

One of the impressive things about Roland Graeme as a hero is that he does achieve independence, even though it is more delicately balanced than he would have believed possible during his intolerant adolescence. His position, in terms of the political and religious conflicts of the day, has been ambivalent from the beginning of the book, since he is the grandchild of a pious papist, brought up in a Protestant household; quietly telling his beads during Henry Warden's sermons, and receiving private 'instruction' from Edward Glendinning, now the Abbot of Kennaquair. Later, when he is employed by the Regent Murray to be a page to the imprisoned Queen on Lochleven, this ambivalence increases. He is already in love with Catherine Seyton, the Queen's maid, and the daughter of a great Catholic house; and he is as completely enchanted by the Queen's beauty and wit, as he is loyal to the duty of protecting her person. It is he who is largely instrumental in her wonderfully exciting escape from the castle. Yet, as he grows up, he is firmly his own man. The romance of the Stuart cause captivates him completely, but the Protestant preacher Elias Henderson, chaplain to the household on Lochleven, convinces him of the errors of popery. It is all very much less casual than the way in which Waverley had been enchanted by the romance of the Jacobite cause but, for the purposes of real life, could return to England as a loyal Hanoverian. In Roland Graeme's case, the hero eventually becomes the master of his own destiny through acts of personal choice. Of course, he would not be a Scott hero if it were not revealed in the dénouement that he was of much higher birth than had been originally supposed, and that his real name was Roland Avenel. Halbert Glendinning, the hero of *The Monastery*, is a self-made man, and proud of it, and in the sequel he makes this the excuse for spending so little time at home: 'Those who are born noble may slumber out their lives within the walls of their castles and manor-houses; but he who hath achieved nobility by his own deeds must ever be in the saddle, to show that he merits his advancement.' As such, Scott presents him as a prototype of Protestant virtue, a sixteenth-century equivalent of Nicol Jarvie, who in *Rob Roy* achieves by mercantile endeavour what men of an older time brought about by deeds of chivalry. Roland Graeme is a much subtler creation, one of Scott's most carefully worked and cleverly portrayed heroes. Cocky, indeed tiresome, to the end, the circumstances of his birth and life have compelled him to come to terms with those tragic historic perspectives which are Scott's peculiar preserve: the awkwardness of victory, the sense of loss which comes to the victorious man when he contemplates the nobility and attractiveness of the defeated side. Almost anyone else writing *The Abbot* would have failed to introduce these complications. Roland Graeme, born a Catholic, in love with a Catholic girl, scornful of the ranting of Protestant preachers, and entrusted to the service of the most romantic of all Catholic monarchs, would scarcely have been stirred to a painful recognition of Protestant truth. Yet it makes a much better story that he should have been; and the pathos and complexity of that era come before us much more vividly than if it had been no more than an adventure story about recusants.

Scott's own firmly held religious opinions govern the complexity of the novel. It is his Protestantism which makes his sympathetic portraits of the Abbot and Mary Queen of Scots so powerful: for it is these figures, the leaders of the defeated cause, who engage our attention. Edward Glendinning's gentle introspection has developed into a quiet courage when, as Father Ambrose, he is elected to the abbacy. But Scott is interested in him as the defender of something which was wrong:

He on whom the office of the Abbot of Saint Mary's was now conferred, had a mind fitted for the situation to which he was called. Bold and enthusiastic, yet generous and forgiving—wise and skilful, yet zealous and prompt—he wanted but a better cause than the support of a decaying superstition, to have raised him to the rank of a truly great man. But, as the end crowns the work, it also forms the rule by which it must ultimately be judged; and those, who, with sincerity and generosity, fight and fall in an evil cause, posterity can only compassionate as victims of a generous but fatal error. Amongst these we must rank Ambrosius, the last Abbot of Kennaquair, whose designs must be condemned, as their success would have rivetted on Scotland the chains of antiquated superstition and spiritual tyranny; but whose talents commanded respect and whose virtues, even from the enemies of his faith, extorted esteem.

(Chapter XIII)

But for all this—and Scott takes equal pains to remind us of the wrongness of Mary's life and cause—*The Abbot* gives the devil all the best tunes. With the exception of the quiet, saintly Elias Henderson, who takes up very little part in the story, the Protestants are disagreeable people. As a literary portrait, the most brilliant of them must be the Lady of Lochleven herself. Bitter, ugly, pathetic, but never likeable, she can never overcome her resentment of the fact that James V had not made her his wife—as a result of which her son, the Regent, cannot succeed to the throne, and she can never be called the Queen Mother. The tension between herself and Queen Mary is sustained magnificently. And yet even when Mary makes her cruellest taunts about Lady Douglas's irregular status in the royal family, we never quite sympathize with her. Still less can we be attracted to the terrible fanaticism of Dryfesdale, the Anabaptist, who makes an unsuccessful attempt to poison the Queen's food. In this figure, we can discern Scott's grave distrust of Protestant fanaticism, something which he held in far greater abhorrence than the dark superstitions of an earlier age. It has already been observed how, in life, this developed into an obsession with him, and how he came to hold the firm conviction that the extreme forms of Protestantism were indistinguishable from revolutionary sentiments. His most burning satire is always reserved for such figures. One thinks of the terrifying meeting of Anabaptists in *Peveril of the Peak*, where 'the torrent of mystical yet animating eloquence of the preacher—an old grey-haired man, whom zeal seemed to supply with the powers of voice and action, of which years had deprived him—was suited to the taste of his audience, but could not be transferred to these pages without scandal and impropriety'.[19] Or, in lighter and completely Dickensian mood, one remembers the dreadful fanatic Mr Holdenough at the beginning of *Woodstock*, whose 'grizzled hair was cut as short as shears could perform the feat, and covered with a black silk skull-cap, which stuck so close to the head, that the two ears expanded from under it as if they had been intended as handles by which to lift the whole person'.[20]

As Scott's life progressed, the Protestants in his books became increasingly contemptible. Emotionally, *The Abbot* seems to be slanted almost entirely in a Catholic direction. When Newman, in the pages of the *Apologia Pro Vita Sua*, tells us that he cannot understand how, as a boy who had no contact with Roman Catholicism, he came to be doodling pictures of crucifixes and rosaries in his exercise book, the answer is not far to seek: for we remember also that he waited patiently by his bedroom window at Alton for the dawn to rise, so that he would have light enough to read the Waverley Novels.

I thought of these things, emerging into the drizzle at Abbotsford from the little oratory where Newman had said mass. My companion, a minister of the suffering and Episcopal Church, murmured gloomily, 'I suppose, had he lived fifty years later, Scott himself would have "poped".' I could not agree. It would be too hard to reconcile this view with, for instance, his thoughts on Catholic Emancipation in 1829:

I hold popery to be such a mean and depriving superstition that I am not clear I could have found myself liberal enough for voting for the repeal of them as they existed before 1780. They must and would in course of time have smothered popery and I confess I should have see[n] the old Lady of Babylon's mouth stopd with pleasure.[21]

The fact that he embraced Episcopalianism distanced him from the faith of nearly all his countrymen, and gave him the detachment which was necessary to describe the turmoils of the sixteenth and seventeenth centuries. He was impatient of sectarianism, and he makes his own views abundantly clear in *A Legend of Montrose*:

The Prelatists and Presbyterians of the more violent kind became as illiberal as the Papists, and would scarcely allow the possibility of salvation beyond the pale of their respective churches. It was in vain remarked to these zealots that had the Author of our holy religion considered any form of church government as essential to salvation, it would have been revealed with the same precision as under the Old Testament dispensation. Both parties continued as violent as if they could have pleaded the distinct commands of Heaven to justify their intolerance.[22]

It was such a horror of religious bigotry which led him to Episcopalianism which, in Scott's day, was scarcely existent, and gave him the excuse of almost never going to church: 'the shadow of a shade, now, and fortunately so'. Yet although he hated bigotry, he was fascinated by it. And he never rejected the memory of what was good about his Presbyterian past. Perhaps the most unaffected description of religious emotion in his novels is the scene in Glasgow cathedral at the time of evening prayer in *Rob Roy*. The great kirk, we are told, 'is the only metropolitan church in Scotland, excepting . . . the cathedral of Kirkwall in the Orkneys, which remained uninjured at the Reformation'; so that here, like Pleydell in *Guy Mannering*, the Episcopalian could pray where his fathers had prayed before him 'without thinking of the Presbyterian forms'. Frank Osbaldistone follows the worshippers into the cathedral and hears their voices reverberating to the harmony of some metrical psalm:

The sound of so many voices, united by the distance into one harmony, and freed from those harsh discordances which jar the ear when heard more near, combining with the murmuring brook, and the wind which sung from the old firs, affected me with a sense of sublimity. All nature, as invoked by the Psalmist whose verses they chanted, seemed united in offering that solemn praise in which trembling is mixed with joy as she addresses her Maker. I had heard the service of high mass in France, celebrated with all the eclat which the choicest music, the richest dresses, the most imposing ceremonies, could confer on it; yet it fell short in effect of the simplicity of the Presbyterian worship.

(Chapter XX)

Here, the voices of controversy, satire, and detachment are dumb. Scott is not constructing an argument, nor even, particularly, advancing a point of view. He is not really asking us to compare the experience of evensong with high mass in any objective terms to see which is the more sublime. It is an expression of sentiment, not of opinion, and all the more powerful for that. The many contrasts which contribute to Scott's genius, historian and entertainer, eighteenth-century rationalist and nineteenth-century romantic, lawyer and countryman, are held in balance. But they are not central to the purposes of *Rob Roy*. They reach their most complex, sustained, and poignant brilliance in *Old Mortality*.

CHAPTER SIX

Old Mortality and The Heart of Midlothian

There was a blended vision of horror before him.

(Old Mortality)

I

Old Mortality, of all the Waverley Novels, seems the most infused with a point of view; an idea of history, but, more fundamentally, an idea about human nature. Although it was written at prodigious speed (four wet days finished half of one volume), it is very carefully constructed and deeply studied. Its controversial interpretation of events was quite deliberate.

The action of the novel is largely confined to three months during the summer of 1679, in the south-west regions of Scotland, and it describes the rebellion of the Covenanters against the government of Charles II. For nearly twenty years, the restored government of the monarch had enforced measures on the Scots which were not merely generally unpopular, but also contrary to pledges and promises given at the time of the Restoration. Most detested of all was the betrayal of the Solemn League and Covenant, whose adherents formed themselves into numerous splinter-groups and off-shoots. Charles I had gone to war with the Scots to make them accept Episcopal government of the Church. Too late in his career, he had revoked this attempt and promised to allow Presbyterian forms of polity and worship. He had even agreed to negotiate the establishment of a limited, experimental Presbyterianism in England as well. Charles II, going several stages further in order to ensure the devotion of the Scots after his father's execution, actually submitted to the Covenant. But after the Restoration, it was made clear that the government wanted the Scots to conform to English ways.

James Sharp, Professor of Philosophy at St. Andrews, and minister of Crail in Fife, had become generally recognized as the leader of moderate opinion during the 1650s. He was a natural ally of Monk's, and it was fitting that he should have gone to London at the beginning

of 1660, as he had done several times during the Protectorate, to plead
for the maintenance of the Presbyterian system. When he returned
the next year as Archbishop of St. Andrews and Primate of Scotland,
it was natural that he should have been regarded as a traitor to the
Presbyterian cause. How far his acceptance of the episcopate indicated a naturally diplomatic temper, how much personal ambition or
absence of principle, it is hard to say. But he was much hated for his
attempts to impose on his old allies conformity to the Episcopal
system. There were numerous attempts on his life.[1]

The shades of opinion among the Presbyterian ranks were various
in the degrees of their fanaticism, ranging from those who merely
objected to episcopacy, to persons who were in effect revolutionaries
and anarchists. But all were united in the sense that their political
liberty as subjects was being infringed by the high-handed way in
which the government not only insisted on religious conformity, but
also appointed ministers to spy on their own congregations.

Matters came to a head in the summer of 1679, when a group of
embittered lairds and farmers encountered Archbishop Sharp's
coach on Magus Moor, and felt persuaded that he had been delivered
into their hands by Providence. They murdered him in front of his
daughter, and mutilated his body. It seemed the moment for action.
When John Grahame of Claverhouse ('Bonnie Dundee') came north
to put down the rebellious factions, all Whiggish parties resisted him.
For a brief interlude, it looked as if they were to be successful.
Claverhouse, with a highly trained body of soldiers, was out-
numbered and put to flight in a skirmish at Drumclog. Scott would
have us believe that Cornet Grahame, who was shot dead in cold
blood while he was holding up a flag of truce, was Claverhouse's
nephew.

The triumph of Drumclog was short-lived. Not only had old vete-
rans of Civil War days, like the proverbially cruel Dalzell, joined
forces with Claverhouse: new regiments under the command of the
Duke of Monmouth secured a victory for the government over the
Covenanting forces (now much divided against themselves) at the
battle of Bothwell Bridge. Monmouth, who always had the gift of
inspiring popularity, sensed the mood in Scotland, and the trials
which followed the battle were (for those days) comparatively
clement.

Yet the slaughter, by Claverhouse's troops, of innocent people after
Bothwell Bridge lived in popular memory for many decades. In his

tale *The Brownie of Bodsbeck* (written as an answer to *Old Mortality*),
Hogg gives the popular view of the matter: 'If through all the histories
of that suffering period, I had discovered one redeeming quality about
Clavers, I would have brought it forward, but I found none. He had
the nature of a wolf and the bravery of a bull-dog.'[2] To make this point
more strongly, Hogg sets the story after the Battle of Bothwell Bridge,
when the Covenanters were really no more than a scattered remnant,
with no power to fight back. Clavers is a sadistic bully, and we see him
and his soldiers shooting, pillaging, raping and torturing the peasan-
try of Ettrick Forest indiscriminately, on the chance that they might
be harbouring Covenanters on their land. The details of their brutality remain in the mind. They force a terrified farmer's wife to throw
her Bible on to the fire to prove that she is not a sympathizer with the
rebels; they extricate a confession from a shepherd that his employer
had used the phrase 'the bond of the Everlasting Covenant' in his
prayers, and for giving this information, the old man is rewarded by
having one ear cut off and his cheek burnt with a hot iron. There are
many other examples, such as old Nanny lifting her cap to reveal the
marks of the brands. When one has read Hogg, it would seem that any
book which defends Claverhouse's handling of the affair must read
like a defence of the Gestapo. Yet, of course, Hogg's story, though
representing the popular Scottish tradition, was not the only one. The
Tory account would see the whole affair as the suppression of dangerous fanatics and revolutionaries by the only means which lay in the
government's power. This point of view is tinged with romance in the
light of the tragedy of Claverhouse's later career; and it is, substantially, that given by Hume in his *History of Great Britain*. A. O. J.
Cockshut has doubted 'whether Scott's aims or his achievements in
uniting the seventeenth century can be fully understood' without
reading Hume.[3] There is probably a large measure of truth in this, but
it is surprising that Cockshut appears to imply that Scott wrote *Old
Mortality* to correct the views of Hume.

The key point . . . is Hume's use of the word 'fanatic', which he . . . would
have happily applied to almost all the rebels in *Old Mortality*. It is important to
remember that 'everybody' read Hume, and, down to the time of Carlyle at
least, most people agreed with him. Now the striking thing about Hume's use
of the word 'fanatic' is that it invariably signals a fixed judgement and a
closed question . . . Scott in *Old Mortality* was reopening the supposedly closed
question, 'What is fanaticism?'[4]

Admirers of Cockshut's book must, like myself, be puzzled by this position. One wonders why Hume, either as a philosopher or as an historian, should be expected to approve of, even to comprehend, fanaticism. Tory bias there certainly is in Hume's account, but nothing of which Scott would have disapproved: 'The passion for liberty was at this time totally extinguished in Scotland: There was only preserved a spirit of mutiny and sedition, encouraged by a mistaken zeal for religion.' Yet, in a later passage, he concedes that the fanatics were heroic. Writing of Cameron and Cargill, who died rather than say 'God save the King', he said, 'Such unhappy delusion is an object rather of commiseration than of anger: And it is almost impossible, that men could have been carried to such a degree of frenzy, unless provoked by a long train of violence and oppression.'[5] This nicely balanced viewpoint—a horror of ugly fanaticism, but a recognition that many of the rebels were brave men provoked beyond endurance by a cruel and unreasoning government—is precisely the attitude of *Old Mortality*.

Nor can it have been the case, as Cockshut asserts, that 'everyone read Hume', or that his was a popular view of events. Scott wrote *Old Mortality* less to counteract the Augustan view of Hume than to balance the extreme Whig view of the Covenanting rebellions which Hogg was later to propound in *The Brownie of Bodsbeck*. This emphasis is made clear by Lockhart's account of the genesis of the novel, when Joseph Train visited Scott in his Edinburgh house:

He found him at work in his library, and surveyed with enthusiastic curiosity the furniture of the room, especially its only picture, a portrait of Graham of Claverhouse. Train expressed the surprise with which everyone who had known Dundee only in the pages of the Presbyterian Annalists, must see for the first time that beautiful and melancholy visage, worthy of the most pathetic dreams of romance. Scott replied, 'that no character had been so foully traduced as the Viscount of Dundee—that thanks to Wodrow, Cruickshanks, and such chroniclers, he, who was every inch a soldier and a gentleman still passed among the Scottish vulgar for a ruffian desperado, who rode a goblin horse, was proof against shot, and in league with the Devil'.[6]

This attitude is also to be seen in Hogg's anecdote about Scott's disapproval of *The Brownie of Bodsbeck*. Who can say how much truth there was in any of Hogg's stories? Hogg himself provides a good vignette of the storms to be encountered in trying to preserve a friendship with the Ettrick shepherd, as Scott did for twenty years:

I called on him after his return from the Parliament House, on pretence of asking his advice about some very important affair, but in fact to hear his sentiments of my new work. His shaggy eye-brows were hanging very low, a bad prelude, which I knew too well. 'I have read your new work, Mr Hogg,' said he, 'and I must tell you downright plainly, as I always do, that I like it very ill—very ill indeed.'

'What for, Mr Scott?'

'Because it is a false picture of the times and the existing characters, altogether an exaggerated and unfair picture.'

'I dinna ken, Mr Scott. It is the picture I have been bred up in the belief o' sin' ever I was born, and I had it frae them whom I was most bound to honour and believe. And mair nor that, there is not one single incident in the tale—not one—which I cannot prove from history to be literally and positively true. I was obliged sometimes to change the situations to make one part coalesce with another, but in no one instance have I related a story of a cruelty or a murder which is not literally true. An' that's a great deal mair than you can say for your tale o' Auld Mortality.'[7]

Scott was a much finer historian than Hogg, but they diverged from each other less over the interpretation of individual historical facts than in their entire outlook. For Scott, of course, Bonnie Dundee was the first of many Jacobite heroes, Bothwell Bridge and its aftermath only an interlude in his career before his espousal of the Stuart cause and his tragic death as a rebel in the reign of William and Mary. Yet although Bonnie Dundee was a hero to him, and his portrait was the only picture hanging on the walls of the library in Castle Street, Scott did not blind himself to the cruelty of either party when he came to write his book. The Covenanters have slowly and deliberately murdered Archbishop Sharp before the action starts, and they shoot down young Cornet Grahame when he is carrying a flag of truce. In both cases, not content to kill their enemies, they also mutilate the bodies. Yet it must be said—and Scott says it—that they are fighting against a government which extracts information from its prisoners with thumbscrews and 'iron boots' and parades not only its victims' heads through the streets on pikes, but also their hands, pushed together in mock attitudes of prayer.

Old Mortality is a bloody, violent book, depicting a bloody and violent world; and the violence is in no small part the result of religious enthusiasm. One of the most terrifying features of this world is the way in which moderation itself has ceased to work. Henry Morton, the hero, who never fails to be horrified by the extremists of

both parties, is driven into rebellion precisely because of his moderation. He is, as it were, a moderate of the 'left', forced into a revolutionary position in 1679 because the government has abused its power
over individual liberties; just as Lord Evandale, a moderate of the
'right', is forced into rebellion in 1688 for very similar reasons.
Because of this, some readers have written of the book as if it were a
sort of Whig manifesto, a demonstration of the fact that rebellion
against an unjust regime is the only way of securing individual
liberties. But this is a perverse reading. At no point does Henry
Morton rejoice that he is involved with roughnecks and maniacs in an
act of revolution. He only becomes involved with them in the first
place because he is giving shelter to one of their leaders for the purely
private motive that he was a man who had saved his own father's life:
he is not particularly inspired by the rebels' aims or politics. And if
some sort of peace seems to descend on the book by the end, it is more
because the major trouble-makers are dead than because we are being
asked to believe that the Prince of Orange had brought the ideal form
of government to these shores. Most schemes of political improve-
ment are very laughable things: that hard, Johnsonian view of things
fits the mood of this novel.

Scott was in love with the Tory legends of Bonnie Dundee, but
there is much more to the figure of Claverhouse in *Old Mortality* than
that. Scott accepted that his hero was a cruel man, even at times a
brutal man; but he himself believed that violent measures were the
only effective check on revolutionaries. He applauded Peterloo, it will
be remembered. When Lord Evandale pleads for Henry Morton's
life, urged on by Major Bellenden and Edith, Claverhouse grants it,
but unwillingly: he had been in favour of shooting the young man
merely on suspicion of having harboured a rebel for one night in his
uncle's barn.

'Be it so, then . . . but, young man, should you wish in your future life to rise
to eminence in the service of your king and country, let it be your first task to
subject to the public interest, and to the discharge of your duty, your private
affections, passions, and feelings. These are not times to sacrifice to the dotage
of greybeards, or the tears of silly women, the measures of salutary severity
which the dangers around us compel us to adopt.

(Chapter XIII)

The language is curiously like Scott's own, or that of any Augustan moralist, when discussing the inner life: passion is subdued to duty, and to a sense of the general good. Yet, as Lord Evandale has the chance to say at a later stage, too extreme a severity on the part of the government can create just those popular risings which it fears and seeks to avoid:

I have been for some time of opinion that our politicians and prelates have driven matters to a painful extremity in this country, and have alienated, by violence of various kinds, not only the lower classes, but all those in the upper ranks, whom strong party feeling, or a desire of court interest, does not attach to their standard.

(Chapter XXV)

Yet the ethos of the book is detached from a specifically political viewpoint. In the sublunary world, one must only expect life to bring reversals, for the government of today to become the disaffected party of rebellion in a matter of years. The narrative voice suggests a kind of Boethian detachment: it is uninterested in politics, except in so far as politics are affected by personal morality. *Old Mortality* is less about movements than about individuals caught up in the chaos of events, and the questions it raises are the ultimately moral ones of how far we should allow passion and feeling to affect our judgements. Henry Morton, though a Presbyterian, is really a rationalist of the Bishop Butler mould: indeed, his initial conversations with Burley read almost like a parody of the Bishop of Durham's famous colloquy with John Wesley. When Burley claims to have been divinely inspired to commit his political murders, Morton replies 'I own I should strongly doubt the origin of any inspiration which seemed to dictate a line of conduct contrary to those feelings of natural humanity, which Heaven has assigned to us as the general law of our conduct.' This is the language of *The Analogy of Religion*.

Enough has probably been said already to indicate how peculiarly this book matches the mood of our own world, and how sagely it anticipates problems which we associate with modern Africa, Ireland or urban terrorism, worlds in which only extremists appear to have a voice. But the book is not a tract but a novel, and its glories are the quality of its prose and the realism of its characters. Hogg's Covenanters are too busy hiding in the mist or being mistaken for Brownies to emerge as very recognizable figures: not so, Scott's. One of the most impressive things about them is that they are at once comic and truly terrible. Moroever, Scott distinguishes between their varying degrees of fanaticism with an almost loving touch, that fully allows them to come before us with their own ghastly points of view. One remembers the ludicrous Kettledrummle and his homily attacking Charles II, preached after Drumclog:

He went at some length through the life and conversation of that joyous prince, few parts of which, it must be owned, were qualified to stand the rough handling of so uncourtly an orator, who conferred on him the hard names of Jeraboam, Omri, Ahab, Shallum, Pekah, and every other evil monarch recorded in the Chronicles, and concluded with a round application of the Scripture, 'Tophet is ordained of old; yea, for the KING it is provided: he hath made it deep and large; the pile thereof is fire and much wood: the breath of the Lord, like a stream of brimstone, doth kindle it.'

(Chapter XVIII)

But this absurd sermon is followed by one by the enthusiastic young MacBriar which is genuinely moving. MacBriar is youthful and in frail health; he is terribly emaciated, hardly able to stand, and unable to project his voice very loudly:

When he spoke, his faint and broken voice seemed at first inadequate to express his conceptions. But the deep silence of the assembly, the eagerness with which the ear gathered every word, as the famished Israelites collected the heavenly manna, had a corresponding effect upon the preacher himself. His words became more distinct, his manner more earnest and energetic; it seemed as if religious zeal was triumphing over bodily weakness and infir-mity. His natural eloquence was not altogether untainted with the coarseness of his sect; and yet, by the influence of a good natural taste, it was freed from the grosser and more ludicrous errors of his contemporaries; and the language of Scripture, which in their mouths was sometimes degraded by misapplica-tion, gave, in MacBriar's exhortation, a rich and solemn effect, like that which is produced by the beams of the sun streaming through the storied representation of saints and martyrs on the Gothic window of some ancient cathedral.

(Chapter XVII)

Yet although MacBriar is always an impressive figure—and dies with great dignity and courage at the end of the book—his fanaticism is, for that reason, all the more terrifying. When Morton is incarcerated with the rebels in a cottage after Bothwell Bridge, MacBriar unites with the lunatic Mucklewrath in wanting to kill him merely because Morton has mumbled an imprecation from the Book of Common Prayer. It is by depicting so faithfully the nobility of the fanatics that Scott is so devastating about them. If they were all obvious madmen or rogues and nothing more, there would be little to fear from them. But they traffic in good and sublime notions—political freedom, personal salvation—and it is this which lends such intensity to their deeds of horrifying violence. However admirable they may be, they are all casebook examples of what Hume was talking about, in his essay 'On Superstition and Enthusiasm', when he described the character of the enthusiast:

In a little while, the inspired person comes to regard himself as a distinguished favourite of the Divinity; and when this frenzy once takes place, which is the summit of enthusiasm, every whimsy is consecrated: Human reason, and even morality, are rejected as fallacious guides: And the fanatic madman delivers himself over blindly and without reserve, to the supposed illapses of the spirit, and to inspiration from above.

In the figure of Morton, the moderate Presbyterian, the book becomes a sort of object lesson: it is impossible to touch the pitch of enthusiasm without being defiled. As a logical consequence of their deep faith, the men with whom he has thrown in his lot want to destroy the stability and order without which personal virtue is impossible. No wonder that when he goes to sleep after his first evening with Burley, an assassin of Archbishop Sharp, Morton has uneasy dreams—'There was a blended vision of horror before him.'

Tracing carefully round the events of Drumclog, Bothwell Bridge, and their aftermath, the novel makes a pattern. It starts as a comedy, with the mock conflicts of the 'wappenshaw', originally a feudal display of arms, now merely games to which the Tory government has insisted that each landowner in the district should send a contingent. Here the dark divisions which pervade the book are seen only at a minor, grotesque level in the ludicrous quarrels which the wappenshaw has caused in Tillietudlem Castle. Lady Margaret Bellenden, who cannot open her mouth without recalling the morning when his sacred majesty took his disjune at her table, has attempted to enlist her largely Whiggish retainers for the wappenshaw. But the sweet, weak-willed Cuddie Headrigg has been kept away by his fanatical mother Mause. Although Mause does not want to lose her position at the castle, and Cuddie, throughout the book, tries to silence her enthusiastic utterances, she feels called upon to 'testify'. Mause ventures to tell Lady Margaret that she considers the wappenshaw unlawful:

'Unlawfu'!' exclaimed her mistress; 'the cause to which you are called by your lawful leddy and mistress—by the command of the king—by the writ of the privy council—by the order of the lord lieutenant—by the warrant of the sherriff?'

'Ay, my leddy, nae doubt; but no to displeasure you leddyship, ye'll mind that there was ance a king in Scripture they ca'd Nebuchadnezzar, and he set up a golden image in the plain o' Dura, as it might be in the haugh yonder by the water side, where the array was warned to meet yesterday, and the governors and the captains, and the judges themsells, forby the treasurers, the counsellors, and the sherrifs, were warned to the dedication thereof, and commanded to fall down and worship at the sound of the cornet, flute, harp, sackbut, psaltery and allkinds of music.'

'And what of a' this, ye fule wife! Or what had Nebuchadnezzar to do with the wappenschaw of the Upper Ward of Clydesdale?'

'Only this far, my leddy,' continued Mause firmly, 'that prelacy is like the great golden image in the plain of Dura, and like as Shadrach, Meshach and Abednego, were borne out in refusing to bow down and worship, so neither shall Cuddie Headrigg, your leddyship's poor ploughman, at least wi' his auld mither's consent, make murgeons or jennyflections as they ca' them, in the house of the prelates and curates, nor gird him wi' armour to fight in their cause, either at the sound of kettledrums, organs, bagpipes or ony kind of music whatever.'

Lady Margaret Bellenden heard this exposition of Scripture with the greatest possible indignation as well as surprise.

'I see which way the wind blaws,' she exclaimed, after a pause of astonishment; 'the evil spirit of the year sixteen hundred and forty-twa is at wark again as merrily as ever.' . . .

(Chapter VI)

It is a brilliant exchange. No one could take either Mause or Lady Margaret seriously, yet their differences introduce us to the major conflicts of the period. Both sides are capable of extremism; both of absurdity. Yet Scott's generosity as an artist allows them both their full weight and complexity, so that when we come to the great central section of the book, starting with the conflict at Drumclog, we can understand something of the mystery whereby absurd and wicked deeds are not always performed by fools and villains; and desperate times make heroes out of maniacs while perverting noble and strong men into positions of savagery.

Some authors would have ended the book after the Battle of Bothwell Bridge. Law has just about been restored. Morton, having attempted to reconcile the rebels with the government, gets off quite lightly for his part in the affair and is exiled. The story could finish here with some neatness. Instead, Scott takes the great risk of allowing ten years to pass, and his hero to return to Scotland. The risk of over-indulgence in such a highly 'professional' writer as Scott was hard to avoid here. The set-pieces are too perfect. There is the comic pastoral of Morton's reunion with Cuddie Headrigg, now being bossed about (his mother in the grave) by a bonny young wife. There is the genuine pathos of Henry's return to Milnwood, his old home, and his meeting with Mrs Wilson, the housekeeper. There is the operatic melodrama of Edith Bellenden breaking off her engagement with Lord Evandale when she spies Henry Morton through a window and realizes that her old lover is not, as she supposed, dead. And there is the great meeting between Morton and Burley, now a semi-lunatic recluse among crags and caves—their quarrel, the crashing of the great oak to the ground, Morton's leap over a dangerous chasm. In a way, the obviousness of all this is too slick; it reminds one of a great fictional detective summoning all the suspects to the library and putting them through their paces for one last time before the book can end. Of course, the plot is competently handled. Burley conveniently murders Lord Evandale in the closing pages, leaving Edith free to marry Henry Morton: not for nothing was one of Scott's favourite sayings 'Patience, cousin, and shuffle the cards'. Yet it seems, by the very end, as though the seriousness of the book is being deliberately cast aside by gratuitous 'novel-writing': a Miss Buskbody, who has read all the novels in the circulating library at Gandercleugh and its environs, taxes the narrator with the unsatisfactoriness of his conclusion, and makes him tell us how each of the surviving characters lived happily ever after.

But, of course, the perspective which ten years give to the events of 1679 is an important one to be left with. We see what paradoxes the enthusiast can be forced into. Burley and Claverhouse, the two chief 'extremists' of the book, are, by the end, both allies in arms against the Whig government of William and Mary.

For all its over-competence, it is one of the finest books in the language. Its set-pieces are justly famous: Bothwell's dying words;

Claverhouse's speech about the ideal death of a hero; the suspense of Morton's incarceration in the cottage, when, in a few minutes, midnight will strike, or Mucklewrath will move the clock forward, the Sabbath will be over, and they can all stick their swords into their captive:

'I take up my song against him!' exclaimed the maniac. 'As the sun went back on the dial ten degrees for intimating the recovery of Hezekiah, so shall it now go forward, that the wicked may be taken away from among the people, and the Covenant established in its purity.'

He sprang to a chair with an attitude of frenzy in order to anticipate the fatal moment by putting the index forward; and several of the party began to make ready their slaughter-weapons for immediate execution, when Mucklewrath's hand was arrested by one of his companions.

'Hist!' he said—'I hear a distant noise.'

'It is the rush of the brook over the pebbles,' said one.

'It is the sough of the wind among the bracken,' said another.

'It is the galloping of horse', said Morton to himself, his sense of hearing rendered acute by the dreadful situation in which he stood—'God grant they may come as my deliverers!'

(Chapter XXXII)

Yet these thrilling and carefully wrought set-pieces would be a good deal less effective without the realistic domestic comedy which throws them into relief. Scott is always brilliant, for instance, in his descriptions of food, particularly of that uniquely bad food which can only be found in Scotland. One thinks of the burning hot porridge which scalds the throat of old Morton of Milnwood ('The pain occasioned by its descent down his throat and into his stomach, inflamed the ill-humour with which he was already prepared to meet his kinsman'). Later, in the same dining-room, the butler 'placed upon the table an immense charger of broth, thickened with oat-meal and colewort in which ocean of liquid was indistinctly discovered, by close observers, two or three short ribs of lean mutton sailing to and fro'. In the touching reconciliation scene at the end, when Henry Morton is scarcely recognized by old Alison Wilson, she is still boiling up the same thin unpalatable stews. It is details such as this which hold the novel together quite as much as the grand themes. Mrs Wilson is one of Scott's great comic creations, yet her homely stubbornness actually increases the pathos of events. At the beginning of the book, she refers to the Duke as 'That was him that lost his head at London—folk said it wasna a very gude ane, but it was aye sair loss to him, puir gentleman.' The remark is made on a level of pure comic fantasy, like the harsh zany pronouncements of Mr F's aunt in *Little Dorrit*. By the time Morton meets her again at the end of the book, he has seen dozens of heads shot off, or paraded on pikestaffs, battered and bleeding. It is poor people like Mrs Wilson and Cuddie Headrigg whose lives are torn apart by the harsh actions of Burley and Claverhouse, and who frequently rise to the occasion with great dignity and courage. Only a consummate artist could make that point without being sugary. Scott trod the delicate border between farce and sentimentality with great delicacy and precision; Dickens, who happily sploshes about on either side of it, is scarcely aware of its dangers. Scott's facility in this respect is a direct consequence of his Augustan sense of moderation, his Shakespearean belief in *degree*:

'Alas, what are we,' said Morton, 'that our best and most praiseworthy feelings can thus be debased and depraved—that honourable pride can sink into haughty and desperate indifference for general opinion, and the sorrow of blighted affection inhabit the same bosom which license, revenge and rapine, have chosen for their citadel? But it is the same throughout; the liberal principles of one man sink into cold and unfeeling indifference, the religious zeal of another hurries him into frantic and savage enthusiasm. Our resolutions, our passions, are like the waves of the sea, and without the aid of Him who formed the human breast, we cannot say to its tides, Thus far shall ye come and no farther.'

(Chapter XXVI)

Such a central intelligence could never feel much confidence that liberty or individualism or the march of progress could improve the human lot. As we have seen, mobs were to shout out 'Burke Sir Walter!' when Scott tried to explain this to them. (Burke was a murderer who had given his name to the method by which he disposed of his victims—by squashing or strangulation—before selling them to the dissecting-rooms.) At the time of Burke's hanging, Scott had written in gloomy terms to his friend Morritt of Rokeby. His feelings of pity for the condemned man and his horror of the hysteria of the mob, are very characteristic:

Our murders have gone on to a point where all must have supd full with horrors. Yet our gentlemen of the press want not indeed to start a new hare, but to have a new course at the old hare, a wretch who was to be sure a most abandoned villain but to whom the publick faith was pledged and to whose evidence specially given under promise of life it was owing that they convicted the murderer who was hanged. However the Court of Justiciary has refused to continue his confinement. You will have heard how we bestialized ourselves by shouts and insults even when the wretch that suffered was in his devotions. Moreover Sanders was ass enough to purchase the rope he was hanged with at half-a crown an inch. Item, the hangman became a sort of favourite and was invited into a house and treated with liquor for having done his miserable duty on such a villain. And all this is in the full march of intellect. It is remarkable Burke was far from being an ignorant man. He wrote a good hand reckond readily and read a good deal chiefly religious tracts and works of controversy of which he could give some account. And with all these advantages he became a human carcase butcher by wholesale.

It is endless speculating upon these things. . . .[8]

2

The gallows and the mob come terrifyingly to our attention in the Second Series of *Tales of My Landlord*. No one who reads *The Heart of Midlothian* will ever forget its opening passages: the greatness of the writing, the sheer energy and ugliness of the mob scenes, the exactitude with which the descriptions of a vast, angry urban riot prepare us for the infinitely private moral drama which is the book's main concern.

If the novel were to arrive unsolicited on the desk of a London publisher for the first time today, there can be no doubt that he would want it to be heavily cut. Even if we skip the Introduction of 1830, explaining how Scott had heard the story from Helen Walker, the original of Jeanie Deans, there is still much to 'get through' before we come to the meat of the story. There is the fiction of the 'Tales of My Landlord', according to which the whole story has been passed on to us by Jedediah Cleishbotham, a schoolmaster of Gandercleugh, from the manuscript of his usher, Peter Pattieson. There is the opening chapter, describing how a coach is overturned by the bridge at Gandercleugh, and how three passengers are persuaded to break their journey at the old Wallace Inn. Two of them are young lawyers, and the third, a much older man, is a victim of the law's delays, who has become bankrupt. Conversation turns on prisons, and particularly on that jail which stood at the very centre of Edinburgh and was known as the Heart of Midlothian. Dunover, the older man, persuades the young men to work for his cause, and later, we learn, he returns to his former prosperity, which he traces 'to his having had the good fortune to be flung from the top of a mail-coach into the river Gander, in company with an advocate and a writer to the signet. The reader will not perhaps deem himself equally obliged to the accident, since it brings before him the following narrative, founded upon the conversation of the evening.'[9]

All this has the slightly horrific air of a bore who has got us into a corner and will not release us until his story is done. The story of *The Heart of Midlothian* is familiar enough: how a cruel law in Scotland decreed that if a woman concealed the birth of a child she could be hanged for murder-presumptive, whether or not she was guilty of the crime; how Effie Deans, a pretty, flighty young girl is arrested on this charge because she dare not confess her shame to her strict Presbyterian father; how her elder sister Jeanie could save her life if she was prepared to tell a single white lie and testify that she knew of Effie's pregnancy; how she refuses to perjure herself; how Effie is condemned to be hanged; and how Jeanie walks to London to plead for the royal pardon, which is granted. We have been told by Scott's admirers that he tells this story with great brilliance, and that it is thought by many critics to be his best novel. And we want him to get on with it. The first chapter, with its schoolmasters and lawyers and carriage accidents which have nothing to do with the plot has taken up thirty pages. But perhaps the second chapter will get the story moving.

Not a bit of it. Scott realizes that, in order to really appreciate the story, we must know about the Porteous riots. Andrew Wilson, a popular Scotch criminal, has been hanged, and the soldier presiding over his execution, Captain Porteous, has behaved with great brutality. Wilson had won the respect of the crowds because, on the previous Sunday, during divine service at the Tolbooth Church, he had set upon his guards simply in order to allow his accomplice, one George Robertson, to escape. This act of daring puts the mob on his side, and they are incensed when Porteous ill-treats him on the scaffold, interrupting his devotions and forcing handcuffs on to him which are too small for his wrists. At their protest, Porteous fires into the crowd and kills half-a-dozen people. This senseless brutality causes such ill-feeling that Porteous himself is arrested and condemned for murder, but at the last minute he receives a royal reprieve. Queen Caroline is known to be violently anti-Scotch, and this pardon is seen as an insult against justice and against the citizens of Edinburgh. A mob collects and makes its way towards the Heart of Midlothian. They storm the prison, dragging a young Presbyterian minister with them. They force him to act as chaplain to the unfortunate Porteous, who is treated with the same cruelty that he had afforded to Andrew Wilson. In the morning, the body of Porteous is seen hanging from the gallows in the Grassmarket.

The writing in these opening chapters is of the highest quality. 'Though a quarrel in the streets is a thing to be hated, the energies displayed in it are fine', Keats wrote in one of his letters;[10] and the full terrifying excitement of the riot is the main source of the book's energy at this stage. At the same time, it is all done with magnificent intelligence. We feel that Scott is completely in command of his material. He possesses not only the romantic ability to convey the energy of the riots—the lanterns carried through darkened streets, the shouts of triumph and terror, the muddle and exultation as prisoners are released from their bondage, the sheer bloodiness of Porteous's end—he also conveys, with the eye of an analytical historian, not only how the riots happened, but why they happened, and why otherwise respectable and law-loving citizens were glad of them. It is a great achievement; and his portraits of Wilson and Porteous have all the energetic magic, the light and shade, of a sketch by Goya.

But fifty pages have passed by now; and we are still waiting to read the story of Jeanie Deans. Our London editor, we can imagine, is in despair: this is no way to write a novel. And, of course, he would be perfectly right if it were true, as most of us now believe, that all the best novels start *in medias res*, with there being no possibility of taking a walk that day, or with Mrs Dalloway buying the flowers herself. Yet when we have come to the end of *The Heart of Midlothian*, a re-reading of those opening chapters shows us how wrong it would be to want a fast opening to the story. The horse-cart with which the narrative opens is slow, and Scott acknowledges that it is out-of-date; in both England and Scotland, 'these ancient, slow and sure modes of conveyance are now alike unknown'. But he knew what he was about in shaping the novel as he did.

Of course, many strands of information which come our way during the Porteous Riots are central to the story of Effie Deans. She is a prisoner in the Heart of Midlothian when it is stormed. The man who leads the mob over the barricades—'George Robertson', 'Wildfire', later revealed to be George Staunton—is the confederate of

Wilson's who escaped hanging because of his friend's courage; he is also the father of Effie's lost child. Reuben Butler, the young minister who is dragged along by the mob to act as chaplain to Porteous on the scaffold, is Jeanie Deans's childhood sweetheart.

Not only have the violently exciting opening scenes unobtrusively introduced us to all the main characters in the story without our recognizing it: they have also presented them to us in a situation of great moral complexity. No one hated mobs more than Scott did, yet his presentation of the Porteous riots is entirely sympathetic to the demonstrators. Porteous's end is dreadful, but he gets what he deserves. The anger of the crowd is explicable, even if it is not to be justified. Probably no novelist has been personally responsible for sending more people to prison than Scott; it was part of his job as a magistrate. And yet the Heart of Midlothian is a hated thing, and the laws it apparently stands for are reversed and challenged. Most of Scott's novels involve the hero going to prison or being incarcerated against his will: it is pertinent to the whole notion of the impotence of the will in Scott's moral outlook. Edward Waverley is held hostage by Jacobites and locked up by Hanoverians: Henry Bertram is arrested for attempted murder, and so is Lovel; Darsie Latimer is bound over by the magistrates in Cumberland; the privilege of free action belongs to no mortal, says Redgauntlet. But in this novel we see the prison being stormed. Reuben Butler, of course, is locked up for a short period when it is discovered that he has been involved in the riots—he would not be a Scott hero if he had not 'done time', however briefly. But the emphasis of the opening of *The Heart of Midlothian* is not on imprisonment, but on prison-breaking. This is not a prison that stands for stern but necessary justice; it is an embodiment of moral anarchy. The turnkey is a hardened criminal; Porteous is well-treated here, and gets a reprieve, when we have seen him to be guilty of gross and violent crimes; poor Effie Deans, languishing there in shame and weakness, is going to be hanged for a crime she did not commit.

This is not what we should expect from the pen of a professional lawyer and a hardened Tory. And yet it is entirely consistent with everything that follows. Effie's former employers, the Saddletrees, provide a grotesque commentary on the whole affair. Saddletree neglects his leather business for a passionate devotion to the *minutiae* of Scotch law and enjoys explaining to his wife why Porteous, an actual murderer, can be spared by the law while Effie, who is inno-cent, will be condemned. 'Then if the law makes murders,' says Mrs

Saddletree, 'the law should be hanged for them; or if they wad hang a lawyer instead, the country wad find nae faut.'

This is all doubtless true. But it is not the whole truth. By the end of the book, we come to feel that those tempestuous, chaotic, terrifying opening passages were appropriate scenes in which to encounter Effie and Staunton for the first time. They are both prisoners of the passions. And one sees in the obviously Byronic figure of Staunton—boasting that 'I am the devil' among the shadows of the Salisbury Crags—that passion is infectious. His reckless desire to live the life of a libertine and a bandit is responsible for all the chaos and torment of the book. Knowing his comparatively noble birth, Wilson saves him and is treated with particular savagery in consequence by Porteous, who is angry to have lost a prisoner. Staunton leads the mob to take their revenge; all the chaos and bloodshed of the beginning originated, indirectly, with Staunton. Across the pages of the book swirls the tall lunatic Madge Wildfire, another of Staunton's discarded mistresses. Like Effie, she has borne him a child; but it died, and the experience turned her brain. Effie's child has been lodged with Madge and her mother. In the first half of the story, Madge's lunacy seems like a Dickensian irrelevance—brilliantly sustained and alarmingly mad, as only a sane writer could describe madness. Her songs, her snatches of wisdom, the fundamental violence of her nature are all well evoked. But all this mental and moral chaos, we learn much later, results from Staunton's irresponsible behaviour.

No character could possibly bear the flattering degree of obloquy which Scott heaps on his Byronic anti-hero. Staunton as a character is the major flaw of the book. But there is no denying the stylistic panache by which he unifies the plot. He is not believable in himself, but he lends credibility to all the other characters. As a device, he is excellent.

It is also rather hard to believe that, when he has married Effie and inherited his father's estate in Lincolnshire, he can succeed in passing her off as a lady of fashion. Readers may remember the melodramatic scene in which Effie, now Lady Staunton, goes to the theatre and finds herself sitting next to the Duke of Argyle. Years have passed since the Porteous riots, yet something in the play reminds him of the heroic journey of Jeanie Deans and, having no idea of Effie's true identity, he tells Lady Staunton the story. Afterwards she writes a letter to Jeanie describing the incident: 'I suffered with courage like an Indian at the stake, while they are rending his fibres and boring his eyes, and while he smiles applause at each well-imagined contrivance of his torturers. It was too much for me at last, Jeanie—I fainted.' (Chapter XLVIII.) The high-flown simile suggests that Scott knew he was straining our credulity a little, but it is a memorable incident. Surely the play that put the Duke in mind of Jeanie Deans was *Measure for Measure*. All the chapter headings at the climax of the story are taken from that play, and the similarities and differences between Isabella's moral plight and Jeanie's have been plotted by the scholars.[11] A cruel law, designed to check sexual license and its unhappy consequences, is being enforced on a young exuberant person, passionate perhaps, but by most standards innocent enough. Only one thing could save her life, and that involves a moral compromise on the part of her sister. But the sister is a pattern of moral correctness and will not yield.

> —Sweet sister let me live!
> What sin you do to save a brother's life,
> Nature dispenses with the deed so far,
> That it becomes a virtue.[12]

Scott quotes this as the heading for Chapter XX.

But for Jeanie Deans this is simply not true. She is asked to say that Effie had told her about her pregnancy—it could then be said in court that Effie had not concealed the pregnancy and was not technically guilty of murder-presumptive. But Effie had not confided in Jeanie, and it would be a lie to say that she had:

'I wad ware the best blood in my body to keep her skaithless,' said Jeanie, weeping in bitter agony, 'but I canna change right into wrang, or make that true which is false.'

(Chapter XV)

'Things and actions are what they are and the consequences of them will be what they will be; why, therefore, desire ye to be deceived?' It is appropriate that Jeanie should marry a man called Butler.

From our first introduction to her, we realize that Jeanie is a pattern of those moderate virtues which Scott regarded as indispensable to the good life. Since their childhood, she and Butler have been hoping to marry; yet 'fortunately for the lovers, their passion was of no ardent or enthusiastic cast'. Her character shines out of her dumpy little countenance:

She was short, and rather too stoutly made for her size, had grey eyes, light coloured hair, a round good-humoured face, much tanned with the sun, and her only particular charm was an air of inexpressible serenity, which a good conscience, kind feelings, contented temper, and a regular discharge of all her duties, spread over her features.

(Chapter IX)

Their aged father, Douce Davie Deans, is a veteran of the Covenanting Wars who had fought at Bothwell Bridge; and it was he, one might feel initially, who had instilled into one daughter such a profound veneration for virtue and truth and, into another, the inevitable libertine reaction against it. But Jeanie's cast of mind, her spiritual serenity, is in point of fact very different from that of her father. While he likes to keep alive the fires of ecclesiastical controversy, she prefers to ignore them. While his instinct is simply to reject Effie as a harlot, Jeanie, no less shocked by her sister's fall from virtue, sees the need for mercy. Her rather alarming firmness of character is infused with courage and pity, but above all by Bishop Butler's 'cool self-love'. She would never have fallen a victim of Effie's passions because she has the common sense to realize that they only lead to misery. It is not her chastity which is tried, as in *Measure for Measure*, but the truth itself. 'You, my dear Jeanie,' says Lady Staunton, 'have been truth itself from your cradle upwards; but you must remember that I am a liar of fifteen years' standing.' And look at them.

It would be rather absurd to suggest that Jeanie Deans was anything but the most confirmed Presbyterian. She is the daughter of a rigidly Calvinistic father and she marries a minister. Yet one feels it is appropriate that, during her journey to London, she should form so very favourable an impression of the Church of England. She and Madge Wildfire—what more incongruous companions could be imagined?—are sitting together in a churchyard, having escaped Madge's mother and her vagabond friends: 'It was one of those old-fashioned Gothic parish churches which are frequent in England, the most cleanly, decent, and reverential places of worship that are, perhaps, anywhere to be found in the Christian world.' (Chapter XXXI.) Madge Wildfire scampers madly into mattins and Jeanie follows her. The form of service is strange to her and she is struck by the fact that the parson reads his sermon rather than relying on the inspiration of the moment:

Jeanie, though her mind in her own despite sometimes reverted to her situation, compelled herself to give attention to a sensible, energetic and well-composed discourse, upon the practical doctrines of Christianity, which she could not help approving, although it was delivered in a tone and gesture very different from those of Boanerges Stormheaven who was her father's favourite preacher.

The coincidence of this preacher turning out to be George Staunton's father is implausible. We can only wonder that Hardy imitated this pattern in the plot of *Tess of the D'Urbervilles*, when Tess encounters old Mr Clare. But the tone it sets is unmistakable.

Of course, Jeanie Deans could have told a lie to save her sister's life. But one only has to consider the mountains of literature attempting to explain *Measure for Measure* to see where this sort of moral confusion would lead. If Isabella has such a high regard for virtue, how can she enter into the deception of sending Mariana to Angelo's bed; and if she is so determined to be celibate, why does she marry the Duke? This is not the place to enter into a discussion of these problems. Perhaps the simplest answer is to recognize that *Measure for Measure* never quite ceases to be a fairy story, and it has all the arbitrariness and amorality of that world. *The Heart of Midlothian* is very far from being a fairy story, yet it seems to have a very simple moral. Lady Staunton is a liar of fifteen years' standing, and she is not happy; Jeanie Deans always tells the truth, and she is happy. 'The paths of virtue,' the conclusion tells us, 'though seldom those of worldly greatness, are always those of pleasantness and peace.'

It may seem a very bold thing to construct so morally complex a thing as a modern novel on so childlike a proposition. And the idea that anyone who sounds (indeed, who *is*) as priggish as Jeanie could be an attractive heroine staggers belief. Yet the greatness of Scott derives from this simplicity. There is a further paradox, of course, in his own elaborate deceitfulness about the authorship of the Waverley Novels, a paradox which he liked to emphasize by quoting Falstaff's outrageous rhetorical question, 'Is not the truth the truth?' Yet there is a great appropriateness in the fact that even those who have never read a line of Scott all know the most famous couplet in *Marmion*:

O what a tangled web we weave
When first we practise to deceive!

The tangle which ensnared the Author of Waverley as novelist, businessman, and publisher was of nightmarish proportions, but it never infects his art. Even if the magnificent stylishness of the plot occasionally strains our credulity, it is impossible to finish *The Heart of Midlothian* without the sure sense that its author has had his finger on the pulse of truth.

The sixth of Scott's novels, it breathes a wonderful certainty of touch. The great themes of the book are all blended together, inviting musical analogy. The upset mail coach at the opening of the book foreshadows Jeanie's coach journey at its centre. The unyielding hostility of Queen Caroline to the Scots, hinted at the beginning of the novel, is challenged by her interview with Jeanie in Chapter XXXVII. The violent hangings at the beginning are echoed in the hideous but distant glimpse of Madge Wildfire's mother on the gallows as Jeanie passes through Carlisle with Mrs Dutton on her way back from London:

The postilions drove on, wheeling as the Penrith road led them, round the verge of the rising ground. Yet still the eyes of Mrs Dolly Dutton which, with the head and substantial person to which they belonged, were all turned towards the scene of action, could plainly discern the outline of the gallows-tree, relieved against the clear sky, the dark shade formed by the persons of the executioner and the criminal upon the light rounds of the tall aerial ladder, until one of the objects, launched into the air, gave unequivocal signs of mortal agony, though appearing in the distance not larger than a spider dependent at the extremity of his invisible thread, while the remaining form descended from its elevated situation, and regained with all speed an undistinguished place among the crowd . . . Jeanie turned her head in the same direction.

The sight of a female culprit in the act of undergoing the fatal punishment from which her beloved sister had been so recently rescued was too much, not perhaps for her nerves, but for her mind and feelings. She turned her head to the other side of the carriage, with a sensation of sickness, of loathing, and of fainting. . . .

(Chapter XL)

How characteristic that the sight of a hanging revolts Jeanie's *mind*. Further echoes of Effie's sad story are heard quite soon afterwards, when Jeanie witnesses the death of Madge Wildfire. Her dying song, one of the most perfect short poems in the language, is only one of many instances of the book's lyricism, of the way in which it is held together not only by the solidity of its moral outlook and the reality of its characters—undeniable as these both are—but by an underlying delicacy of language:

> Proud Maisie is in the wood,
>   Walking so early;
> Sweet Robin sits on the bush,
>   Singing so rarely.
>
> 'Tell me, thou bonny bird,
>   When shall I marry me?'
> 'When six braw gentlemen
>   Kirkward shall carry ye.'
>
> 'Who makes the bridal bed,
>   Birdie, say truly?'
> 'The grey-haired sexton,
>   That delves the grave duly.
>
> 'The glow worm o'er grave and stone
>   Shall light thee steady.
> The owl from the steeple sing,
>   "Welcome, proud lady."'

(Chapter XL)

Of course, it has all the poignancy which surrounds the utterances of the mad. It is in fact Madge's own story; but how much she recognizes this, it is impossible to say. Yet that is only part of the magic of 'Proud Maisie'. If it were possible to define what is so haunting and so pertinent about it, it would not be so powerful; but it seems to tie the tale quite appropriately into the savage tradition of folk song, where we so often encounter the jilted bride, the gallows and the grave.

Although inimitable and uniquely itself, *The Heart of Midlothian* is a prototype of many other nineteenth-century novels, a model which few Victorian writers could match, since the necessity of serial writing destroyed the firm shape which, writing volume by volume, Scott was able to impose on his stories. It is not merely the violent energy of that mob, reminding us of the storming of Newgate Prison in *Barnaby*

Rudge, which makes us feel that this is a novel which seems to anticipate Dickens, nor even the individual episodes which one can imagine Dickens enjoying. One can imagine Mrs Glass, the tobacconist with whom Jeanie lodges when in London, cropping up in any Dickens novel, and taking up more space than she does in *The Heart of Midlothian*. There is something Dickensian, too, about the pathetic absurdity which breaks through when Jeanie questions the boy who, in killing George Staunton, has been unconsciously guilty of parricide:

He stretched out his hands, still smeared with blood, perhaps that of this father, and he ate voraciously and in silence.
    'What is your first name?' said Jeanie, by way of opening the conversation.
    'The Whistler.'
    'But your Christian name, by which you were baptized?'
    'I never was baptized that I know of—I have no other name than the Whistler.'

(Chapter LII)

This could be an exchange in Fagin's lair; and Jo the crossing-sweeper in *Bleak House* is not far away.

But it is something bigger and more nebulous which makes one feel some affinity between Scott and Dickens. It is something to do with the *size* of *The Heart of Midlothian*: the whole city, initially at least, is the subject of this novel; a great image, the prison at the centre of it, governs our view of it. This is the practice of the later Dickens.

It is tendentious to look for 'influences' of one writer's work on another's. Dickens's wholly idiosyncratic genius would have blossomed if Sir Walter Scott had never written a line. Yet if there are no obvious influences, there are many affinities; perhaps the most striking of which is that, however large the scene before us, our eyes are always drawn to the individual examples of human oddity within that scene. And then, very often, the artist moves even closer to focus on individual physical characteristics—arms which resemble lobsters, protruding ears which look as though they were designed as handles.

In *The Heart of Midlothian*, this close focus is done with delicacy and pathos. There is much less obvious humour here than in, say, *The Antiquary*. Perhaps Jeanie's rather stiff view of life comes to govern the whole atmosphere of the book. Certainly, for Scott, she was the book's glory—'The lass kept tugging at my heart-strings.' The year before he died, he paid for the erection of a memorial to Helen Walker, the original of Jeanie Deans. The gesture was typical. Old Mortality's chisel, preserving the names of the dead on their tombstones, was doing the same work as Scott's pen. In both cases, one sees that much more was involved than a love of the past.

CHAPTER SEVEN

Scott's Heroines
The Bride of Lammermoor and *Kenilworth*

... many a flawless lyric may be due
Not to a lover's broken heart, but 'flu.

W. H. Auden: *Letter to Lord Byron*.

The mythology of Shakespeare's life, like the multiplicity of interpretations of Christ's personality by agnostics such as Strauss and Renan, knew its full flowering in the nineteenth century. This was so not merely in the numerous fanciful biographies which appeared, but in the lives of literary men themselves. Shakespeare dominated every idol, coloured every 'life'. One sees this process at work in Sidney Lee's delightful *Life of Shakespeare*, which concludes with the bard's re-establishment as a successful bourgeois in his native town.

His extant work attests his 'copious' and continuous industry, and with his literary power and sociability there clearly went the shrewd capacity of the man of business. Pope had just warrant for the surmise that he

For gain not glory winged his roving flight,
And grew immortal in his own despite.

His literary attainments and successes were chiefly valued as serving the prosaic end of providing permanently for himself and his daughters . . . Ideals so homely are reckoned rare among poets, but Chaucer and Sir Walter Scott among writers of exalted genius, vie with Shakespeare in the sobriety of their personal aims and in the sanity of their mental attitude towards life's ordinary incidents.[1]

Scott's attitude to literature was, of course, entirely consistent with this picture of apparent domestic common sense, the precise opposite of Byron's and Shelley's aristocratic bohemianism. But, also, it must be said that the Victorian Scott who emerges from such an iconography probably bears no more relation to the real Laird of Abbotsford than Sidney Lee's Shakespeare does to the Swan of Avon.

The prosaic end of providing for himself and his daughters was not

something that Scott sniffed at, however. Daughters were an important part of the nineteenth-century household, and it is this which
gives Lockhart's *Life* its richly Victorian flavour. Indeed it could
almost have been called *Wives and Daughters*, his own wife never
abandoning her position as primarily the daughter of Scott, her role
as Mrs Lockhart coming a good way second.

The facts of Scott's life fit the parlour image pretty well; indeed,
helped to contribute to the cult of the daughter which was to console
so many nineteenth-century women for the less gallant cult of the
aunt which would meet them whenever siblings married. Scott's
relationship with Anne and Sophia, his two daughters, was very close,
and he showed a gentleness of touch in their upbringing which was
largely lacking in his dealing with his sons. For instance, describing
Sophia to Joanna Baillie, he wrote,

She is an excellent good child sufficiently sensible, very affectionate not
without perception of character—but the Gods have not made her poetical
and I hope she will never attempt to act the part which nature has not called
her to . . . I am therefore particularly anxious to store the heads of my young
damsels with something better than the tags of rhimes.[2]

This letter provides a useful gloss to the story of Ballantyne asking
Sophia, when a child of twelve, her opinion of *The Lady of the Lake*—to
receive the reply, 'Oh, I have not read it: papa says there is nothing so
bad for young people as reading bad poetry.'[3] Only the most obtuse
critic would take this as a serious reflection on Scott's poetry. It is
really evidence of Scott's desire to protect Sophia from being 'a poet's
child'. Whatever mistakes he and Lady Scott made as parents, at least
they avoided rearing a creature so unfit for existence as Pen Browning.

Everyone liked Sophia, who married Lockhart in 1820. The marriage was a blow to Scott because, in spite of his caution during her
childhood, she had developed a passion for Scotch songs and ballads.
Evenings at Abbotsford were spent listening to her renderings of
them. Anne did not share this enthusiasm to the same degree, and
Scott was not one to pretend that he liked a thing when he did not. Her
attempts to fill the gap left by Sophia's departure were, at least in the
field of song and recitation, unsatisfactory. She was a 'difficult'
character. When Miss Edgeworth eventually visited Abbotsford, she
found the girl tart and did not like her, though she was won round in

the end. This was a common experience. Anne had the sort of shyness which was initially rebarbative. Scott himself was often embarrassed by her satirical tongue, but he was proud of it too. 'Did it ever strike you,' he wrote to Miss Edgeworth, 'that Anne has an odd cast of Beatrice's humour about her?'[4] This had its social drawbacks, though it made her lively company. She saw no reason to pretend to be charmed by Wordsworth, and sharply upbraided him for his portentous dismissal of Crabbe. On more than one occasion, she nearly disclosed, to uninitiated company, the identity of the Author of Waverley. She was sharp, charming, but distant.

She had inherited her mother's good looks and the portrait at Abbotsford, depicting her in Spanish dress, could, appropriately, represent the heroine of a Scott opera. She had the glossy black hair and eyes of her mother; but, alas, the same high temper, depressions and fits of hysteria. She was the sort of girl to whom accidents were always happening. In 1822, when she stood with her father watching the restoration of Mons Meg, the great cannon, to the battery of Edinburgh Castle, there was a celebratory burst of rockets. One of the fireworks landed on her bonnet, and it was some time before she or anyone noticed that her hat was in flames. 'She neither screamed nor ran,' Scott was proud to relate. 'All who saw her, especially the friendly Celts, gave her merit for her steadiness, and said she came of good blood.'[5]

The same was not always the case. When her mother died, Anne was hysterical for a week. Much of the burden of nursing Lady Scott had fallen on her, Sophia being in London by that stage with Lockhart. Perhaps the younger daughter now sensed that she was to be Scott's chief companion. His own health was not good, and his sunny temperament had begun to degenerate into prematurely senile irritability. They were extremely close, but Anne had to bear all the weight of his rages when household accounts were in a muddle or servants became disorderly or guests got out of control. Moreover, she was a conscientious aunt, and helped Sophia nurse her little son, Johnny Lockhart—the dedicatee of *Tales of a Grandfather*—until his pathetic death at the age of ten. Shortly after, Scott's own health began to collapse completely.

'He is irritable to a degree that is dreadful,' she complained bitterly to her brothers and sisters when they failed to relieve her from her task.[6] Much later, after his strokes, she recorded, 'He has screamed without ceasing *six and twenty hours*.'[7]

Worse than this, in the short period when the strokes deranged his mind Scott believed himself to be King Lear. In his madness, he saw neither of his daughters as Cordelia, even though, by then, Anne had earned the title. They seemed tigers, not daughters, and both Anne and Sophia had to be kept from him, since he became violent if he so much as knew they were in the room. He only admitted business colleagues into his presence, saluting those two old swindlers Ballantyne and Cadell as 'my two learned Thebans'.

The mad phase passed, of course, but it is hard to forget it. For Anne, her father's last illness and death were altogether too much. She only survived him by six months, dying in June 1833. She was thirty. Her elder sister followed her four years later, aged thirty-eight.

There is no doubt something consciously Shakespearean about the fact that so many of Scott's heroines are the daughters of widowed fathers, or of fathers whose wives play no noticeably important part in their lives. Rosa Bradwardine is the first in a long line of this type, her cosy relationship with her ageing father the Baron anticipating Julia Mannering, Isabella Wardour, Diana Vernon, Edith Bellenden, Jeanie Deans, Rebecca the Jewess, Amy Robsart, Alice Lee, Catherine Glover, and Menie Gray (a list which is by no means exhaustive), all of whom conform to this pattern.

It is natural, too, quite apart from Shakespearean precedent, that a man who started writing novels when he had two daughters approaching womanhood should see his heroines as daughters to a much greater degree than as mistresses or wives. But it would be perverse to go further than that. In spite of the traditional identification of Alice Lee in *Woodstock* with Anne Scott, one would be unwise to draw any conclusions about Scott's relationship with his daughters from a reading of the novels.

One striking thing about his heroines, though, is that the two most notable for having mothers and fathers who are still alive are those who come to tragic ends. In nearly all the other stories, a slightly ageing father overcomes his objections to a possible son-in-law when the young man turns out to have some hitherto unrevealed quality of birth and character, and the trio settle down to existence together. But the two girls with living parents—Clara Mowbray and Lucy Ashton—are both forced into marriages which they dislike after being forbidden by domineering families to marry the man they love. The end is lunacy, despair, and, of course, in the case of Scott's most famous bride, bloodshed.

The legend of how *The Bride of Lammermoor* came to be written would be too familiar to be worth repeating were it not for the obvious inconsistencies which it contains. The tradition on which the novel is based must have been familiar to Scott ever since he entered the legal profession, since Janet Dalrymple, the original of the Bride, was a seventeenth-century forebear of one of the leading legal families in Scotland, the head of whom, Lord Stair, was a friend of Scott's. Scott did not, therefore, as in some of his novels, have to wrestle with the actual composition of the *story* as he went along; and this perhaps explains why he was able to produce it without having to write it down himself.

One of the delights which the book's publication provided Scott was that it was generally assumed that he could not possibly have written it. Gossip had by this date identified 'the Author of Waverley' almost conclusively. Yet all Scott's legal acquaintances and literary friends knew that, when *The Bride of Lammermoor* was being composed, he was much too ill to work. Indeed, during the early summer of 1819, he was prostrate with gallstones and jaundice. Although he had crawled to his writing-desk and tried to force himself to start the novel, his pen would not move at a satisfactory speed and he was at length prevailed upon to use secretaries. Lockhart describes it well:

His amanuenses were William Laidlaw and John Ballantyne;—of whom he preferred the latter, on account of the superior rapidity of his pen; and also because John kept his pen to his paper without interruption, and though with many an arch twinkle in his eyes, and now and then an audible smack of his lips, had resolution to work on like a well-trained clerk; whereas good Laidlaw entered with such keen zest into the interest of the story as it flowed from the author's lips, that he could not resist exclamations of surprise and delight—'Gude keep us a'!'—'the like o' that!'—'eh sirs! eh sirs!'—and so forth—which did not promote despatch. I have often, however, in the sequel heard both these secretaries describe the astonishment with which they were equally affected when Scott began this experiment. The affectionate Laidlaw beseeching him to stop dictating, when his audible suffering filled every pause. 'Nay, Willie,' he answered, 'only see that the doors are fast. I would fain keep all the cry as well as all the wool to ourselves; but as to giving over work, that can only be when I am in woollen.' John Ballantyne told me that after the first few days, he always took care to have a dozen pens made before he seated himself opposite the sofa on which Scott lay, and that though he often turned himself on his pillow with a groan of torment, he usually continued the sentence in the same breath. But when dialogue of peculiar animation was in progress, spirit seemed to triumph altogether over matter—he arose from his couch and walked up and down the room, raising and lowering his voice, and as it were acting the parts. . . .[8]

There are few better illustrations of the way Lockhart makes Scott into the Romantic man of genius, his art pouring out of him, a bard who never needs to blot a line. Yet although it is obviously modelled on a Shakespearean pattern, it seems wholly plausible. Even allowing for the fact that Lockhart and Laidlaw want to make a good story, one can believe the almost mystical detachment from self which overcame Scott when he inhabited his own fictions. When the book finally went to press, the legend goes on, he could not remember a word of his novel. It had vanished from his mind with the fever.

Similarly, one may believe that the words 'Go, bid the soldiers shoot' had no sooner been scratched on some actor's copy, than Shakespeare never gave the character of Hamlet another thought. Yet, this part of the Scott legend, if not actually incompatible with the famous conversation in Italy with Don Luigi Santa Croce, at any rate sits oddly beside it. Don Luigi, it will be remembered, had protested against the harshness of the ending of *St. Ronan's Well*. Scott replied that 'of all the murders that I have committed in that way . . . there is none which went so much to my heart as the poor Bride of Lammermoor; but it could not be helped—it is all true.'[9] One cannot readily tell from this whether he meant that he could not depart from the original historical story of Janet Dalrymple, or whether he felt an inner compulsion to finish the story as he did. Laidlaw's account of its composition would make the latter more likely. So, on the one hand, in 1819, Scott claims total detachment from the work; yet ten years later, he appears to admit such total commitment to its subject matter that 'it could not be helped'.

The paradox of the book is unintentionally emphasized by Andrew Lang's introduction to the Border Edition. He recounts the legend of its composition, and piously adds 'thus among the many lessons of Scott's life he taught by example, the possibility of overcoming pain through courage and succeeded in doing what the Stoics vaunted that their ideal Wise Man could achieve.'[10]

No one would deny the extraordinary stoicism of doing any-thing—let alone write a novel—in the condition which afflicted Scott in April 1819. His courage is not in question. But there seems an irony in invoking the Stoics to commend a production such as *The Bride of*

Lammermoor. It is not merely the most passionate and erotic novel which he ever wrote: it appears to contradict what he had written earlier about the nature of passion and moderation, and about self-control, for it is self-control which drives Lucy Ashton mad. Her father, Sir William, and her lover, the Master of Ravenswood, are both too concerned with their own melodramas, and their own feelings about Lucy, to notice how strongly the tensions between their two houses are working on the girl. Nor, of course, have either of them reckoned on the terrifying forcefulness of Lady Ashton's personality, or of the jealous feelings of Lucy's brothers. The dénouement at the end, when Lucy stabs her bridegroom, is as full-blown as it could be: 'Here they found the unfortunate girl, seated, or rather couched like a hare upon its form—her head-gear dishevelled; her night-clothes torn and dabbled with blood—her eyes glazed, and her features convulsed into a wild paroxysm of insanity.' (Chapter XXXIII.) It is so shocking because it has been worked up to so gently. As Hardy observed, '*The Bride of Lammermoor* is an almost perfect specimen of form.'[11] It is brilliantly put together. And this is all the more remarkable when we remember the circumstances in which it was made. It shows that Scott did not need to construct carefully. Unlike Newman, who could not think 'without a pen in his hand', Scott conceived his greatest books whole, and merely needed, like Milton, to be 'milked'.

The figure of Caleb Balderstone should be mentioned here. He is, of course, the type of bad Scotch servant with whom we are familiar in the Waverley Novels, as insolent as Andrew Fairservice, as parsimonious as Alison Wilson. But his role in the book is much more important than that of a clown providing a little routine knockabout, as when he steals a hot dinner from the local inn to feed the Master of Ravenswood's guests. Nor, as the magnificence of the last scene shows, is Caleb's position anything like as simple as a phrase like 'comic relief' would suggest. But one very important function he plays in the earlier parts of the book is that his presence keeps the temperature low. Passion is at the book's core, but it is always being held in check, and this is what makes it all the more poignant when it bursts. Donizetti's opera is quite unlike the novel in this respect. *Hamlet* and *King Lear* are the plays behind the novel; *Romeo and Juliet* is the key of the opera. The book concerns the love of children for their parents and *vice versa*—Edgar's insulted rage at the interruption of his father's funeral; Sir William Ashton's terrified devotion to his only daughter; Lucy's inability to make either her father or her mother aware of her own feelings—but the opera concentrates on the lovers themselves, banishing Lucia's parents altogether. An early scene refers to her weeping at her mother's grave. But, even apart from this, *Lucia di Lammermoor* is quite unlike the novel in texture because of its deliberate exclusion of comic or light touches. It plunges us straight into intense high feeling. When Enrico is exclaiming

> Mi fa gelare e fremer, solleva in fonte in crito
> Colema di tanto opprobria, chi suora a me nascea

in the first quarter of an hour, the outbursts of passion at the end do not provide any great contrast with the sense of frustration which had been built up at the beginning of Scott's story but is absent from Donizetti's opera.

It is after the quietness of the opening of the novel, the bull-headed insensitivity of Lucy's family, that her end is so effective. Edgar, of course, has always lived in an atmosphere of wounded honour and high love and rage. But his menage at Wolf's Crag is absurd. The fact that Caleb has been so persistently irritating, and deflated Edgar's domestic dignity so persistently throughout the book, makes the Master's last ride such an impressive piece of writing. Lucy's elder brother waits for Edgar to appear for a duel at dawn. At the back of our minds, we recall the prophecy that the Master of Ravenswood will meet his death in the quicksands of Kelpie's Flow:

Colonel Ashton, frantic for revenge, was already in the field, pacing the turf with eagerness, and looking with impatience towards the tower for the arrival of his antagonist. The sun had now risen, and showed its broad disk above the eastern sea, so that he could easily discern the horseman who rode towards him with speed which argued impatience equal to his own. At once the figure became invisible, as if it had melted into the air. He rubbed his eyes, as if he had witnessed an apparition, and then hastened to the spot, near which he was met by Balderstone, who came from the opposite direction. No trace whatever of horse or rider could be discerned; it only appeared, that the late winds and high tides had greatly extended the usual bounds of the quicksand, and that the unfortunate horseman, as appeared from the hoof-tracks, in his precipitated haste, had not attended to keep on the firm sands of the foot of the rock, but had taken the shortest and most dangerous course. One only vestige of his fate appeared. A large sable feather had been detached from his hat, and the rippling waves of the rising tide wafted it to Caleb's feet. The old man took it up, dried it, and placed it in his own bosom.

(Chapter XXXIV)

Effects such as this, the last glimpse through the mist as Edgar rides to
his predestined end in the Kelpie Flow, could never have been captured on stage. And there are many features of Scott's literary manner—his facility to convey authentic dialogue, and his analytical
historical sense, to name two obvious ones—which are lost in any
operatic rendering of his books. Yet it remains appropriate that so
many operas[12] have been inspired by Scott—and by *The Bride of
Lammermoor* in particular. Before Donizetti's masterpiece in 1835,
there had been at least five others: *Le Caleb de Walter Scott*, a comic
pasticcio which appeared in Paris in 1827; Michele Carafa's *Le Nozze
di Lammermoor* of 1829; Rieschi's *La Fidanzata di Lammermoor* in 1831
(another opera with the same title was to appear in 1834, by
Mazzucato); and, in 1832, *Bruden fra Lammermoor* by the Danish
composer Ivar Frederick Bredal, with a libretto by Hans Christian
Andersen.

Although so astonishingly well-composed as a novel, it is really
little more than an extension of the familiar motive of much folk-song:
the star-crossed lovers and the enmity of two households; a bloody
wedding-day; the mysterious fulfilment of a sybil's prophecies.
Moreoever, in Lucy Ashton's song, one feels that the book is almost
resolving itself into another *genre*; for, having grown out of folk-song
material, the essential points of the plot seem capable of resolution
into lyric:

> Look not thou on beauty's charming,
> Sit thou still when kings are arming,
> Taste not when the wine-cup glistens,
> Speak not when the people listens,
> Stop thine ear against the singer,
> From the red gold keep thy finger;
> Vacant heart and hand and eye,
> Easy live and quiet die.

While she is singing, her father enters her apartments and overhears
the lyric, but before Scott allows either of them to speak, he tells us of
the absence of sympathy between Lucy and her mother. Lady Ashton
thinks that she can manipulate Lucy; and so she can, but only with
the most disastrous consequences:

Like many a parent of hot and impatient character, she was mistaken in
estimating the feelings of her daughter, who, under a semblance of extreme

indifference, nourished the germ of those passions which sometimes spring up in one night, like the gourd of the prophet, and astonish the observer by their unexpected ardour and intensity. In fact, Lucy's sentiments seemed chill because nothing had occurred to interest or awaken them. . . .

                                                                (Chapter II)

This is the central fact about Lucy—the central point, indeed, of the book—and, as Miss Lamont makes clear in a most attractive lecture on the poetry of the early Waverley Novels,[13] it is all contained within the song itself. In the drama which is about to enfold them neither her lover nor Lucy herself can follow the stern advice of the lyric, nor stop their ears against the siren voices of the singer. Nor has anyone in the book—which places it worlds apart from, say, *The Anti-quary*—developed the notion of how to 'easy live and quiet die'. The lyric remains fixed in our minds not merely because it is exquisite (though unoriginal), but because there is no song after Chapter II, when Lucy has been introduced.[14] It is the first song we hear from her lips. The poems of that chapter are not just tags of verse put in to decorate the prose: the prose grows out of the song. And although most, perhaps all, of its subtlety is lost in opera, the novel itself is, at the same time, almost visibly heaving itself into operatic positions at various points.

The prophecies of blind Alice, Edgar's speeches about the honour of his family, and the absurd antics of Caleb in the kitchen are all, in their way, equally operatic material. But it is not merely the 'operatic moments' which make the novels such obvious fodder for the librettist (Meg Merrilies's 'Ride your ways, Ellangowan', Balfour of Burley's 'Fearing nothing', or Lord Glenallan's account of his broken love-affair with Eveline are almost arias already): one finds, as Scott's powers as a novelist declined, that he conceived of his characters in increasingly stagey and externalized terms. Consider Fenella in *Peveril of the Peak*. Based on Mignon in Goethe's *Wilhelm Meister's Lehrjahre*, she pretends to be a deaf mute in order to spy on the Countess of Derby. In reality, she is the daughter of the villain, Edward Christian. She is one of the most powerfully erotic figures Scott ever conceived, with her thick, abundant hair covering a tiny little body like a mane. One can imagine how vividly Dickens would have conveyed her inner oddity and *haecceitas* as he did with, say, the Marchioness in *The Old Curiosity Shop*, whose relationship with Quilp clearly owes something to Fenella and Christian. But, for Scott, having brought the character forward, she becomes simply a device: partly one of plot—to explain how Christian gets so much of his information—but chiefly one of *effect*. She exists in the book not for what she is but for the various lights in which the novelist can display her, like a wax-work with feelings—her unrequited love for young Peveril, her miserable history, the flamboyant disclosure that she is not a deaf mute after all: in all these scenes she is conceived as a series of carefully stage-managed manifestations or displays rather than as a continuously observed character. She is, in effect, a character in opera; the librettist, unlike the novelist, being under no compulsion to suggest human personality in the round.

In *The Romantic Survival*, John Bayley, reflecting on the Shelleyan view of poetry as a force which infuses all forms of art and science, rightly pointed out that this is a definition which defeats its own purpose:

Instead of helping to universalize the idea of poetry it only tends to provincialize the idea of verse. Just as bad money drives out good, so prose will drive out verse. Since those who use prose will do so all the more readily now that Romantic theory assures them that they can do so poetically. The form of verse will now seem more specialized and artificial, less readily to be turned to by the average writer. Scott turns from verse to prose; George Eliot who—had she lived fifty years earlier—would certainly have written in verse, is a novelist first and a versifier a long way second.[15]

From this conception of Romantic formlessness, the novel develops as a perfect artistic portmanteau whose essentially fluid character can be adapted to suit the changing requirements of any practitioner.

Peter Conrad, a pupil of Professor Bayley's, extends the argument of *The Romantic Survival* to the point at which all artistic forms in the nineteenth century are aspiring to the condition of each other; in particular, he sees the Romantic opera as attempting all the time to turn into a novel: 'In setting words, opera obscures them by transmuting them into notes. In providing music to accompany a drama, it subverts that drama into a sentimental or psychological novel.'[16]

It could be objected to Mr Conrad's use of the word *novel*, as to Shelley's use of the word *poetry*, that its limits, in such a definition, had been stretched beyond the bounds of sense. But there is no accident, surely, in the fact that Romantic opera and novel both reached their fullest flowering at roughly the same stage of nineteenth-century history. *Romantic Opera and Literary Form* is a gay, paradoxical essay, itself delighting by its romantic oddity; few beside its author can ever have felt, while sitting through *The Ring*, that 'Wagner's epic is a novel in code.' But many must have felt when reading Scott, particularly the later Scott, the reverse tendency at work, with the novels dissolving into a series of operatic scenes.

In many ways so similar in theme and atmosphere to *The Bride of Lammermoor*, *Kenilworth* (1821) is a case in point. As with *The Bride*, one feels that the story is conceived on the simple level of folk-song—or, at its most sophisticated level, of narrative verse. Scott says as much in his Introduction:

The reader will find I have borrowed several incidents as well as names from Ashmole, and the more early authorities; but my first acquaintance with the history was through the more pleasing medium of verse. There is a period in youth when the mere power of numbers has a more strong effect on ear and imagination than in more advanced life. At this season of immature taste, the Author was greatly delighted with the poems of Mickle and Langhorne, poets who, though by no means deficient in the higher branches of their art, were eminent for their powers of verbal melody above most who have practised this department of poetry. One of those pieces of Mickle, which the author was particularly pleased with, is a ballad, or rather a species of elegy, on the subject of Cumnor Hall, which, with others by the same author, were to be found in Evans's *Ancient Ballads* (Volume iv, page 130) to which work Mickle made liberal contributions. The first stanza had a peculiar species of enchantment for the youthful ear of the Author, the force of which is not even now entirely spent. . . .

For fullness, one should read the whole poem, much of which, as Scott admits, is 'sufficiently prosaic'; it throws a fascinating light on the way in which *Kenilworth* was conceived and composed. But the favourite first stanza gives the flavour:

> The dews of summer night did fall,
>   The moon, sweet regent of the sky,
> Silver'd the walls of Cumnor Hall,
>   And many an oak that grew thereby.

For what it is, one cannot imagine Mickle's poem being bettered. But it is a peculiar inspiration for a fiction. *Kenilworth* is a splendid book, but it is not exactly speaking a novel. It is a poem set to prose, a series of scenes divided by historical tableaux and pageants. The inconsequential quality of Donizetti's opera title—*Elisabetta al Castello di Kenilworth*—exactly captures the type of book it is. Unlike the portrait of Queen Mary of Scotland in *The Abbot*, to which in a way it is designed as a companion piece, that of Queen Elizabeth seems to be designed for scenic effect rather than because of its relevance to the plot. The overpowering sexual possessiveness of the Queen—which of course has direct importance in the tale of Amy Robsart—is not brought before our attention in any exchange so brilliant as, say, those jealous *fracas* between Queen Mary and the Regent's mother in *The Abbot*. It is really a Mrs Skewton's-eye view of Tudor England which is presented in *Kenilworth*. Walter Raleigh's throwing his cloak in the mud, for instance, has nothing to do with the tragedy of Amy Robsart—indeed, it would have been very surprising if Raleigh had come to court by the time of Leicester's illicit marriage. But Scott cannot resist bringing it in. We are not being presented with a realistic portrait of the Queen, like that of Queen Mary in *The Abbot* or of James I in the *Fortunes of Nigel*, but with Good Queen Bess as her image is fixed in the popular imagination, a figure who requires as little explanation as Bluff King Hal, or Robin Hood, or Father Christmas, or Dick Whittington.

This does not, I think, make *Kenilworth* a bad book, but it makes it different from, say, *Old Mortality*, in which familiar historical scenes and characters are all moulded into the interests of the plot, and are all interpreted afresh as they take their place in the author's imagination. They are conceived as fictional realities, not as historical stereotypes. Many people have a distaste for Scott's later fiction and think of it as thin, slapdash, even meretricious. This is not a view I share—partly because he is so interested in human character and, simply, so good at writing novels, that even the most hastily composed of his later works cannot fail to display merit, often of an unexpected kind, in one way or another. But, without fully realizing what he was doing, he began after 1820 gradually to abandon the novelistic techniques which he had perfected and to go back to writing narrative poetry. If read in the same way that one reads *The Lady of the Lake*, *Kenilworth* is an experience that few could fail to enjoy.

What makes the great narrative poems of Scott so memorable is their colourful, boldly designed scenes, which are probably only held together by the slenderest thread of logical narrative and will often be interrupted by verse epistles to Scott's friends, reflections on scenery or politics, or addresses to the reader. We do not expect *Marmion* to be coherently bound together like a novel. It does not much matter how all the characters relate or even who they are. What we remember is the intensity with which the great scenes are built up to, and described: a stranger arriving at a castle; a shrieking girl walled up in an island convent; the pageantry and array of Flodden Field.

Oddly, it is this tendency of Scott's later fiction to resemble the disparately connected scenes of his narrative verse which is one of his most influential contributions to the shape of the nineteenth-century novel, or rather to its lack of shape. It is not merely that his most formless works, the historical romances of his later period, were by far the most popular of the Waverley Novels in the nineteenth century. More than that, their popularity stood as an object lesson to the novelists who followed.

Henry James remarked of *Middlemarch* that it was 'a treasure-house of detail but an indifferent whole'. The same could be said of any of the great novels in the earlier part of that century—and, most obviously, those of Dickens and Thackeray. The chief historical reason for this was that the serial form, designed to be read in weekly instalments, provided a much less rigid structure for fiction than that adhered to by eighteenth-century and Regency novels, which were conceived in volumes, and where the structure of the story is frequently patterned by the volumes which contain it. *Old Mortality*, for instance, can be seen to centre round three occasions of combat: the mock combat in the Festival of the Popinjay, which opens the first volume of the story; the triumph of the Covenanters at Drumclog, which dominates the second volume; and their defeat at Bothwell Bridge which is the business of the third. It cannot be an accident that the story takes this neat shape. By adopting a much less rigid structure in his later stories, Scott was paving the way for these vast expansive Victorian novels which made no claim to have any 'shape' in this formal sense. Dickens, like Scott himself, followed the chaotic formlessness of the eighteenth-century picaresque tradition. But it is unlikely that he would have done so, after the formal interregnum of carefully structured Regency novels, without Scott's lead. The structure of the later Waverley Novels reverts, both to the increasingly formless patterns of Romantic poetry, and to the undisciplined narrative techniques of Fielding. This is what James called 'an indifferent whole'. But until James himself developed his own richly delicate formalism, the treasure-house ran riot.

CHAPTER EIGHT

Scott's Medievalism

'Lord deliver me from this Gothic generation,' exclaimed the
Antiquary.

At least six dramatic productions based on *Ivanhoe* were performed on
the London stage within a year of the book's publication; and there
were many more within the course of the century. One of the most
striking must have been *The Maid of Judah, or the Knights Templar*. It
was first acted at Covent Garden on 7 March 1829, with music by
Rossini and words by M. Rophino Lacy, Esq., author of *The Turkish
Lovers*, *The Two Friends* and *Love in Wrinkles*. The printed version
describes it as 'a serious opera in three acts', and the illustrated
frontispiece by Cruikshank makes Rebecca and Sir Brian de Bois-
Guilbert look as though they are being played by Mr Lenville and the
Infant Phenomenon in Mr Vincent Crummles's theatrical company.
Sir Brian de Bois-Guilbert stepping onto the boards was to be seen
dressed 'in white scaled armour suit,—scarlet full-skirted tunic, with
short sleeves, trimmed with black velvet—the Templar's cloak over
it'. Rebecca herself wore a 'scarlet and gold under-petticoat, trimmed
with gold, over it—white trousers—scarlet and gold turban—drapery
trimmed with amber and black—white silk stockings—flesh colour
and black shoes'. It must have been very beautiful.

The plot is simplified a good deal. Rowena and Athelstane do not
come into the story at all. Anticipating Thackeray's desire to marry
off Ivanhoe to the Jewess,[1] M. R. Lacy concluded his piece with
Ivanhoe, having victoriously fought on Rebecca's behalf in trial by
combat, singing

> The help thy danger crav'd
>   With joy was given by me.
> The conflict which I brav'd
>   I fought and won for thee.

Scott appeared to have very little objection to these popular distor-
tions of his work. Three years before the appearance of *The Maid of
Judah*, he had greatly enjoyed Rossini's *Ivanhoe* (on which it was
based), which he saw in Paris on 31 October 1826.

'It was superbly got up,' he recorded in his Journal,

the normal soldiers wearing pointed helmets and what resembled much
hauberks of mail which lookd very well. The number of the attendants and
the skill with which they are moved and grouped on the stage is well worthy of
notice. It was an opera and of course the story greatly mangled and the
dialogue in great part nonsense. Yet it was strange to hear anything like the
words which I (then in an agony of pain with spasms in my stomach) dictated
to William Laidlaw at Abbotsford now recited in a foreign tongue and for the
amusement of a strange people. I little thought to have survived the complet-
ing of this novel.[2]

He did not have a chance to see any of the other adaptations, the
most lavish of which was Sir Arthur Sullivan's *Ivanhoe* in 1891, nearly
sixty years after Scott's death, and surely one of the Scott operas
which deserves to be revived. For my part, though, I should have
preferred to see the rather earlier *Ivanhoe* by Fox Cooper, performed at
Astley's Theatre on Easter Monday 1869, in which Mr Brandon Ellis
played Sir Brian de Bois-Guilbert and Ivanhoe, wearing 'brilliant
steel armour with helmet etc.—scarlet surcoat, trimmed with gold . . .
plume—sword, etc', was played by Miss Agnes Cameron.

The most rumbustious production of all was at Astley's Royal
National Amphitheatre of the Arts, when Andrew Ducrow, the fore-
most circus ringmaster in Europe, staged a re-enactment of the
tournament at Ashby-de-la-Zouche. The spectacle was hugely popular. Not only did it run to packed houses for more than fifty perfor-
mances in its first summer in 1839, but it remained a standard part of
the repertory at the amphitheatre until its final closure in 1895. Here,
in the large arena, built as a riding-school, the public could see the
tournament enacted with real armour, horses, lances, pavilions, and
pageantry.

It was very vulgar, of course. The more discerning might have
preferred to read the book itself, or to see the paintings inspired by it
in the Royal Academy. For twenty years after the first publication of
Ivanhoe, at least two such paintings were shown in the annual Summer
Exhibition; and these, of course, were only a fragment of the number
of paintings inspired by the whole Scott *œuvre*, well over a thousand of
which were produced and exhibited in the course of the century.
Ivanhoe touched a deeper vein than most of Scott's other novels—and a
vein too profound to dismiss as mere fantasy.

In 1839, not long after the presentations of the tournament began at

Astley's Amphitheatre, a group of rich young men, centred around
Lord Eglinton in his castle in Ayrshire, determined to have a real
tournament of their own.* It is a story of enormous and fantastic
expense. The combatants fitted themselves out in suits of armour
provided by Pratt of Bond Street. Since no one had the slightest idea
how a medieval tournament was fought, still less of the distinctions
between different types of tournament, they relied fairly heavily for
their inspiration on *Ivanhoe*. Alas, like so many good things designed to
take place in Scotland, the event itself was completely ruined by the
weather. The lists were flooded by a river that had burst its banks; the
medieval banquet was almost literally washed away; and the numerous spectators, rain seeping through the samite and chain mail to the
back of their necks, were turned away soaked and hungry in the dark,
after a deluge severe even by the standards of the western counties of
Scotland.

Scott, of course, was not solely responsible for the medievalism of
the last century, nor is *Ivanhoe* the first attempt at medieval romance.
There had been Walpole's *Castle of Otranto* and Thomas Leland's
monumentally dull *Longsword* in the eighteenth century; there had
been 'Monk' Lewis and the school of horror, which Scott had grown
up on; there had been Chatterton and Coleridge's *Christabel*. But
Ivanhoe is one of those books which is important not only in itself but
for the way in which it caught the mood of its generation so perfectly.
In Memoriam, *The Waste Land*, and *Look Back in Anger* occupy similar
positions in literary history. They could not be ignored even if one
considered them to be indifferent works of art. In some nebulous way,
they spoke for their time.

Lofty, realistic minds would describe the Eglinton tournament or
Astley's Amphitheatre as the merest escapism. That hardly seems the
point. The Gothic mood suffuses the last century so completely that it
is hard to know where fantasy ends and 'real life' begins. Since life
always imitates art, the pageants which Scott's contemporaries saw in
their art galleries and theatres were soon to become part of their
visible world. The opera of *Kenilworth*, for instance, had the most
magnificent sets seen in London for decades. They were designed by a
brilliant, highly idiosyncratic eighteen-year-old called Augustus
Welby Pugin.[3] Pugin acknowledged that *Ivanhoe* had been for him, as
for so many of his generation, an epiphany. Like all men devoted to a

---

* For an excellent account of this extraordinary affair, the reader is referred to that
delightful book by Ian Anstruther, *The Knight and the Umbrella* (London, 1963).

theory, he was doomed to disappointment. Perhaps now we can only admire individual buildings—the Houses of Parliament, the Abbey at Ramsgate, St. Giles's Cheadle—rather than the passionate view of things which created them. But Pugin's *Contrasts* is a work that shows us that the Gothic revival was much more than an aesthetic ideal divorced from life.[4] Rather, it shows that aesthetic considerations are among the most important in life, and neglect of them socially disastrous.

Contrasts is one of the most brilliantly sustained pieces of argument in the language, and the illustrations by the author are exquisite. Here we see Ely House, Dover Street, with its sensible town-house facade, its gentle front steps and nursery windows, its classical architraves. 'This house has been built with due regard to the modern style of episcopal establishments', comments the author ironically. And then, beneath, we see the magnificent Ely Palace, Holborn, destroyed in 1776. A clerke in cap and robes wanders in its holy shades, reading an olde tome—a Breviarie, perhaps, or a Romaunce. Behind and above him, spindly crosses and spires point upwards to the sky. Turn the page, and we see a Catholic town in 1440, and, beneath, the same town in 1840. The spires are greatly diminished and replaced by chimneys. The ecclesiastical architecture which remains has been 'spoilt' in the eighteenth century. Most of the Gothic buildings have gone. Here, instead, is an 'Iron Works and ruins of St. Marie's Abbey'; on the site of St. Olave's Church stands the Socialist Hall of Science. There is a new town hall; chapels for Baptists, Unitarians and Wesleyans; a new jail, and a lunatic asylum.

It is hard to appreciate now the impact of all this on its first readers; just as it would have been impossible to predict, when Scott's father was proudly building his elegant little Georgian house in the 1770s, that a succeeding generation would contrive to make their houses look more like the craggy tower of Smailholm which had inspired the young Wattie's 'childhood hour'. The return to the Middle Ages was much more than an artistic game: it involved an attempt to transform the whole quality of life, and to recover spiritual values in the wreckage of an industrial age. There is not much evidence that Arnold's 'touchstones' from Dante and Homer did much to combat the Philistines. But the Waverley Novels are a different case.

The middle ages were not perfect: they had evils of their own; but they were very unlike what they appeared to the gloomy imagination of a French theophilanthropist. Of the new interest in the middle ages, the pioneer in this century was Sir Walter Scott; his indirect relation to the Oxford movement was often dwelt upon by Pusey in private conversation. That relation consisted not only in the high moral tone which characterized Scott's writings and which marked them off so sharply from the contemporary writers of modern fiction, but also and especially in the interest which he aroused on behalf of ages and persons who had been buried out of sight to an extent that to our generation would appear incredible.[5]

So wrote Canon Liddon in his life of Pusey. Ruskin speaks of Scott in the same terms. The day would dawn, within less than thirty years of Scott's breakfast with Pusey, when monks would once more process through town and cloister as they do at the end of *The Monastery*. At Trinity College, Glenalmond, one evening in the mid-1850s, when some of the boys were crossing the new Gothic quadrangle,* one of them remarked, 'I say, we look just like ye monks of ye nineteenth century processing to ye Vespers.' His companion decided, on the strength of these childish fantasies, to re-establish the Benedictine Order in the Church of England. 'Light words, lightly spoken, and more lightly received,' wrote the Baroness de Bertouch in her inimitable prose, but 'the great bell of the monastic vocation sounded its solemn Angelus in the soul of Leycester Lyne.'[6]

It began as mere play-acting, but it became something much more. Father Ignatius, as Lyne came to be called, was a saint in the fullest medieval sense. His miraculous powers of healing—he raised a girl called Lizzie Meek from the dead—have been doubted, as have his visions of Our Lady in the rhubarb patch at Llanthony Abbey.[7] But what can not be doubted is that crowds of sixty thousand flocked to hear him preach in Lombard Street, in the heart of the City of London, denouncing the prevailing materialism of the age and what he called the worship of the Golden Calf. When one thinks of nineteenth-century 'medievalism', these things must be considered, as well as the Pre-Raphaelite and Arthurian fancies of aesthetes who walked down Piccadilly with a poppy or a lily in their medieval hands.

Scott lived slightly too early to be able to see why or how *Ivanhoe* could affect the generation of Pugin, or to know that his work was to be the most influential bridge between the Gothick of eighteenth-century noblemen and intellectuals and the popular Gothic of the Victorian towns. To the purest taste, medieval Scott will never appeal

* Designed by John Henderson in the English tractarian manner.

as much as *The Monastery* or *Old Mortality*. And it seems somewhat unfair that *Ivanhoe* should be his best-known book, since it does not allow much scope for the qualities which, in his Scotch novels, are used to such purpose and brilliance: his humour, his breadth of sympathy, his finely understood, profoundly learned idea of seventeenth- and eighteenth-century Scotland. But there is no unfairness about the fact that it *was* popular. It is almost as impossible to judge it by purely literary standards as it is to judge Pugin's Houses of Parliament—what Lord Clark has called a 'Waverley novel in stone'[8]—by purely architectural standards. Both, in a way, are not merely works of art, but brilliant pieces of myth-making.

Ivanhoe is brilliant in every sense of the word. The scenes are bright with English sunshine. Composed in the same way, and during the same illness, as *The Bride of Lammermoor*, it carries no trace of the sick-bed. Its picture of medieval life was not, therefore, something which had been carefully worked out with reference books and histories to hand. It reflects a breadth of memory and imagination, and benevolence, at an almost subconscious level. After it was finished, he did not claim to be unable to remember what it was about, as he had done with *The Bride of Lammermoor*. He was confident that it would be popular. 'I am led to expect I[vanhoe] will please the public,' he told John Ballantyne, 'because it is uncommon.' Certainly, even now, when one is wholly familiar with the idea of the book and its thousand imitations, it seems a phenomenon of peculiar brightness and strength. It bears any amount of reading. John Buchan's is the best description I know of what it is like to read:

> . . . a pageant so far-flung and glittering that, in spite of its artificiality, it captivates the fancy. There are no less than one hundred and fifty-three characters at some time or another on the stage. With generous profusion he piles excitement upon excitement, weaving, like his favourite Ariosto, many different narratives into one pattern, and managing it all with such skill that there are no gaps in the web. It is a success—though on a far greater scale—of the same type as Byron's metrical romances. Improbabilities, impossibilities, coincidences are accepted because the reader's mind is beguiled out of scepticism. The scene is so novel, the figures so vivid that we bow to the convention and forebear to doubt.[9]

Anyone who has once been caught by the spell of *Ivanhoe* will never shake off its excitement. Crisis follows upon crisis, nearly always interrupted by the clear notes of the bugle or the horn. Across our gaze flit knights in bright armour, lovely, high-minded girls, gluttonous ecclesiastics, wicked barons. Here are Robin Hood, and Richard the Lionheart and Prince John and Friar Tuck: sturdy Saxons, devious but heroic Normans, grasping but pious Jews. The importance of Jews in this novel will be discussed later on. But pause for a while to contemplate the unforgettable appearance of Ivanhoe in the lists at Ashby-de-la-Zouche:

As the Saracenic music of the challengers concluded one of those long and high flourishes with which they had broken the silence of the lists, it was answered by a solitary trumpet, which breathed a note of defiance from the northern extremity. All eyes were turned to see the new champion which these sounds announced, and no sooner were the barriers opened than he paced into the lists. As far as could be judged of a man sheathed in armour, the new adventurer did not greatly exceed the middle size, and seemed to be rather slender than strongly made. His suit of armour was formed of steel, richly inlaid with gold, and the device on his shield was a young oak-tree pulled up by the roots, with the Spanish word *Desdichado*, signifying Disinherited. He was mounted on a gallant black horse, and as he passed through the lists he gracefully saluted the Prince and ladies by lowering his lance. The dexterity with which he managed his steed, and something of youthful grace which he displayed in his manner, won him the favour of the multitude, which some of the lower classes expressed by calling out, 'Touch Ralph de Vipont's shield—touch the Hospitaller's shield; he has the least sure seat, he is your cheapest bargain.'

The champion, moving onward amid these well-meant hints, ascended the platform by the sloping alley which led to it from the lists, and, to the astonishment of all present, riding straight up to the central pavilion, struck with the sharp end of his spear the shield of Brian de Bois-Guilbert until it rung again. All stood astonished at his presumption, but none more than the redoubted Knight whom he had thus defied to mortal combat, and who, little expecting so rude a challenge, was standing carelessly at the door of the pavilion. . . .

(Chapter VIII)

For some readers, the lack of authenticity and the improbability of many details in the story, will always make it impossible to appreciate. Brian de Bois-Guilbert, for instance, has Negro slaves. Guilelessly, Scott adds a note:

The severe accuracy of some critics has objected to the complexion of the slaves . . . as being totally out of costume and propriety. I remember the same objection being made to a set of sable functionaries whom my friend Mat Lewis introduced as the guards and mischief-doing satellites of the wicked Baron, in his Castle Spectre. Mat treated the objection with great contempt, and averred, in reply, that he made the slaves black in order to obtain a striking effect of contrast, and that, could he have derived a similar advantage from making his heroine blue, blue she should have been.

I do not pretend to plead the immunities of my order so highly as this; but neither will I allow that the author of a modern antique romance is obliged to confine himself to the introduction of those manners only which can be proved to have absolutely existed in the times he is depicting, so that he can restrain himself to such as are plausible and natural, and contain no obvious anachronism.

(Note C)

Even when one has grown accustomed to the absence of historical authenticity in *Ivanhoe*, there are still the wild twists and turns of the plot to be accommodated. Athelstane, for instance, who is stone dead in one chapter, is suddenly brought back to life again. A note adds:

The resuscitation of Athelstane has been much criticised as too violent a breach of probability, even for a work of such fantastic character. It was a tour-de-force, to which the author was compelled to have recourse, by the vehement entreaties of his friend and printer, who was inconsolable on the Saxon being conveyed to the tomb.

From now on, the Waverley Novels were quite blatantly a joint business venture of Scott and Ballantyne's. Scott was unashamedly writing to please his readers, and unashamedly writing in the trashy traditions of the Gothic novel. Yet, as a piece of 'Gothic revival', *Ivanhoe* could hardly be bettered.

The days are over now when people laughed at the great buildings of the nineteenth century. As every town in England has been eroded or destroyed by the planners, neo-Gothic architecture has been redis- covered not merely as a private fad of the Poet Laureate's, but on its own merits. Freed from the Georgian prejudices of the thirties, and from the doctrinal positions of a generation reared on Pevsner and Le Corbusier, we can now see how good the great Victorian architects were: G. E. Street's Law Courts, Bodley's churches at Cowley or Hoar Cross, Butterfield's All Saints' Margaret Street, and Bentley's Roman church at Watford stand quite respectably beside their medieval predecessors, and beside Hawksmoor or Vanbrugh.

A similar recognition has not been afforded to Scott's medieval fiction. Those who appreciate his earlier work are embarrased by it. And yet it was as a medievalist that Scott was most influential. One thinks of Balzac's *Illusions Perdues*, where the French publisher is unable to do any trade because of Sir Walter Scott's popularity. Augustin Thierry's experience must have been common:

Ce fut avec un transport d'enthousiasme que je saluai l'apparition du chef d'œuvre d'*Ivanhoe*. Walter Scott venait de jeter un des regards d'aigle sur la période historique vers laquelle depuis trois ans, se dirigeaient tous les efforts de ma pensée. Avec cette hardiesse d'execution que le caractérise . . . il avait coloré en poète une scène du long drame que je travaillais à construire avec la patience de l'historien.[10]

What Thierry's comment shows, as Dr Pusey's did earlier, is that while we—and Scott himself—might have thought his romance totally fantastic, for his readership it opened up the whole world of the 'real' Middle Ages. Scott could defend his practice by comparing it with that of Matt Lewis, a writer of fantasy. But his readers were of the state of mind which could see that

> Fancy with fact is but one fact the more.[11]

Emotionally, Scott revealed the past to the nineteenth century, less through the novels in which he actually possessed a wealth of historical insight and memory than through the romances; and he did so not merely for the poets, but for the serious historians, the novelists and romancers, and the architects. In France alone, his influence is incalculable. Where would Alfred de Vigny be, or the Hugo of *Notre Dame de Paris*, without Scott? Still more, how we should miss the novels of Dumas had *Ivanhoe* never been written. Even if we have no taste for the book, it surely deserves our attention as a vast monument in the history of literature. Even if we do not believe in what is supposed to have happened there, a shrine acquires sanctity from the tread of pilgrims' feet, and from the number of devotees who journey from distant lands to visit it.

Scott is often accused, rather patronizingly, of not having known enough about the Middle Ages to have been able to write a novel about them. Several things could be said in reply. First, one could say that, just as Bodley is in many ways better than most medieval architects, so *Ivanhoe* is infinitely more ingenious, colourful and read-able than almost all the real Middle English romances. Again, Scott knew far more about the Middle Ages than most people of his genera-tion. True, his sources are chosen in more haphazard a way than his assembly of evidence about the eighteenth century, and Froissart, Sidney, Shakespeare, and Malory are all drawn upon fairly freely, whatever period is in question. But it should not be supposed that he was completely careless. He took immense pains, for instance, to make the unfamiliar landscape authentic in such novels as *Quentin Durward*, *Anne of Geierstein*, and *Castle Dangerous*.

One must add that to expect a man of Scott's generation to have a knowledge of the Middle Ages comparable with our own is anach-ronistic. Modern medievalists now know more about the Middle Ages than any preceding generation, including of course the medievals themselves. We have hinted that this initially resulted from the impetus of the Waverley Novels. But the thoroughness of modern scholarly methods is largely the result of German and English researches towards the end of the last century. The enormous strides made in philology and textual criticism in the last hundred years have opened up medieval language and literature to us in a way which to Scott's generation—even to pedants like Ritson—would have been almost unthinkable. Archaeologists have been similarly diligent. The historians have not only sifted almost every will, parish register, letter and chronicle of medieval times, but have had an astonishing number of them printed and reproduced, so that any student can, by visiting a good library, acquaint himself with more detailed knowl-edge of medieval history in one afternoon than Scott acquired in a decade.

And yet, one is now no nearer 'the Middle Ages', any more than a physicist who knows all that there is to be known about electricity can plumb the mystery of a thunderstorm. Indeed, many medieval scho-lars have no interest in what Scott would have considered 'medieval'. We do not expect medievalists to have hunted with a hawk, or chased the deer, or wasted a fortune on a tournament or a castle. Indeed, the whimsy of some modern medievalists—for instance when trying to reproduce Middle English speech in productions of mystery plays—can be profoundly embarrassing. The function of the modern 'medievalist' is to establish the provenance of manuscripts, to examine the structure and development of language, or to give cauti-ous estimates of, say, how many inhabitants of Ewelme or Exeter or

York were affected by the Black Death. We distrust attempts to recapture the 'ethos' of earlier times.

Yet, on an emotional level, we must all have an 'idea of the past'. Even the scholar has one: for him, the Middle Ages are a scarcely penetrable terrain, only to be attempted with very sure equipment, with glossaries and carbon-dating; a place where any speculation, let alone flights of fancy, will immediately lead to error. For others, the Middle Ages are equally inaccessible, and for that reason profoundly romantic, to be grasped by acts of faith, works of imagination, romance: indeed, 'romance', not 'novel', is how Scott himself described *Ivanhoe* and his subsequent books. They are images of an ideal, largely unreal and barely imaginable world, and any attempt to relate them to the values of our own times swiftly becomes absurd.

Thackeray, as if to show this point very clearly, wrote a romance on a romance, which is both a skit and a continuation of *Ivanhoe*. Most readers of the book will share Thackeray's view that Ivanhoe should have married Rebecca, and not Rowena:

Nor can I ever believe that such a woman, so admirable, so tender, so heroic, so beautiful, could disappear altogether before such another woman as Rowena, that vapid, flaxen-headed creature, who is, in my humble opinion, unworthy of her place as heroine. Had both of them got their rights, it ever seemed to me that Rebecca would have had the husband, and Rowena would have gone off to a convent and shut herself up, where I, for one, would never have taken the trouble of inquiring for her.[12]

In Thackeray's *Rebecca and Rowena*, the Ivanhoe marriage is, of course, unsatisfactory. Rowena becomes increasingly imperious, and is still jealous of her husband's early feeling for Rebecca. Ivanhoe himself starts to drink rather too heavily. All his neighbours have become dull and respectable. Even Robin Hood, as Earl of Hunting-don, has joined the Establishment—'There was no more conscientious magistrate in all the county than his lordship: he was never known to miss church or quarter-sessions; he was the strictest game-proprietor in all the Riding and sent scores of poachers to Botany Bay.'[13] Small wonder that when a chance of going abroad occurs, Ivanhoe seizes it. He fights in Richard the Lionheart's last campaign and is thought dead. Rowena then marries Athelstane and they have a boy called little Cedric. Once they have both been conveniently killed off, Ivanhoe goes to Spain to fight the Saracens, and it is there that he is reunited with Rebecca.

The skit has a perfect final sentence: 'Married I am sure they were, and adopted little Cedric; but I don't think they had any other children, or were subsequently very boisterously happy. Of some sort of happiness melancholy is a characteristic, and I think these were a solemn pair and died rather early.'[14]

As we have seen, Thackeray was not the first to make Ivanhoe marry Rebecca. But, unlike M. R. Lacy, he takes the trouble to have her converted to Christianity. Thackeray, of course, shared Scott's anti-semitism.

When, in 1817, Maria Edgeworth published *Harrington*, her father wrote in the preface that it had been 'occasioned by an extremely well-written letter which Miss Edgeworth received from America, from a Jewish lady, complaining of the illiberality with which the Jewish nation had been treated in some of Miss Edgeworth's works.'[15]

Harrington has a terrifying opening chapter in which a little boy, watching with delight as the lamp-lighter makes his way down the street outside the nursery windows, suddenly sees with horror the figure of Simon the Jew, with his old bag slung over his shoulder. This harmless old man has been built up in the child's mind as a creature of nightmarish cruelty. His nursemaid has persuaded him that old Simon eats children and that his bag contains their limbs. Harrington's father, a Tory of the old school, encourages the boy's hatred of Jews, but when he grows up and goes to Cambridge he changes his mind completely and becomes enamoured with the romance of that race. He meets Jewish intellectuals, and a sophisticated Spanish Jew, a collector of paintings, a *littérateur*, and a man called Montenero with an exotic pedigree and a beautiful daughter. It goes without saying that Harrington falls in love with the beautiful daughter. Marriage is out of the question, until, at the end, it is revealed that Miss Montenero has actually been brought up as an English Protestant, her mother having been the daughter of an English diplomat posted in the peninsular.

'I think Miss Edgeworth's last work delightful,' Scott wrote to Joanna Baillie,

though Jews will always be to me Jews. One does not naturally or easily combine with their habits and pursuits any great liberality of principle although certainly it may and I believe does exist in many individual instances. They are money-makers and money-brokers by profession and it is a trade which narrows the mind. I own I breathed more freely when I found Miss Montenero was not an actual Jewess.[16]

Scott never greatly changed this position. It came as no surprise to him that his least generous creditor after the financial crash was 'Abud the Jew', and he was fond of dismissing mean characters as 'an absolute Hebrew'. Yet he viewed the young Disraeli with amusement rather than contempt.

One cannot twist Scott's views of the matter to make them agreeable to modern liberal sensibility—'Jews will always be to me Jews.' But his attitude needs to be seen in context. *Harrington* is unusual in the extent to which it anticipates British liberal reactions to Jews in the later part of the century. The popularity of Disraeli himself doubtless contributed to this, as did the intensely romantic light in which Browning and George Eliot saw the Jews. Even now a modern Frenchman or Russian is likely to come out with unself-consciously anti-semitic feelings rather in the way that an Englishman might make no bones about disliking the Scots or the French. Scott lived before all these developments, and it is hard to judge him by the morality of a later age. It was as natural for him to be anti-semitic as it was for Shakespeare. He belonged to the same generation as that mild and wholly inoffensive intelligence Charles Lamb, who could write, in his essay *Imperfect Sympathies*,

I have, in the abstract, no disrespect for Jews. They are a piece of stubborn antiquity, compared with which Stonehenge is in its nonage. They date beyond the pyramids. But I should not care to be in habits of familiar intercourse with any of that nation. I confess that I have not the nerves to enter their synagogues. Old prejudices cling about me. I cannot shake off the story of Hugh of Lincoln. Centuries of injury, contempt, and hate, on the one side—of cloaked revenge, dissimulation and hate, on the other, between our and their fathers, must, and ought, to affect the blood of the children. I cannot believe it can run clear and kindly yet; or that a few fine words, such as candour, liberality, the light of a nineteenth century, can close up the breaches of a deadly disunion. A Hebrew is nowhere congenial to me.[17]

What is so interesting about *Ivanhoe* in this respect is that although 'old prejudices' clung about Scott as fiercely as they did about Lamb, in the stuff of his romance he begins to feel much of the new sympathy sweeping over him. Old Isaac is a noble figure, even though, in a predictable way, he worships Mammon. But Rebecca is one of Scott's most charming heroines. During Scott's illness, James Skene had talked to him about the amiable Jews he had met in Germany, and he claimed much of the credit for this change in outlook:

Mr Skene, partly in seriousness, and partly from the mere wish to turn his mind at the moment upon something that might occupy and divert it, suggested that a group of Jews would be an interesting feature if he could contrive to bring them into his next novel. Upon the appearance of *Ivanhoe*, he reminded Mr Skene of this conversation, and said, 'You will find this book owes not a little to your German reminiscences.'[18]

Scott also owed not a little to *Harrington*. The whole picture of the Jews in *Ivanhoe* shows how well Scott almost subconsciously adapted the *ethos* of his romance to the future developments of public sympathy.

The fact that *Ivanhoe* sold better than any previous novel was of course something to be glad of. Scott already had reason to be worried about money; he followed up the success of *Ivanhoe* with a series of novels which were not specifically medieval, but returned to the formula in 1823 with *Quentin Durward*. After his ruin in 1826, the potential earnings from medieval romances became a powerful lure, and only once again did he return to the Scottish eighteenth century as a subject for fiction (the exception being *The Surgeon's Daughter*). Apart from *Woodstock*, which he was writing at the time of the crash, all his last novels are set before the sixteenth century—*The Fair Maid of Perth*, *Anne of Geierstein*, *Count Robert of Paris*, *Castle Dangerous*, and the unfinished novel, *The Siege of Malta*.

His attitude to these novels, as disclosed in the pages of the Journal, is purely mechanical, and sunnily cynical. They are his 'task' which will enable him to acquit himself with honour with his creditors. We find him writing at enormous speed. *The Fair Maid of Perth*, for instance, though written at intervals of about three months while working on other things, was composed at breakneck pace. A not uncharacteristic entry in the Journal reads: 'Feb. 19th, 1828: A day of hard and continued work, the result being eight pages. But then I hardly ever quitted the table save at meal times. So eight pages of my manuscript may be accounted the maximum of my literary labour. It is equal to forty printed pages of the Novels. . . .'[19] Scott seems to have been under few illusions about the quality of the work produced under these conditions. 'By heaven, I will finish *Anne of Geierstein* this day betwixt the two engagements. I don't know why nor wherefore but I hate Anne. . . .' His publishers did not think much of it either, and made him revise it quite heavily. When he rewrote the final version, he admitted in his Journal that it read 'more trashy than I expected'.

But, he adds, with an important proviso, 'when could I ever please myself, even when I have most pleased others'.[20]

Scott only kept his Journal for the years during and after *Woodstock* (1826–32). But there can be little doubt that he would have considered *Rob Roy, The Heart of Midlothian*, or *Waverley* to be equally 'trashy' when talking about them to himself. His own self-deprecation does not entitle us to take it at face value, but it contributes to the complication of our feelings about the medieval novels. To begin with, we approach them through the encrustations of their nineteenth-century imitators and admirers; and then we are faced with the bald and rather disillusioning facts of their composition. They were composed as entertainments, pure and simple, to satisfy Scott's creditors. They were received as entertainments; but, as we have already seen, they were much more. They became part of a national myth, and they were absorbed into the quasi-seriousness of Victorian medievalism.

But how are we to read these novels? We are not entitled to stand in judgement on Scott, or to fling the words he wrote in his Journal at the end of a hard day's work back in his face as literary criticism. On the other hand, since we do not belong to a 'Gothic generation', how can we read and appreciate them? It is often said that it is only possible to do so if they have been absorbed into the system during childhood. One recalls Ruskin's powerful description of *Ivanhoe* (which he disliked) as 'partly boyish, partly feverish';[21] and it could be argued that, without having had the excitement and experience of reading it as a child, one could not, as an adult, escape its 'feverishness'.

Yet, how unlikely this seems as a picture of mid-twentieth-century taste. Children do not, on the whole, lose themselves endlessly in the Waverley Novels; and it is unlikely that grown-ups pretend to them that they should. I must belong to the last generation to have Scott forced on them at school. At ten, we were made to read *The Talisman* and *Ivanhoe* and thought them both extremely boring. At twelve, one was presented with *Quentin Durward*: I admire it enormously now, but no child could appreciate the subtle and essentially grown-up portrait of Louis XI, or the deft but marked way in which Quentin Durward's developing sexual awareness is suggested to the reader. It could hardly be said that I grew up with a prejudice in favour of Scott—the sort of prejudice E. M. Forster ascribed (probably quite rightly) to his own generation in the Clark Lectures.

Yet, oddly, a recommendation to read *Anne of Geierstein* from an undergraduate contemporary made me an addict of the Waverley

Novels. It is a novel which has all the merits and most of the defects of Scott's medieval fiction. The narrative carries us into an exotic and only dimly known world: fifteenth-century Switzerland. Two travellers, apparently English merchants by the name of Philipson, are making their way through the Alps. We immediately encounter two of Scott's most repeatedly used pieces of stock-in-trade. The first is the traveller of mysterious identity who turns out to be someone rather grander than at first appears. In this case, one traveller is the Earl of Oxford and the other is his son: in *The Lady of the Lake* the traveller is King James IV; in *Ivanhoe*, the Black Knight is the Lionheart; in *The Talisman* the disguised figure is Saladin; and in *Quentin Durward*, 'Maître Pierre' turns out to be Louis XI. If one reads a great deal of Scott at a stretch, one grows weary of this trick. But encountered afresh, it is a powerful narrative device which never fails to hold the attention; even when we have guessed that the hooded stranger is more than he at first appeared, the disguise must be unravelled and the traveller's true identity discovered.

The second device is the immediate involvement of the characters in the drama of landscape. In *Anne of Geierstein*, torrents threaten to break through the dark clouds as the travellers pass through a gloomy pass and come within sight of Mount Pilatus:

The young merchant addressed himself to the Swiss lad who acted as their attendant, desiring to know the name of the gloomy height which, at that quarter, seems the leviathan of the huge congregation of mountains assembled about Lucerne.

The lad crossed himself devoutly, as he recounted the popular legend, that the wicked Pontius Pilate, Proconsul of Judaea, had here found the termination of his impious life having, after spending years in the recesses of that mountain which bears his name, at length, in remorse and despair rather than in penitence, plunged into the dismal lake which occupies the summit. Whether water refused to do the executioner's duty upon such a wretch, or whether, his body being drowned, his vexed spirit continued to haunt the place where he committed suicide, Antonio did not pretend to explain. But a form was often, he said, seen to emerge from the gloomy waters, and go through the action of washing his hands; and when he did so, dark clouds of mist gathering first round the bosom of the Infernal Lake (such it had been styled of old) and then wrapping the whole upper part of the mountain in darkness presaged a tempest or hurricane, which was sure to follow in a short space. . . .

(Chapter I)

Sure enough, a dramatic storm blows up in the next few pages. This is all very routine Scott. One can see him using these devices to much better effect elsewhere—the storm in *The Antiquary* is much better, the disguised stranger is more exciting in *Redgauntlet*, and the quality of the writing is at moments almost insolently careless, shapeless sentences accumulating subordinate clauses in every line and padded out with unnecessary parentheses. Only a man being paid by the word would bother to tell us that Pontius Pilate had been Proconsul of Judaea.

Yet *Anne of Geierstein* is very competently handled. If one had read no great Scott, one would find much to admire here, and would sense, however faintly, the taste of what great Scott would be like.

One could list features of *Anne of Geierstein* which are redolent of the conveyor-belt in the fiction-factory—the little journey made into the Duke of Burgundy's lands by the Philipsons and the Swiss; their capture by Archibald de Hagenbach; the young hero being thrown into prison, 'one of those gloomy caverns which cry shame on the inhumanity of our ancestors'—yet here again one encounters a very characteristic quality of Scott. In the medieval novels, as in all he wrote, there is a frankness and goodness which he does not forsake even at his most pot-boiling. Characters might be larger, scenes brighter, than in life. But human values remain intact. Duelling is thought to be wrong in the early nineteenth century; in *The Fair Maid of Perth* it is also shown to have been wrong in the fifteenth century. In all the medieval novels the cult of violence and the adulterous cultivation of *amour courtois* are condemned. Scott takes the same moral position as he did when he wrote the 'Essay on Chivalry'. When reading any of Scott's novels, we do not take a moral holiday, as we do when reading Matt Lewis, or, to a lesser extent, Mrs Radcliffe.

Anne of Geierstein is full of great set-pieces, some of which reflect the quality and breadth of Scott's reading. There is the exciting conclave of the Vehm-gericht, based on Goethe's 'Goetz von Berlichingen', which Scott had translated when he was a young man. The Earl of Oxford is brought before the conclave on a stretcher, his hands bound with rope. But their threats do not daunt him: 'Cords and daggers are not calculated to strike terror into those who have seen swords and lances. My answer to the accusation is that I am an Englishman. . . .'

Other great set-pieces appear in King René's poetical court in Aix-en-Provence and on the battlements of the monastery of Mont Ste. Victoire, where we encounter Margaret of Anjou for the last time.

Much of the power of this character depends on our remembering her from Shakespeare's history plays. 'We cannot describe the appearance of her noble and beautiful, yet ghastly and wasted features, agitated strongly by anxious hesitation and conflicting thoughts, unless to those of our readers, who have had the advantage of having seen our inimitable Siddons in such a character as this': for all that, some of the magic of Shakespeare and the inimitable Siddons leads to a moment which is pure Scott at his histrionic best:

As Margaret spoke, she tore from her hair the sable feather and rose which the tempest had detached from the circlet in which they were placed, and tossed them from the battlement with a gesture of wild energy. They were instantly whirled off in a bickering eddy of the agitated clouds, which swept the feather far distant into the empty space, through which the eye could not pursue it. But while that of Arthur involuntarily strove to follow its course, a contrary gust of wind caught the red rose and drove it back against his breast, so that it was easy for him to catch hold of and retain it.

(Chapter XXX)

Colour, excitement, moral beauty and the 'Big Bow wow strain'; these Scott retained to the last. What his final novels lack, of course, is comedy. It is the ingredient present in all his great novels, and which reveals his closeness to Shakespeare in the fullest way. The medieval novels have knockabout—Wamba the Jester makes jokes and is biffed about by Gurth—but the stories do not pause long enough for their characters to be fully comprehended, and there is always something thin about them as a result. They lack the completely real quality of Alison Wilson, or the Bailie, or Meg Dods, or James VI or Baron Bradwardine. There are stray moments of realism and humour in these books, but nothing sustained. That side of Scott's genius, the Shakespearean comedian, had dried up after 1825.

CHAPTER NINE

The Gurnal*

And he has paid the rescue shot,
  Baith wi' goud, and white monie;
And at the burial o' Willie Scott,
  I wat was mony a weeping ee.

'Jamie Telfer of the Fair Dodhead':
from *The Minstrelsy of the Scottish Border*.

The iconography of Sir Walter Scott could itself form the subject of a book, if it were fully treated. There is the early, rather pudgy innocence of the portrait by William Nicholson. The early Raeburn of 1808—complete with boots, dog and ruins—presents the border minstrel, his hair awry, dramatic clouds in the background, his eyes straining into some distant scene

For old, unhappy, far-off things,
And battles long ago.

The later Raeburn (1822) shows the hair brushed and the cravat in place. Only the well-groomed head and shoulders are presented. It is a respectable citizen of Edinburgh; the eyes gaze outwards, now a little nervously, perhaps, towards the future. The bust by Sir Francis Chantrey (1828), with a plaid cast round a naked sholder like a toga, suggests an imperial severity; whereas Sir David Wilkie's 'Abbotsford Family' of nine years earlier had depicted a Squire Allworthy, almost a domestic clown, with an old hat perched on the back of his head and grinning rustics in attendance. In the one, Scott is almost Octavius; in the other, Duke Senior. The paintings and busts and statues went on being produced long after Scott's death, ranging from the flamboyance of the memorial in Princes Street to the homeliness of imagined scenes like William Borthwick Johnstone's 'Robert Burns in James Sibbald's Circulating Library', which shows the young Scott gazing up from his book in the direction of the poet.

* 'A hard word so spelld on Authority of Miss Scott now Mrs. Lockhart' (MS).

In May 1828, Scott was in London and sat for Northcote; like Hazlitt—who made a delightful book out of them—he was enchanted by the old man's recollections of the companionship of Reynolds and Johnson.

Another long sitting to the old wizzard Northcote. He really resembles an animated mummy. He has alterd my ideas of Sir Joshua Reynolds who from the expressions used by Goldsmith, Johnson, and others, I used to think an amiable and benevolent character. But though not void of generosity he was cold, unfeeling and indifferent to his family. So much so that his sister Miss Reynolds after expressing her wonder at the general acceptance which Sir Joshua met with in society concluded with—'For me, I only see in him a dark gloomy tyrant.' I own this view of his character hurt me by depriving me of a pleasing vision of the highest talents united with the kindest temper. . . .[1]

Such disillusion is often in store when one probes beneath the surface of an artist's life. Highest talents united with the kindest temper are not often to be found. It is hard to see why this should matter in the case of novelists—their fictions, and not they themselves, are on display. Hardy's compassionate *persona* as an artist is not really destroyed by the biographical revelations of petty snobbery and domestic callousness. Those with a taste for D. H. Lawrence's orgiastic fantasies would be naive if they were surprised at his sexual impotence. And it hardly affects our feeling about Paul Dombey or Little Nell to discover that Dickens found his own children tiresome and irritating. Yet such feelings of disillusionment remain, and it would spoil our pleasure in the Waverley Novels if we learnt that Scott's life did not match them in some way.

Mr Quayle has unconvincingly tried to make out that Scott was financially dishonourable.[2] Hogg tells us of his fits of bad temper. Most commentators feel that they must condemn his extravagance, adding the charge of snobbery which is usually applied to those who have friends among the aristocracy and a taste for living in the country. No one has ever attributed to him cowardice or impurity. It would be disillusioning if they had, because part of the pleasure of reading Scott seems to be in the gradual absorption of a point of view.

A taste for Scott begins, perhaps, by reading a handful of the Waverley Novels. Different qualities of genius emerge with each volume, and with each re-reading. Perhaps what attracted us at first was his understanding of history; or the wide variety of human types depicted in his pages; or his exact feeling for place. Gradually, our imagination feasts not only on these things, but something more. We grow increasingly in awe of the sheer range of his knowledge. It is deeply ingrained, lightly worn. Evidence of it shoots out from every book like sparks from a bonfire. The range and depth of knowledge required to create the character of the Antiquary alone is not something easily found in a novelist. In the English tradition, perhaps only George Eliot and Mrs Humphry Ward were comparably well-informed; and, as the comparison suggests, great knowledge is not always conducive to great fiction. The most carefully researched, and the best-informed of George Eliot's is obviously *Romola*; a point which speaks for itself.

Not only was Scott a man with a wide range of information: he was also someone who could have been—indeed was—successful in other areas of life, as historian, poet, literary critic and lawyer. But the love of Scott, while feasting on his breadth and his erudition, depends on something more. Increasingly, one begins to realize that one is admiring not merely a set of artefacts but a whole vision of life, the product of a whole man. It is a mind which delights in the vagaries of human eccentricity; which loves, in the full sense in which Keats used it of Shakespeare's 'love' for Imogen and Iago, the villains as well as the heroes. But it is a mind firmly placed in a moral universe in which courage and honesty and sound judgement are esteemed almost more highly than love itself.

Consider, for instance, the rather harsh heroism expressed at the beginning of Chapter XVIII of *Rob Roy*: 'There is one advantage in an accumulation of evils, differing in cause and character, that the distraction which they afford by their contradictory operation prevents the patient from being overwhelmed by either. . . .'

There is an intellectual neatness about this proposition; it is analogous, obviously, to Johnson's dictum about a man who knows he is to be hanged in a fortnight. What lends weight to both these stoical jokes is the knowledge that, in both cases, it would truly apply to their authors. Johnson's mind really would have been concentrated by the prospect of hanging. The accumulation of evils in the last five years of Scott's life really did prevent the patient being overwhelmed by either. It is this which makes the Journal such remarkable reading. The stoical adage comes first; calamity made Scott determine to act upon it.

The novels were not, we have suggested, a vehicle for Scott to parade his personal sorrows. On the contrary, such personal allusions as can be found in them emerge from so unconscious a part of his imagination that they become pushed to the borders of fantasy. The reality of his fictions is to be found not in Scott himself, but in the world and the characters he observed. They seem rooted in reality by virtue of the stiffness of the moral world they inhabit. Uncompromisingly themselves, Jeanie Deans, Nicol Jarvie, Meg Dods, Redgauntlet and the rest, all recognize, or come to recognize, the larger reality outside themselves. Just as Scott is the least self-regarding of novelists, so his greatest characters are markedly lacking in self-analysis, even when they are total egotists. The impression built up, therefore, is one of a firm moral universe which we all inhabit; a place in which stern sayings such as that quoted above do not seem out of place. Burley can die saying that he fears nothing; Brian de Bois-Guilbert that 'many a law, many a commandment have I broken, but my word, never'; Jeanie Deans cannot tell a lie. In many fictitious worlds, the virtuous characters are the weakest and the least convincing. Thackeray, for instance, can depict the self-disgust of Pendennis; but his conversion into a life of domestic rectitude, however delightful as a period piece, is not something which the author's tone can sustain. Scott has more in common with Jane Austen, in whose novels the good, like Edmund Bertram and Mr Knightley, are always wise and strong, whilst those with moral failings are shown up as fools. Yet in the later fiction, Jane Austen shows her hand. The savage attacks on poor Mrs Musgrove in *Persuasion*—who is not allowed by her creator to weep for a dead son on the grounds that she is fat—demonstrate Jane Austen's moral ambivalance; as does the crude hilarity of *Sanditon*. It is no surprise to find, in her letters, that she had much more in common with the vulgar, silly and selfish people in her books than she did with the moral heroes and heroines. The engaging and perpetual malice of the letters reflect what was, after all, delightful about the novels.

Scott's Journal similarly confirms the *persona* we have grown used to in the fiction; but in his case the position is reversed. There is nothing in his novels to suggest moral ambivalence, and their extraordinary combination of benignity and good humour with moral sternness is entirely compatible with the self-portrait of the Journal. Of course, much less is given away in a diary than in a letter. The diarist only records what is compatible with his vision of himself, whereas the letter-writer is subjecting himself to the scrutiny of another. Moreover, Scott almost certainly intended the Journal for publication—or at least for use by a future biographer. Were the picture it presented quite incompatible with his letters or the reminiscences of his friends, it could be read as a piece of whitewashing or, at worst, of harmless egotism. But the Journal is more subtle than that. There is nothing in it which can be contradicted by other biographical evidence. It is all substantially true. Yet there is something extremely *conscious* about it. It is far more than a work of art. Scott was not making himself out to be someone that he was not; rather, the Journal is his record of how he made himself conform to the heroic standards of his own fictions. In so far as his disappointments and sorrows are reflected in the novels, they assume fantastic forms; but by the end of his life, when they became the material for the Journal, Scott was intent on facing them with the bravado of Burley and the stubbornness of Jeanie Deans. It was not, in other words, merely a case of his moral world being real and sincere in the novels: it was something which he felt constrained to prove to himself. Life, once again, was forced to imitate art.

He began writing his Journal in imitation of Lord Byron:

I have bethought me on seeing lately some volumes of Byron's notes that he had probably hit upon the right way of keeping such a memorandum-book by throwing aside all pretence to regularity and order and marking down events just as they occurd to recollection. I will try this plan and behold I have a handsome lockd volume such as might serve for a Lady's Album.[3]

This being its purpose, he began in a desultory way, recording memories of a recent holiday in Ireland and recollections of Moore and Byron. The worst family crisis to be recorded occurred when Lockhart left for London to become editor of the *Quarterly*, taking with him his wife Sophia, Scott's favourite daughter. Characteristically, Scott stayed in his bedroom on the morning of their departure, and did not bid them farewell:

When I arose at eight o'clock they were *Gone*. This was very right. I hate red eyes and blowing of noses. *Agere et pati Romanum est*. Of all schools commend me to the Stoicks. We cannot indeed overcome our affections nor ought if we could, but we repress them within due bounds and avoid coaxing them to make fools of those who should be their masters.[4]

As we have already noticed in discussing his novels, this attitude was deeply real to Scott. But, fascinatingly, one can see that it is the very

artificiality of writing it down which makes it real. It was his strong
sense of how one should behave which enabled him to behave as he
did. In our times, *natural* behaviour is so highly esteemed that it has
become almost a moral orthodoxy for us that honesty is only compatible with frank displays of self. Scott's Journal can hardly recommend
itself to a generation like our own which over-values self-expression.
Honesty, in Scott's world, has nothing to do with the discovery of
'self'. In this, of course, he contrasts strongly with Byron, who is an
appropriately popular author at the moment. There can be cases, the
Journal would seem to imply, where the expression of every impulse
or characteristic lurking beneath the surface of a man's nature can be
a positive evil. His attitude to the disgrace of Richard Heber is a case
in point. Heber, half-brother of the bishop who wrote 'From Green-
land's icy mountains', 'Brightest and best of the sons of the morning'
and other hymns, was a friend of Scott's youth. He had one of the
largest private libraries of the age, shared Scott's antiquarian interests, and was the dedicatee of one of the verse epistles in *Marmion*. In
June 1826, Scott learnt that Heber, who was then Member of Parliament for the University of Oxford, had resigned his seat and fled
abroad owing 'to his having been detected in unnatural practices'.[5]
'These things,' Scott added in a later entry, 'worse than loss of fortune
or even loss of friends, make a man sick of this worldly [scene] where
the fairest outsides so often cover the foulest vices.'[6] On a different
occasion, Scott wrote, perhaps of Heber, perhaps of someone else,*

I had a long conversation about D. with Lockhart.—All that is whisperd is
true—a sign how much better our domestics are acquainted with the private
affairs of our neighbours than we are. A dreadful tale of incest and seduction
and nearly of blood also—horrible beyond expression in its complications
and events—'And yet the end is not'—And this man was amiable and seemd
the soul of honour—laughd too and was the soul of society. It is a mercy our
thoughts are concealed from each other. O if at our social table we could see
what passes in each bosom around we would seek dens and caverns to shun
human society. To see the projector trembling for his falling speculations, the
voluptuary ruing the event of his debauchery, the miser wearing out his soul
for the loss of a guinea—all—all bent upon vain hopes and vainer regrets—we
should not need to go to the hall of the Caliph Vathek to see men's hearts
broiling under their black veils. Lord keep us from all temptation for we
cannot be our own shepherd.[7]

* W. R. Spencer.

This point of view lends a tone of perfectly justifiable pride to the Journal when disaster did actually strike, and provides one of the best expressions of what Bishop Butler had meant by cool self-love. Virtue really is shown to be its own consolation. Although Scott does congratulate himself, the tone of the Journal is oddly lacking in self-conceit. He has set out to live by a set of rules, and he finds that they work. It is almost as prosaic as that. When he wrote 'of all schools commend me to the Stoicks' on 5 December 1825, he had, almost consciously, been rehearsing for the part for the last fifty years. Illness had been the chief thing to be stoical about; yet at the time they may have seemed easy enough words to write. He was one of the richest men of letters who had ever lived, and had certainly made more money by his pen than any previous author. He was one of the most respected figures in Scotch and English high society. He enjoyed an international reputation. His beloved Abbotsford was finished to his satisfaction and, like Sir Arthur Wardour, he could dream of 'buying contiguous estates that would have led him from one side of the island to another'. His health had to a large degree recovered from the agonizing torments of gallstones in his late forties. His life seemed set fair. But, ten days later, the miserable spectre of bankruptcy haunts the pages.

Who will ever know whether Scott's ruin was avoidable, or to what extent he was personally responsible for it?[8] It happened as a result of the financial crash which ruined many investors in London at the end of 1825. Scott, it will be remembered, owned a large share in the Ballantyne brothers' printing company, which was responsible for producing his books. He also invested money with Constable, his publisher. This meant that if things went well he would benefit from his books not merely as author but as a partner of the publishers. Every book, therefore, could make him two or three times more rich than if he were merely receiving royalties; and these were considerable enough. But, inevitably, it also meant that, if the publishing firm failed, he could not merely take his books somewhere else. Even he, however, did not realize until the time of the crash the extent of his financial commitment to Constable and the Ballantynes.

By the standards of the day, or at least by the standards as understood by Scott, it was essential to keep his business interests secret; he considered it inappropriate for a Clerk to the Court of Sessions and a Sheriff to have business interests at all. This is partly why he kept the authorship of the novels secret, too. The crash, of course, made everything quite public. But when it came, his pride forbade him to take the comparatively easy path (for himself, and his creditors) of sequestration, which would have given him an absolute discharge for as little as seven shillings in the pound. His reasons for doing so were largely because to accept sequestration would have been to admit that his wealth had come to him through 'trade'. Sequestration was what bankrupt shopkeepers used. But there were other reasons, the chief of which was the desire to save Abbotsford.

What happened was this. Scott found that his own borrowings had almost no capital to support them apart from Abbotsford. His involvement in Constable's collapse and the financial chaos surrounding the Ballantynes resulted in debts standing at something near £130,000.

Sequestration being rejected, there remained the possibility of *cessio bonorum*, by which an insolvent debtor could, if his creditors agreed, put all his goods at their disposal. But this again would have involved the loss of his house and lands. As he reiterated strongly in the Journal, he felt not only a sense of personal loss as his dreams lay in ruins, but a sense of responsibility towards his tenants and employees. Indeed, his initial fear was that the loss of Abbotsford would have been inevitable, and he realized that he had not the strength to face seeing it again:

This news will make sad hearts at Darnick and in the cottages of Abbotsford which I do not nourish the least hope of preserving. It has been my Dalilah and so I have often termd it—and now—the recollection of the extensive woods I have planted and the walks I have formed from which strangers must derive both the pleasure and the profit will excite feelings likely to sober my gayest moments. I have half resolved never to see the place again—how could I tread my hall with such a diminishd crest? How live a poor indebted man where I was once the wealthy, the honourd? My children are provided—thank God for that. I was to have gone there on Saturday in joy and prosperity to receive my friends—my dogs will wait for me in vain—it is foolish—but the thoughts of parting from these dumb creatures have moved me more than any of the painful reflections I have put down—poor things I must get them kind masters. There may be yet those who loving me may love my dog because it has been mine. I must end this or I shall lose the tone of mind with which men should meet distress. I find my dogs' feet on my knees—I hear them whining and seeking me everywhere—this is nonsense but it is what they would do could they know how things are—poor Will Laidlaw—poor Tom Purdie—this will bring news to wring your heart and many a poor fellow's besides to whom my prosperity was daily bread.[9]

What makes this so moving is that, although so conscious of 'the tone of mind with which men should meet distress', Scott actually met it in a very different way. He tried to respond with a Johnsonian detachment, but in reality he anticipated the mood of a picture by Landseer. The last century in which Boethius was a popular writer had passed: we haved moved into an era which was to produce Queen Victoria's *Journal* and parlour songs like 'Do they miss me at home, do they miss me—'Twould be an assurance most dear'.

Given his intense feeling about Abbotsford, it was not surprising that he should look for a third way out of his difficulties, through the establishment of a trust deed. He was asked by his trustees to sell 39 Castle Street, his house in Edinburgh; they in turn would give him a salary to live on while he undertook to pay off his debts by the labours of his pen:

I the said Walter Scott have resolved to employ my time and talents on the production of such literary works as shall seem to me most likely to promote the ends I have in view, the sums arising from such works I am also desirous to devote to the payment of the debts owing by me as a Partner of the said Company and as an individual.[10]

The moment for which all his life he had been preparing, had arrived. He was at last in the position of a hero who can only be saved by his own efforts. But, like the Bailie who in *Rob Roy* supported the Highland warriors by giving them grants from his counting house, Scott was obliged to exert a true heroism in the world of commerce in order to preserve the fantastic heroic world which his 'Dalilah' had made for him. There is an understandable note of triumph in the Journal as he recognizes the challenge:

My mind to me a Kingdom is,

he quoted in May 1826, when things had gone from bad to worse, his health had collapsed, and his wife had died: 'I am rightful monarch and God to aid I will not be dethroned by any rebellious passion that may rear its standard against me. . . .'[11]

True to form, he managed to do it. He saw it as his life's work; two years later, he imagined his fame resting not on his books but on the heroism with which he met his financial disasters:

Abbotsford. 24th December 1827 . . . My reflections at entring my own gate were of a very different and more pleasing cast than those with which I left my house about six weeks ago. I was then in doubt whether I should fly my country or become avowedly bankrupt and surrender up my library and household furniture with the life rent of my estate to sale. A man of the world will say I had better done so. No doubt had I taken this course at once I might have employd the £25,000 which I made since the insolvency of Constable and Robinson's house in compounding my debts—But I could not have slept sound as I now can under the comfortable impression of receiving the thanks of my creditors and the conscious feeling of discharging my duty like a man of honour and honesty. I see before me a long tedious and dark path but it leads to true Fame and stainless reputation. If I die in the harrows as is very likely I shall die with honour. . . .[12]

The heroism and diligence he displayed is undeniable. In less than six years he had made more than £50,000 for his creditors and something in the region of £6,000 for himself. By the time of his death, there was no difficulty in paying off the remaining debts. Cadell did so on the family's behalf, buying the copyright of all Scott's works for £10,000. It made his fortune.

In the short period covered by the Journal, Scott wrote *Woodstock*, a seven-volume life of Napoleon, *The Fair Maid of Perth*, *Anne of Geier-stein*, *Count Robert of Paris*, *The Surgeon's Daughter* and *Castle Dangerous*, in addition to the *Tales of a Grandfather*, a child's history of Scotland. He also prepared the notes and introductions to a complete edition of his works; and prepared the Miscellaneous Prose Works for the press. This would have been hard enough work even in the days of his vigour. If the Journal were only a record of how a man discharged himself of a vast debt in the most honourable way known to him, it would be a fascinating achievement; but, like Boethius or the Book of Job, the more nobly the central figure behaves, the more fiercely he is tried. Not only did he have to work harder than he had ever done in a hard-working life, but his health began to collapse, his wife died, his friends died or fell into disgrace, his beloved grandson died at the age of ten, and the world he had known and loved and approved of appeared to have fallen into ruins. It was against this background that Scott took a pride in maintaining an urbane cheerfulness. Although he had lost all interest in 'society', he still mixed in the world as much as his work would permit. More and more time, though, was spent at Abbotsford—the place for which he slaved and the people on whose behalf he worked himself into the grave. Will

Laidlaw, the factor, remained with him to the end; Tom Purdie, the poacher turned gamekeeper, who was, in many ways, the best friend Scott ever had, predeceased his master. Occasionally Edinburgh friends came to stay, the Skenes being the most welcome. But, for the most part, Scott stayed at home, rising early to sit at the desk in his tiny study; 'wrought', 'finishd my task', are such familiar entries as almost to seem mere punctuation. Scott's study still has a miserable atmosphere. It feels more like a condemned cell than a place where great works of art have been produced; and, indeed, all his best works were written in Edinburgh.

The core of the Journal is hard work and intense, undeserved, and meaningless suffering. Many of its greatest passages reflect this, such as the entry in which he describes the corpse of his wife:

I have seen her—The figure I beheld is and is not my Charlotte—my thirty years' companion—There is the same symmetry of form though those limbs are rigid which were once so gracefully elastic—but that yellow masque with pinchd features which seems to mock life rather than emulate it, can it be the face that was once so full of lively expression? I will not look on it again. Anne thinks her little changed because the latest idea she had formed of her mother is as she appeard under circumstances of sickness and pain. Mine go back to a period of comparative health. If I write in this way I shall write down my resolution which I should rather write up if I could. I wonder how I shall do with the large portion of thoughts which were hers for thirty years. I suspect they will be hers for a long time at least. But I will not blaze cambrick and crape in the publick eye like a disconsolate widower, that most affected of all characters.[13]

Perhaps no passage in the fiction matches this—and there are many others like it. For all its painful stoicism—his resolution to 'write up' rather than 'write down'—there could not be a less 'stiff' book than the Journal. One keeps turning to it as to the company of a delightful and talkative friend. As his letters show to much better effect, Scott had a genius for friendship, and with a huge variety of people: people as different as Skene and Byron, Tom Purdie and Joanna Baillie, Heber and Ballantyne, Lady Louisa Stuart and 'Christopher North', Hogg and Maria Edgeworth. Reading the Journal one can see why. The useful Italian word *simpatico* exactly fits it. It reflects a mind bubbling over with impressions: quotations, anecdotes, snatches of old songs burst into every entry.

Long life to thy fame and peace to thy soul, Rob Burns. When I want a phrase
to express a sentiment which I feel strongly, I find the phrase in Shakespeare
or thee.[14]

This is largely true. But there are so many other sources of memory as
well: ballad and folk-tale; Jacobean drama; Prior, Otway, Swift,
Dryden, Coleridge are often quoted. *Don Quixote*, appropriately, is a
favourite book. How often he likes to quote 'Patience, cousin, and
shuffle the cards'.[15]

It is not, particularly, a 'writer's diary': we do not feel, after reading
it, that we understand more about Scott's books, or how he composed
them. But one does feel, satisfyingly, that the character portrayed in
the Journal is quite compatible with the impression we have formed of
the Author of Waverley. There are, above all, two characteristics
which, perhaps, are essential to a great writer and which he shows
repeatedly. The first is an inability to be bored.

Few men leading a quiet life and without any strong or varied change of
circumstances have seen more of Society than I have—few have enjoyd it
more or been *bored* as it [is] calld less by the company of tiresome people. I
have rarely if ever found any one out of whom I could not extract amusement
or edification and were I obliged to account for hints offerd on such occasions
I should make an ample deduction from my inventive powers. Still, however,
from the earliest time I can remember, I preferd the pleasures of being alone
to waiting for visitors, and have often taken a bannock and a bit of cheese to
the wood or hill to avoid dining with company. As I grew from boyhood to
manhood I saw this would not do and that to gain a place in men's esteem I
must mix and bustle with them. Pride and excitation of spirits supplied the
real pleasure which others seem to feel in society and certainly upon many
occasions it was real. Still if the question was eternal company with the power
of retiring within yourself or Solitary confinement for life I should say,
'Turnkey, Lock the cell'. My life has been a sort of dream spent in

Chewing the cud of sweet and bitter fancy.[16]

This is a very revealing passage, and puts us firmly in our place as we
finger the pages of his private reflections. The intense amusement he
derived from the grotesque varieties of human types explains his
almost endless taste for society. And, of course, we know that Scott
was fairly shameless about using real characters and events in his
fictions. One has, for instance, Hogg's account of the 'long sheep' joke
in *The Black Dwarf*:

During the sociality of the evening, the discourse ran very much on different breeds of sheep, that everlasting drawback on the community of Ettrick Forest. The original black-faced forest breed always denominated the *short sheep*, and the Cheviot breed the *long sheep*. The disputes at that time ran very high about the practicable profits of each. Mr Scott, who had come into that remote district to visit a bard of Nature's own making and preserve what little fragments remained of the country's legendary lore, felt himself rather bored with the everlasting question of the long and short sheep. So at length, putting on his most serious calculating face, he turned to Mr Walter Brydon and said, 'I am rather at a loss regarding the merits of this *very* important question. How long must a sheep actually measure to come under the denomination of a *long sheep*?'

Mr Brydon, who, in the simplicity of his heart, neither perceived the quiz nor the reproof, fell to answer with great sincerity, 'It's the woo', sir; it's the woo' that maks the difference, the lang sheep hae the lang thing, an' these are just kind o' names we gie them, ye see.'

Laidlaw got up a great guffaw, on which Scott could not preserve his face of strict calculation any longer; it went gradually awry, and a hearty laugh followed. When I saw the very same words, repeated near the beginning of the *Black Dwarf*, how could I be mistaken of the author?[17]

This shows the truth of Scott's admission that 'I have rarely if ever found any one out of whom I could not extract amusement or edification and were I obliged to account for hints offerd on such occasions I should make an ample deduction from my inventive powers.'[18] The social Scott—the observer of so many of the 'Scott originals'—is readily imaginable. One can trace hundreds of examples of what Hogg is describing. But Scott's private self—the solitude which he enjoyed when he took a bannock and a piece of cheese to the wood—is unimaginable: and perhaps one of the qualities which distinguish men and women of genius from the rest of their kind is that they are in the last resort completely unknowable. The Journal gives us no more hint about the workings of Scott's imagination than any external accounts by his friends. We know from reading the private journals of Virginia Woolf and Arnold Bennett exactly what they were like, and how they wrote their novels. But the flood of biographical information which we possess about Scott—as in the case of Tolstoy—brings us no nearer an understanding of his mystery.

Of course, Tolstoy's interminable chronicling of passing moods, crazes and opinions, and his alarming habit of sharing domestic 'confidences', brought him no nearer to self-knowledge. Indeed, it was his preoccupation with himself and the rightness of his own views which destroyed his art and made him abandon fiction in favour of self-improvement. Scott, on the other hand, was strikingly unegotistical.

The remark needs qualification, of course. Although Scott was the more stoical and humorous, his preoccupation with his bowels at times almost seems to anticipate the chief absorption of Tolstoy's later years. But he always tries to dismiss his obsession:

Almost sick with pain—and it stops everything. I shall tire of my journal if it is to contain nothing but biles and piles and plaisters and unguents. In my better days I had stories to tell but death has closed the long dark avenue upon loves and friendships and I can only look at them as through the grated door of a long burial place filld with monuments of those who were once dear to me . . . My pains were then of the heart . . . Still Colon has his rights. As Jeffrey said in a clever parody

> Whether we board a Berwick smack
> Or take the mail or mount a hack
> None leaves his a—e behind.

The least honourd—the most indispensable part of our body corporate is sure to keep its place. I am always horrified to think how the reverend Lord of the trouser may be treated by and by if this goes on.

> Ah dextrous Chirurgeons, mitigate your plan:
> Slice bullock's rumps—but spare the rump of man.[19]

The essential point is that Scott resented the way in which illness intruded these unwelcome details into his consciousness; Tolstoy, on the other hand, sometimes saw the chief function of his diary to be a log-book of his bowel functions.

From time to time, Scott actually abandoned the Journal. Sometimes he was simply too ill to write; and, as he remarked about smoking, 'I despise custom'.[20] He lacks the unashamed egotism which often makes diaries such absorbing reading—'Johnson advises Boswell to keep a diary but to omit registers of the weather and like trumpery. I am resolved in future not to register what is yet more futile—my gleams of bright and clouded temper.'[21] For all that, many of the most telling passages describe the trivial irritations of everyday life. We do not penetrate the mystery of his mind at work, but we observe the chaotic effects which ensue while it is so disengaged. He is always losing things: '. . . assorting papers and so forth. I never could help admiring the concatenation between Achitophel's setting his house in order and hanging himself. The one seems to me to follow the other as a matter of course.'[22] Or again, 'This a morning of fidgetty nervous confusion. I sought successively my box of Bramah pens, my proof sheets and last, not least anxiously, my spe[c]tacles. I am convinced I lost a full hour in these various chases.'[23] 'The strange contradictory mode of papers hiding themselves that you wish to see and others thrusting themselves into your hand to confuse and bewilder you' is not, perhaps, what one might expect in Scott, with his fierce office training.

These, of course, are among the most trivial entries in the Journal. One of Scott's gifts it shows to best advantage is his passion for anecdote, and the largely humorous way in which he viewed his friends and the human condition:

His Lordship's funeral took place in a chapell amongst the ruins. His body was in the grave with its feet pointing westward. My cousin Maxpopple was for taking notice of it but I assured him that a man who had been wrong in the head all his life would scarce become right headed after death.[24]

It is possible to take too solemn a view of the Journal. On one level, it is one of the saddest books that was ever written. The catalogue of calamities is unending, and the heroism and detachment which he attempts to practise break down. Syntax and handwriting finally collapse altogether, as can now be appreciated in Mr Anderson's faithful edition of the manuscript. Yet, although the comparisons made earlier in this chapter with Boethius and the Book of Job are not out of place in terms of Scott's suffering, nor of his courage, they quite disguise the tone of the Journal. Cheerfulness keeps breaking through, and sunny episodes occur even in the later stages—one recalls the happy morning spent with Rogers, the banker poet, in London:

The freshness of the air, the singing of the birds, the beautiful aspect of nature, the size of the venerable trees, gave me all a delightful feeling this morning. It seemd there was pleasure even in living and breathing without anything else. We (i.e. Rogers and I) wanderd into a green lane borderd with fine trees which might have been twenty miles from a town.[25]

Such untroubled pleasures became rarer in the last three years of his life, but they never leave us in any doubt that they embody the real Scott. What he missed in Northcote's recollections of Sir Joshua Reynolds is abundant in the Journal—'a pleasing vision of the highest talents united with the kindest temper'.

It is not the diary of a saint. Scott could, at times, be petulant, disagreeable, and stubborn. Against this, we notice that he was never mean, and that his extravagance always extended itself into generosity. Even after his ruin, he freely gave away sums of money: 'A distressing letter from Haydon [the painter]—imprudent probably, but who has not [been], and a man of rare genius. What a pity I gave that £10 to Craig. But I have plenty of ten pounds sure and I may make it something better.'[26] They are rather splendid words for a bankrupt to have written.   John Buchan described the Journal as 'one of the most complete expressions of a human soul that we possess'.[27] He went on to say that 'the greatest figure he ever drew is in the Journal.' Its greatness does not obscure the greatness of much of the later fiction, but actually explains it. The detachment of his greatest fiction gives expression to a fine comic realism, making *The Antiquary*, for all its faults, one of the most ambitious and accomplished novels which he wrote. Jonathan Oldbuck, the Antiquary, is an affectionate portrait of George Constable, the old man who introduced Scott to the works of Shakespeare as a boy. But, as we observed in Chapter Four, he is much more than that. He is a full-blooded embodiment of the type of man Scott would like to have been himself. The Journal is a perfect complement to the novel, a companion-piece to Oldbuck's qualities of desultory, but enormous, learning, companionability, endurance, and good humour.

CHAPTER TEN

Scott and the Critics

Pearson: Sad to think that no one nowadays reads Scott except you, me and Sidney Webb.
Kingsmill: Webb?
Pearson: Yes. Kitty Muggeridge told me that she was staying with him not very long ago, and the following remarks passed between them—

> 'How do you occupy your time, Uncle Sidney?'
> 'I read one novel a day.'
> 'What are your reading now?'
> 'I am reading the novels of Sir Walter Scott.'
> 'Do you like them?'
> 'No.'

Talking of Whittington, by Hesketh Pearson
and Hugh Kingsmill.

It is strange to think of Sidney Webb, the admirer of Stalin, and one of the founding fathers of modern British socialism, devoting his last days to a perusal of the Waverley Novels. But it is no surprise that he did not like them. Scott's fundamental Toryism, combined with the highest powers of imagination and intelligence, can hardly have been congenial to him.

Yet much of the best criticism of Scott has come from the Marxist critics, most notably in Georg Lukacs's monumental study, *The Historical Novel*. Lukacs demonstrates more forcefully than any other critic in this century how the triumph of Scott's art was its marriage of psychological realism with an idea of history. Scott 'never modernizes the psychology of his characters . . . The historical novel . . . has to demonstrate by artistic means that historical circumstances and characters existed in precisely such and such a way. What in Scott has been called very superficially "authenticity of local colour" is in actual fact this artistic demonstration of historical reality.'[1] As such, for Lukacs, Scott was the first historical novelist, and one of the greatest.

This is little more than a nineteenth-century commonplace about

Scott. It is Carlyle's tribute to the Waverley Novels[2]—even, in a different form, Dr Pusey's[3]—that they change our idea of history by showing us how it affected real people: 'Scott portrays the great transformations of history as transformations of popular life.'[4] One sees this not only in the great novels of eighteenth-century life—*Rob Roy*, *Waverley* and *Redgauntlet*—but also in stories of earlier periods like *The Abbot*.

For Lukacs, as a Marxist, the popularity of the Waverley Novels was itself one of the testimonies to 'the truthfulness of historical atmosphere'[5] which we find in them. And it is here, perhaps, that the dispassionate non-Marxist first begins to sense that what Lukacs is offering is less criticism than doctrine. Scott's most popular work, after all, was *Ivanhoe* and it was the novel which he himself acknowledged to be the most lacking in 'truthfulness of historical atmosphere'. Lukacs has to resolve this difficulty by suggesting that the minor characters in the book, most notably peasants like Wamba and popular heroes like Robin Hood, overshadow Ivanhoe himself: but this takes us nowhere closer to understanding why *Ivanhoe* was popular, and with whom. It would be perverse to read it as a serious account of the class struggle, and Lukacs shies away from doing so. But he is left with a problem. Scott, as he has said, possesses, in his greatest books, the art of showing us the processes of history actually at work. Yet, far from being a revolutionary or a radical figure in the literary scene, he was a stubborn old Tory landlord, a magistrate who believed in firing shot into mobs and sending rebellious loom-workers to Botany Bay.

Hazlitt, a radical writing a hundred years before Lukacs, was disturbed by the same problem, and so divides his essay on Scott into two parts.[6] In the first, he recognizes that 'his works (taken together) are almost like a new edition of human nature'; that Scott's 'worst is better than any other person's best'. But at the same time, he feels constrained to assault Scott's political position, representing him as one who has 'supported the worst abuses of authority in the worst spirit'. Lukacs feels no acrimony towards Scott personally and so falls back on the ingenious suggestion that 'Scott ranks among those great writers whose depth is manifest mainly in their work, a depth which they often do not understand themselves, because it has sprung from a truly realistic mastery of their material in conflict with their personal views and prejudices.'[7]

This point of view is expanded later in the chapter, in which Lukacs admits that Balzac and Tolstoy had the same difficulty. He sees at work 'Engels's triumph of realism' over 'Sir Walter Scott, the Scottish petty aristocrat'; a triumph which is manifested in the works of 'Scott the writer'.[8]

This book has been an attempt to trace the relationship between 'Scott the writer' and 'Sir Walter Scott the Scottish petty aristocrat'. Sometimes we have looked inward, and tried to see what of his own life he carried into his fiction. At other times, particularly in the last chapter, we have tried to see how his life matched the ideals and images of his art.

The lives of men of genius are always, as in Matthew Arnold's sonnet on Shakespeare, quite impenetrable. One can accumulate documentation for almost all their waking hours; in the case of Scott, this can be found in innumerable biographical studies, and in compilations of his letters and journals. After he reached manhood, hardly a day of his life has escaped the notice of scholars. And yet, when all is done, the first part of Lukacs's statement is true. Scott's depth is mainly manifest in his work; and it is a depth which Scott evidently did not understand himself. No one can ever comprehend, least of all the artist himself, the ultimate mystery of how great works of art come into being.

Yet this is only true of the 'greatness', the sublimity of art at its most nebulous level. An artist's point of view, the general movement of his mind, seems as easily traceable as the books he read, the friendships he made, and the attitudes he adopted in ordinary conversation. And this is supremely true of Scott. The investigations and suggestions in this book have been, of necessity, haphazard and slight: a complete survey of the relationship between Scott's mind and art, his life and his fiction, would take up many volumes. And I have been openly subjective in my choice of examples and the emphasis which I have placed upon them. This is a region where certainty would be improper. Yet a survey of the biographical material seems to suggest that Scott's life and art are of a piece. The early poetry springs completely from Scott's absorption in local history, ballad and anecdote—as Coleridge observed, in a passage already quoted, 'No insect was ever more like in the colour of its skin and juices to the leaf it fed on, than Scott's muse is to Scott himself'[9]—and what is true of the poetry is even truer of the novels. On a trivial level, one feels that their genial, decent honesty reflects his own personal goodness of heart. But, more seriously than that, in so far as they represent a point of view, it is clearly Scott's own. They are not the novels of a man who secretly thought like Engels, penned, as if by spirit-writing, by 'a Scottish petty aristocrat'. They *are* the novels of a Scottish petty aristocrat. Lukacs cannot allow himself to believe that such a person could be as intelligent or subtle as the Author of Waverley evidently was; and so, prompted by Scott's example, he invents a literary *persona*, 'Scott the writer'. And yet, in the novels in which Scott is being most serious, we see the hand of the 'petty Scottish aristocrat' most clearly. Scott's Toryism in *The Antiquary*, *Old Mortality* and *Redgauntlet* is not of an unreasoning kind. He is able to see that history defeats those, like Redgauntlet, Lady Margaret Bellenden or Lord Glenallan, who make their spiritual homes in the last ditch. But this point would be too obvious to be worth making if it were not complemented by another. Those who die in the last ditch become indistinguishable from their radical opponents; though both are treated by Scott with full artistic sympathy, and given great dignity. One thinks of the fanatics in *Old Mortality*, or the subdued heroism of the Jacobites at the end of *Waverley*. Yet always, in these books, another way is posited: the path of private virtue. Manifestly, at the beginning of *The Heart of Midlothian*, the prison is corrupt, the military commanded by sadists and the government both oppressive and inept; but, equally, its opponents, with the exception of Wilson, are fanatical egotists. Exactly the same pattern can be found in *Old Mortality*, in which the heavy-handedness of government fully explains, but does not justify, the outrageous rebels. Scott does not seem to be making a primarily political point here. He is not, in spite of himself, showing governments up to be cruel and corrupt. It was no part of his creed that they were. Nor is he suggesting that rebellions against such governments are ever particularly effective, still less determined by any pattern of history. In all phases of history, rather, we can discern the possibility of leading a life of private virtue: that of Jeanie Deans with her husband, of the Antiquary, of Henry Morton after his return from exile, or of Edward Waverley after his pardon. There are many ways of leading privately virtuous lives, but for Scott the sanctity of such lives was self-evident: his faith, his life, his art all testify to it.

In politics, it led him to the conviction that any infringement of civil order and any threat to domestic stability were to be resisted. It was this which made him volunteer to fight against Napoleon, and made him a hard-working local magistrate and a devoted son, father and grandfather. And it was also what made him a novelist. It seems perverse to think that he who prided himself on 'the Big Bow wow strain' should have been the prophet of the quiet life. Yet the conclusion to *The Heart of Midlothian* strikes a note which runs through all Scott's great fiction: 'The paths of virtue, though seldom those of worldly greatness, are always those of pleasantness and peace.' If this warm, Victorian glow seems too rosy, one can see nonetheless that it is the intensely felt quality of individual lives which distinguishes Scott's fiction.

Lukacs saw this perfectly clearly, which makes his own criticism so interesting. Scott had a view of man and history in his novels which was entirely consistent with his assertion (not, obviously, quoted by Lukacs) that he would 'if called upon, die a martyr for the Christian religion, so completely is . . . its divine origin proved by its beneficial effects on the state of society.'[10] And since this is obviously not in accordance with 'realism' as Engels understood the term, Lukacs was obliged to search around for some traces of materialist determinism in Scott's treatment of the eighteenth century. He found it in *Rob Roy*.

Lukacs's 'howler' is by now notorious. *Rob Roy* is actually set in 1715, but Lukacs places it at the 'end of the eighteenth century':

With the suppression of the uprising of 1745—which is depicted in *Waverley*—the real downfall of gentile [*sic*—does it mean genteel?] society in Scotland begins, says Engels. Several decades later (in *Rob Roy*) we see the clans already in a state of complete economic dissolution . . . Thus we have here already an element of dissolution, the beginnings of class-uprooting which were as yet absent from the clan picture of *Waverley*.[11]

Anyone can make mistakes, and subsequent critics have perhaps been unduly harsh about this one. 'M. Lukacs . . . proceeds to erect a complicated argument in economic history upon this gross error. M. Lukacs is one of those men who pontificate on books they have not read, and the tendency evident in some quarters to take his book seriously can only be an obstacle to the understanding of Scott,' explodes Mr Cockshut in a footnote.[12] Yet he himself places a very determinist historical interpretation on the absurd rapidity with which the various Osbaldistone brothers die at the end of the novel:

The six sons represent a race that is spiritually dying. They . . . disappear because their way of life is outmoded . . . It is sad to see the author of *Old*

Mortality and *The Heart of Midlothian* treating religion almost as an epiphenomenon of class realities. But this 'Marxist' side of Scott's versatile intelligence was only one, and may be allowed its place.[13]

It sounds superficial to reply that the reason Scott killed off all the Osbaldistones was to allow Frank Osbaldistone, the hero, to inherit their house and marry the heroine, Diana Vernon. But this is manifestly the case. The degree to which Mr Cockshut has absorbed the point of view he was attacking here is a tribute to Lukacs. *Rob Roy* cannot, however, be twisted into a commentary on economic or political affairs in the eighteenth century. It is an adventure story, pure and simple, with a number of characters and scenes far too vivid for the feeble plot which contains them. The critics are simply too clever for it.

Indeed, all modern criticism of Scott is likely to recoil from Scott's obviousness. Literary history since Henry James has led us to assume that human life is almost infinitely mysterious and complicated; and the novelist has conceived it as her, or his, task to obfuscate, to assure us that life is indeed complicated, much more complicated than we at first supposed. 'Back we must go,' wrote Virginia Woolf archly, 'and say to the reader who waits a-tiptoe to know what life is, alas we don't know.'[14] So it is that the critic comes into his own, chipping away at the density of fictitious creations to provide us with an established 'sub-text' to illuminate our search.

Not all novelists play the game, of course, and it could be argued that even James and Virginia Woolf are at their best when creating characters which have all the self-evident haecceity of Chaucer's Canterbury pilgrims. '"Eleanor is not a bad old girl when you get to know her." A statement unquestionably true,' Nick Jenkins snottily observes in Anthony Powell's great sequence, 'but since human life is lived largely at surface level, that encouraging possibility, true or false, did not appreciably lighten the burden of Eleanor's partners.'[15]

Chesterton made this point trenchantly in his essay on Scott. Referring to the instantly moving quality of the great scenes and speeches in the Waverley Novels, he wrote that

The whole question is one of immediate effect of greatness, such as is produced even by fine bombast. It is absurd to call it merely superficial; here there is no question of superficiality; we might as well call a stone that strikes us between the eyes merely superficial. The very word superficial is founded on a fundamental mistake about life, the idea that second thoughts are best. The superficial impression of the world is by far the deepest.[16]

Full of densely observed appreciation of Scott's genius, the whole essay is magnificent, and can be enjoyed even by those with no taste for the absurd acrobatics of Chestertonian rhetoric.

We encounter in Scott's novels the greatest diversity of realistic human characters outside Shakespeare; we discover from reading his biography one of the most genial men who ever lived. It really requires no further comment. The discovery of Scott is like finding oneself in a new landscape, enjoying the sort of experience he himself describes at the beginning of *The Fair Maid of Perth* when he tells us of his first glimpse of the Highlands:

Childish wonder, indeed, was an ingredient in my delight, for I was not above fifteen years old; and as this had been the first excursion I was permitted to make on a pony of my own, I also experienced the glow of independence, mingled with that degree of anxiety which the most conceited boy feels when he is first abandoned to his own undirected counsels. I recollect pulling up the reins without meaning to do so, and gazing on the scene before me as if I had been afraid it would shift like those in a theatre before I could distinctly observe its different parts, or convince myself that what I saw was real.

(Chapter I)

Notes

The titles of works cited in the footnotes are given in full when first mentioned but may be afterwards abbreviated: e.g. Hogg's *Domestic Manners of Sir Walter Scott* becomes 'Hogg'.

The following abbreviations are used throughout for Scott's own works:

MPW: *The Miscellaneous Prose Works of Sir Walter Scott*. Thirty volumes (Edinburgh, 1871).

Letters: *The Letters of Sir Walter Scott*. Edited by Sir Herbert J. C. Grierson, assisted by Davidson Cook, W. M. Parker, and others. Twelve volumes (London, 1932–7). All readers of the letters are indebted to James C. Corson's *Notes and Index* to Grierson's edition (Clarendon Press, 1979).

Journal: *The Journal of Sir Walter Scott*. ed. W. E. K. Anderson (Oxford, 1972). Mr Anderson's work is magnificently informative and I have drawn freely from it.

There are so many editions of Scott's poems and novels that it seems pointless to give page references for citations from them. I have used the Oxford Standard Authors edition of *The Poetical Works of Sir Walter Scott* (1908) and the Centenary Edition of the Waverley Novels (1871) because these are the ones which I happen to possess. I have in general checked quotations beside the first editions, but I do not think that the substance of my arguments would be altered by any textual variants.

Chapter One

1 Mrs Hughes (of Uffington), *Letters and Recollections of Sir Walter Scott* (1904), 338.
2 *Familiar Letters of Sir Walter Scott* (1894), ii 49.
3 Leslie Marchand (ed.), *Born for Opposition: Byron's Letters and Journals* (1978), viii 13.
4 'The Antiquary', *Collected Essays* (1971), i 143.
5 'Gas at Abbotsford', *Collected Essays* (1971), i 134.

Chapter Two

1 Quoted in *Notes and Queries* (1926), cli 60.

2 Thomas M. Raysor (ed.), *Coleridge's Shakespearean Criticism* (1931), ii 231.
3 Quoted in Hesketh Pearson, *Walter Scott: His Life and Personality* (1954), 1.
4 *Letters* (1815–17), iv 301.
5 J. G. Lockhart, *Life of Scott* (1838), iii 128.
6 *ibid*. lv 5 119.
7 *Proceedings of the British Academy* (1961), xlvii 229.
8 Quoted in John O. Hayden (ed.), *Scott: the Critical Heritage* (1970), 39.
9 John Ruskin, *Works* xxxiv 546.
10 *MPW*, vi 3.
11 'On the Old Road': John Ruskin, *Works* xxxiv 386.
12 Lockhart, vii 71.
13 *ibid*., iii 456.
14 Journal (13 May 1829), 401.
15 See Leslie Marchand, *Byron—A Biography* (1957), iii.
16 Journal (9 February 1826).
17 Quoted in Hesketh Pearson, *op. cit.*, 67.
18 Joseph Strutt, *Queenhoo Hall, a romance and Ancient Times, a Drama* (1808). It has not, to my knowledge, been reprinted, though Scott's continuations are usually printed with the Notes of *Waverley*.
19 *Horda Angel-cynnan: or A Compleat view of the manners, customs, arms, habits, &c, of the inhabitants of England from the arrival of the Saxons* (1775).
20 Leslie Marchand (ed.), *So Late into the Night: Byron's Letters and Journals* (1976), v 105.

Chapter Three

1 John Buchan, *Sir Walter Scott* (1932), 42.
2 *Letters* (1817–19), v 200.
3 *Letters* (1819–21), vi 214.
4 *ibid*., 259.
5 James Hogg, *Domestic Manners of Sir Walter Scott* (1909), 107.
6 *Letters* (1819–21), vi 57.
7 *ibid*., 114.
8 *Rob Roy*, Chapter I.
9 Quoted in Edgar Johnson, *The Great Unknown* (1970), 435.
10 'George Eliot', *Collected Essays* (1971), i 201.
11 This, broadly, is the thesis expounded by Alexander Welsh of the University of Pittsburgh in *The Hero of the Waverley Novels* (1963).
12 *cp*. Lockhart, i 44, and *Rob Roy*, i 7.

Chapter Four

1 Lockhart, v 268.
2 *ibid*., v 10 267.
3 Mrs Hughes, 65.
4 Lockhart, v 265–6.
5 Quoted in Edgar Johnson *op. cit.* 1176.

6 Hogg, 117.

7 *MPW*, xxi 4.

8 William Hazlitt, *The Spirit of the Age* (1825).

9 Journal (5 December 1825), 25.

10 Joseph Butler, *Fifteen Sermons Preached at the Rolls Chapel*. Sermon Number 1, paragraph 7.

11 Journal (25 June 1826), 162.

12 There have been at least two books devoted to Scott's relationship with Williamina. Adam Scott's *The Story of Sir Walter Scott's First Love* (1896) is a sentimental treatment; *Sir Walter Scott's Congé* by the Hon. Lord Sands (1929) examines the evidence with a more rigorous legalistic eye.

13 *Letters* (1819–21), vi 506.

14 Journal (16 June 1827), 315.

15 *ibid.*, (25 October 1827), 368.

16 *ibid.*, (7 November 1827), 375.

17 *Guy Mannering*, Chapter LI.

18 *The Surgeon's Daughter*, Chapter XIV.

19 Scott usually misquoted this tag in a variety of ways: it comes from George Villiers, Duke of Buckingham's *The Rehearsal* (1671) III 1. For Scott's application of the term, see Ioan Williams (ed.), *Sir Walter Scott on Novelists and Fiction* (1968), 188, 239, 454.

20 Lockhart, vii 373.

21 E. M. Forster, *Aspects of the Novel* (1927), Chapter 2.

22 Edgar Johnson, *op. cit.*, 538.

23 For example, in the life of *Alain le Sage. MPW*, iii 426.

24 *MPW*, iii 451.

25 *ibid.*, 388.

26 *MPW*, iv 321.

27 Journal (14 March 1826), 114.

28 James Boswell, *Life of Johnson*: 22 March 1776. Oxford Standard Authors edition, 705.

29 *Letters* (1808–11), ii 287.

30 Buchan, *op. cit.*, 267.

31 Quoted in Ioan Williams, *op. cit.*, 260.

32 *Frankenstein*, Oxford English Novels edition, 209.

33 *Melmoth the Wanderer*, Chapter XXXVIII. Oxford English Novels edition, 539.

34 *ibid.*, Chapter XXXIX. Oxford English Novels edition, 540.

Chapter Five

1 *Letters* (1826–8), x 448.

2 *ibid.*, 449.

3 See Henry Parry Liddon DD, *The Life of Edward Bouverie Pusey* (1893), i 144.

4 Wilfrid Ward, *The Life of John Henry, Cardinal Newman* (1912), i 300.

5 Hogg, 110.

6 *ibid.*
7 *Letters* (1787–1807), i 75.
8 *ibid.*, 76.
9 *Letters* (1817–19), v 73.
10 *Guy Mannering*, Chapter XIX.
11 Lockhart, vi 414.
12 Lockhart, vii 387.
13 *ibid.*, 391.
14 Sir Herbert Grierson, *Sir Walter Scott Bart.* (1938), 299.
15 Lockhart, vii 393.
16 Journal (18 December 1827), 399.
17 1832 Introduction to *The Monastery*.
18 *Quarterly Review* xvi (1817).
19 *Peveril of the Peak*, Chapter XXIII.
20 *Woodstock*, Chapter I.
21 Journal (28 February 1829), 525.
22 *A Legend of Montrose*, Chapter VII.

Chapter Six

1 See T. F. Henderson, 'James Sharp', *The Dictionary of National Biography*; Gordon Donaldson, *James V to James VII* (1965) in the Edinburgh History of Scotland, iii 370; Ian Cowan, *The Scottish Covenanters 1660–1688* (1966).
2 *The Works of the Ettrick Shepherd: A New Edition Revised at the Instance of the Author's Family* (1865), i 1–61.
3 A. O. J. Cockshut, *The Achievement of Sir Walter Scott* (1969), 132.
4 *ibid.*
5 David Hume, *A History of Great Britain*, Chapter LXIX. I quote from the edition of 1807, viii 170.
6 Lockhart, vi 206.
7 Hogg, 75.
8 *Letters* (1828–31), xi 131.
9 *The Heart of Midlothian*, Chapter I.
10 Hyder Edward Rollins (ed.), *The Letters of John Keats* (1958), ii 80.
11 E. M. W. Tillyard, *Shakespeare's Problem Plays* (1950). Tillyard's conclusions are elaborated by Miss Lascelles in her book, *Shakespeare's Measure for Measure* (1953).
12 *Measure for Measure*, III. i.

Chapter Seven

1 Sidney Lee, *A Life of William Shakespeare* (1898), 279.
2 *Letters* (1815–17), iv 121.
3 Lockhart, ii 308.
4 *Letters* (1825–6), ix 46.
5 *Letters* (1828–31), xi 150.
6 Edgar Johnson, *op. cit.*, 1163.

7 *ibid.*, 1276.
8 Lockhart, iv 257.
9 Lockhart, vii 373.
10 The Waverley Novels, Border Edition, viii x.
11 Harold Otel (ed.), *Thomas Hardy's Personal Writings* (1967), 121.
12 Jerome Mitchell, *The Walter Scott Operas* (1977).
13 Claire Lamont, 'The Poetry of the Early Waverley Novels', *PBA* lxi (1975), 315.
14 Its debt to Carew is explained in J. C. Maxwell, 'Lucy's Ashton's Song', *Notes and Queries* cxcv (1950), 210.
15 John Bayley, *The Romantic Survival* (1957), 20.
16 Peter Conrad, *Romantic Opera and Literary Form* (1977), 113.

Chapter Eight

1 *Rebecca and Rowena* (1849). Quotations are from the Oxford Thackeray, Volume X.
2 Journal (31 October 1826), 226.
3 Benjamin Ferrey, *Recollections of A. N. Welby Pugin and his Father, Augustus Pugin* (1861), 48.
4 *Contrasts: or A Parallel Between the Noble Edifices of the Fourteenth and Fifteenth Centuries, and Similar Buildings of the Present Day; shewing the Present Decay of Taste: Accompanied by Appropriate Text.* I quote from the second, much revised, edition of 1841. There is a full bibliography of Pugin's works in Phoebe Stanton, *Pugin* (1971).
5 Liddon, *op. cit.*, i 254.
6 The Baroness de Bertouch, *The Life of Fr. Ignatius OSB, the Monk of Llanthony* (1904), 65.
7 For an account of the raising of Lizzie Meek, see the Baroness de Bertouch, *op. cit.*, 116–20. The miracles of the Holy Rhubarb Leaf are recounted on pp. 550 ff.
8 Kenneth Clark, *The Gothic Revival* (1928), 87.
9 Buchan, *op. cit.*, 199.
10 Quoted in E. P. Dargan, 'Scott and the French Romantics', *PMLA* xlix (1934).
11 Robert Browning, *The Ring and the Book*, i 458.
12 *Rebecca and Rowena*, 501.
13 *ibid.*, 507.
14 *ibid.*, 572.
15 Maria Edgeworth, Tales and Novels (1833), xvii.
16 *Letters* (1815–17), iv 478.
17 Charles Lamb, *Essays of Elia*. The World's Classics edition, 82–3.
18 *Ivanhoe*, Note A.
19 Journal (19 February 1828), 429.
20 *ibid.* (29 April 1829), 554.
21 'On the Old Road': John Ruskin, *Works*, xxxiv 290.

Chapter Nine

1 Journal (10 May 1828), 472.
2 Eric Quayle, *The Ruin of Sir Walter Scott* (1968).
3 Journal (20 September 1825), 1.
4 *ibid*. (5 December 1825), 25.
5 *ibid*. (25 November 1826), 162.
6 *ibid*. (10 July 1826), 171.
7 *ibid*. (12 November 1826), 236.
8 There is an excellent summary of Scott's financial position by W. E. K. Anderson in his edition of the Journal (pp. xxiii–xxviii). For a more hostile account, see Eric Quayle, *op. cit*.
9 Journal (18 December 1825), 39.
10 Quoted by W. E. K. Anderson: *ibid*., xxvi.
11 Journal (31 May 1826), 152.
12 *ibid*. (24 December 1827), 403–4.
13 *ibid*. (16 May 1826), 145.
14 *ibid*. (11 December 1826), 252.
15 *ibid*. 41, 267, 528.
16 *ibid*. (27 December 1825), 49–50.
17 Hogg, 54–5.
18 There is a very good account of some of them in W. S. Crockett, *The Scott Originals* (1912). See also Robert Chambers, *Illustrations of the Author of Waverley: being Notices and Anecdotes of Real Characters, Scenes and Incidents supposed to be described in his works* (1825).
19 Journal (18 December 1826), 254–5.
20 *ibid*. (28 February 1827), 283.
21 *ibid*. (26 March 1829), 539.
22 *ibid*. (13 May 1827), 304.
23 *ibid*. (10 August 1827), 338.
24 *ibid*. (25 April 1829), 552.
25 *ibid*. (18 May 1828), 477.
26 *ibid*. (29 June 1827), 322.
27 Buchan, *op. cit*., 277–8.

Chapter Ten

1 Georg Lukacs, *The Historical Novel*, translated from the German by Hannah and Stanley Mitchell (third edition, 1974), 41.
2 *London and Westminster Review* xii (1838).
3 Liddon, *op. cit*., i 254.
4 Lukacs, 39.
5 *ibid*., 48.
6 Hazlitt, *op. cit*.
7 Lukacs, 31.
8 *ibid*., 54.
9 Thomas M. Raysor, *op. cit*.
10 Journal (18 December 1827), 399.

11 Lukacs, 58.
12 Cockshut, *op. cit.*, 159.
13 *ibid.*, 170.
14 *Orlando* (1928), 244.
15 *A Buyer's Market* (1953), 23.
16 *Twelve Types* (1902), 179 ff.

Index